BrightRED Study Guide

CfE HIGHER

RMPS

RELIGIOUS, MORAL AND PHILOSOPHICAL STUDIES

Tim Beattie

First published in 2023 by: **Bright Red Publishing Ltd Mitchelston Drive Business Centre Mitchelston Drive KY1 3NB**

Copyright © Bright Red Publishing Ltd 2023. Cover image © Caleb Rutherford

All rights reserved. No part of this publication may be reproduced, stored in a retrieval system, or transmitted in any form or by any means, electronic, mechanical, photocopying, recording or otherwise, without prior permission in writing from the publisher.

The rights of Tim Beattie to be identified as the author of this work has been asserted by him in accordance with Sections 77 and 78 of the Copyright, Designs and Patents Act 1988.

A CIP record for this book is available from the British Library. ISBN 978-1-906736-87-3

With thanks to: Ian Hamilton (editorial) and PDQ Digital Media Solutions (layout) Cover design and series book design by Caleb Rutherford – e i d e t i c.

Acknowledgements
Every effort has been made to seek all copyright-holders. If any have been overlooked, then Bright Red Publishing will be delighted to make the necessary arrangements. We are grateful for the use of the following:

Image credits
Monkey Business Images/Shutterstock.com (p 4 top); StunningArt/Shutterstock.com (p 4 bottom); Triff/Shutterstock.com (p 5 top); Jorm Sangsorn/Shutterstock.com (p 5 bottom); Iva Vagnerova/Shutterstock.com (p 8); Zolnierek/Shutterstock.com (p 9); rudall30/Shutterstock.com (p 10); Ivanov Oleg/Shutterstock.com (p 18); VMStock/Shutterstock.com (p 19); Quality Stock Arts/Shutterstock.com (p 20); socrates471/Shutterstock.com (p 22); dreamloveyou/Shutterstock.com (p 24); chris piason/Shutterstock.com (p 26); Tanison Pachtanom/Shutterstock.com (p 28); anek.soowannaphoom/Shutterstock.com (p 31); Jozef Klopacka/Shutterstock.com (p 32 top left); Mashosh/Shutterstock.com (p 32 top right); Lerra Anak Bajut/Shutterstock.com (p 32 middle); Zolnierek/Shutterstock.com (p 32 bottom); Romolo Tavani/Shutterstock.com (p 33); FooTToo/Shutterstock.com (p 34); Zvonimir Atletic/Shutterstock.com (p 35); ESB Professional/Shutterstock.com (p 36); Renata Sedmakova/Shutterstock.com (p 37); ArtMediaWorx/Shutterstock.com (p 40); Rachata Sinthopachakul/Shutterstock.com (p 41); Martin Charles Hatch/Shutterstock.com (p 44 top); Bill Perry/Shutterstock.com (p 44 bottom); BlueDesign/Shutterstock.com (p 47); Rawpixel.com/Shutterstock.com (p 48); Gina Vescovi/Shutterstock.com (p 49); Billion Photos/Shutterstock.com (p 51 top); Lightspring/Shutterstock.com (p 51 bottom); richardjohnson/Shutterstock.com (p 52 top); fran_kie/Shutterstock.com (p 52 bottom); alinabuphoto/Shutterstock.com (p 54 top); cornfield/Shutterstock.com (p 54 bottom); TheVisualsYouNeed/Shutterstock.com (p 55); Lightspring/Shutterstock.com (p 58); Morphart Creation/Shutterstock.com (p 59); felipe aparros/Shutterstock.com (p 61); Stock City/Shutterstock.com (p 62 top); Gts/Shutterstock.com (p 62 bottom); dvlcom - www.dvlcom.co.uk/Shutterstock.com (p 64 top); 360b/Shutterstock.com (p 64 bottom); Gagarin Iurii/Shutterstock.com (p 66); TUKiphoto/Shutterstock.com (p 68 top); AVN Photo Lab/Shutterstock.com (p 68 bottom); Kateryna Kon/Shutterstock.com (p 72 top); Lightspring/Shutterstock.com (p 72 bottom); Ditom/Shutterstock.com (p 73); SvetaZi/Shutterstock.com (p 74); Jordan Grinnell/Shutterstock.com (p 78); Krakenimages.com/Shutterstock.com (p 80); Stephen Rees/Shutterstock.com (p 81); vchal/Shutterstock.com (p 82); ricochet64/Shutterstock.com (p 84); cooperr/Shutterstock.com (p 85); Dan Race/Shutterstock.com (p 88); Motortion Films/Shutterstock.com (p 90 top); Ga Fullner/Shutterstock.com (p 90 bottom); sangriana/Shutterstock.com (p 93); dizain/Shutterstock.com (p 100); Lightspring/Shutterstock.com (p 101); Don Artua/Shutterstock.com (p 104); FlashMovie/Shutterstock.com (p 106 top); MUHAMMEDKARSLI/Shutterstock.com (p 106 middle); sakkmesterke/Shutterstock.com (p 106 bottom); VectorMine/Shutterstock.com (p 107); Take Photo/Shutterstock.com (p 109); Uncle Leo/Shutterstock.com (p 111 top); Everett Collection/Shutterstock.com (p 111 bottom); GoodIdeas/Shutterstock.com (p 113); Deer worawut/Shutterstock.com (p 114); German Vizulis/Shutterstock.com (p 118); Freezing Photons/Shutterstock.com (p 119 top); German Vizulis/Shutterstock.com (p 119 bottom); German Vizulis/Shutterstock.com (p 121); dreamy-art/Shutterstock.com (p 122); Kirasolly/Shutterstock.com (p 123).

Text credits
Extract from 'A Sketch of the Buddha's Life: Readings from the Pali Canon', edited by Access to Insight. Access to Insight (BCBS Edition), 30 November 2013, www.accesstoinsight.org/ptf/buddha.html (p 12); Three extracts from *The Dhammapada*, verses 153, 273–6 & 2 © Buddha Dharma Education Association Inc. (pp 19, 22 & 23); Extract from 'Buddhist Studies (Secondary) The Buddha's Wisdom and Compassion', www.buddhanet.net/e-learning/buddhism/bs-s16.htm © Buddha Dharma Education Association Inc. (p 20); Extract transcribed from: www.truetube.co.uk/film/day-life-buddhist-monk. Reproduced by permission of Manapo Bhikkhu (p 27); Scriptures taken from *The Holy Bible*, New International Version®, NIV®. Copyright © 1973, 1978, 1984, 2011 by Biblica, Inc.™ Used by permission of Zondervan. All rights reserved worldwide. www.zondervan.com. The "NIV" and "New International Version" are trademarks registered in the United States Patent and Trademark Office by Biblica, Inc.™ (pp 34, 38, 41–3, 45–6, 48, 57, 60–2, 66, 70, 104–5, 110 & 120); Two scripture quotations taken from the (NASB®) *New American Standard Bible*®, Copyright © 1960, 1971, 1977, 1995, 2020 by The Lockman Foundation. Used by permission. All rights reserved www.lockman.org (pp 43 & 54); Extract from Pope Benedict (Holy Mass on the solemnity of the assumption of the blessed Virgin Mary; Castel Gandolfo, 2010). Copyright 2010 – Libreria Editrice Vaticana (p 43); Contemporary version of 'The Lord's Prayer' © The Archbishops' Council of the Church of England (p 48); Extract from *The Holy Bible*, English Standard Version® (ESV®) Copyright © 2001 by Crossway, a publishing ministry of Good News Publishers. All rights reserved (p 54); Two extracts from 'Justice in Scotland: Vision and Priorities' from www.gov.scot/publications/justice-scotland-vision-priorities/documents/[1] (pp 57 & 69); Extract from The Qur'an (Oxford World's Classics) © M. A. S. Abdel Haleem 2004, 2005. Published by Oxford University Press (p 69); Extract from 'The Death Penalty', published May 2008 by Church and Society Council. Reproduced by permission of The Church of Scotland (p 71); Extract from *Dead Man Walking: The Eyewitness Account of the Death Penalty That Sparked a National Debate* by Helen Prejean, published by Vintage 1994 (p 71); Two extracts from Humanists UK website reproduced by permission of Humanists UK (pp 77 & 85); Extract from *Dignitas Personae* by the Roman Catholic Church, published by Veritas Books (p 79); Extract from 'Presumed vs Expressed Consent in the US and Internationally'. AMA Journal of Ethics, Copyright 2005 American Medical Association. All rights reserved. The AMA Journal of Ethics® is a registered trademark of the American Medical Association (p 82); Extract from *Transplantation – Opting in or presumed consent for organ and tissue donation?* published May 2015 by Church and Society Council. Reproduced by permission of The Church of Scotland (p 84); Extract from 'Gray Areas on Gray Matter: The Ethics of Brain Death' by Melody Stringer, 12 September 2018 from https://thehumanist.com/commentary/gray-areas-on-gray-matter-the-ethics-of-brain-death/ © The American Humanist Association (p 87); Extract from *Sri Guru Granth Sahib (Guru Nanak Dev. SGGS:940)*. Translated by Sant Singh Khalsa and published by SikhNet, Inc (p 96); Extract from 'Anticipatory Care Planning: Frequently Asked Questions' taken from www.gov.scot/publications/anticipatory-care-planning-frequently-asked-questions[1] (p 98); Extract reproduced from 'Palliative care', 5 August 2020 (www.who.int/news-room/fact-sheets/detail/palliative-care) Copyright 2020. Accessed 7/7/2023 (p 99); Two extracts from 'End of Life Issues: A Christian Perspective' taken from www.churchofscotland.org.uk/__data/assets/pdf_file/0008/64772/End-of-Life.pdf. Reproduced by permission of The Church of Scotland (p 100); Extract from *The Kalam Cosmological Argument* by William Lane Craig, published by Macmillan © 1979 by Craig, William Lane (p 117); Extract from *The Question of God: An Introduction and Sourcebook* by Michael Palmer, published by Routledge, an imprint of the Taylor & Francis Group © 2001 Michael Palmer. Reproduced with permission of the Licensor through PLSclear (p 118); Extract from *Xenophon in Seven Volumes: Volume 4*. Translated by E. C. Marchant and O. J. Todd. Published by Harvard University Press, Cambridge, MA and William Heinemann, Ltd., London 1923 (p 120); Extract from *Philosophical Theology: Volume II* by F. R. Tennant, published by Cambridge University Press © 1930 F. R. Tennant. Reproduced with permission of the Licensor through PLSclear (p 122); Extract from William Dembski, www.discovery.org/a/121/. Originally published in *COSMIC PURSUIT: In Pursuit of Answers to Life's Big Questions*, Volume 1, Number 2 (Spring 1998) (p 123); Extract from *Language, Truth, and Logic* by A. J. Ayer. Copyright 1936, 1946 by A. J. Ayer. First published by Victor Gollancz Ltd. 1970. Reprinted by Penguin Books 2001 (p 125).

Printed and bound in the UK.

CONTENTS

INTRODUCTION
Higher RMPS 4
Study Techniques and Things To Do And Think About .. 6

CHAPTER 1 – BUDDHISM
Introducing Buddhism 8
Beliefs
Beliefs about the Buddha 1 10
Beliefs about the Buddha 2 12
The Three Marks of Existence: Anicca; Anatta; Dukkha 14
The nature of human beings: Tanha; Three Root Poisons; Kamma 16
Samsara 18
Nibbana 20
Practices
The Noble Eightfold Path 22
Sila and the Five Precepts 24
The Sangha 26
Meditation 28
Devotion 30

CHAPTER 2 – CHRISTIANITY
Introducing Christianity 32
Beliefs
Beliefs about God 34
The nature of human beings 36
Beliefs about Jesus 38
Jesus' death 40
Judgement; Heaven and Hell 42
Practices
Living according to the Gospels 44
Christian action; the Christian community 46
Worship: Prayer and the Eucharist 48

CHAPTER 3 – MORALITY AND JUSTICE
Understanding moral issues 50
Causes of crime
Environmental influences 52
Religious and non-religious responses 54
Psychological factors 56
Purposes of punishment
Reformation 58
Retribution 60
Protection 62
Deterrence 64

Responses to crime
Custodial sentences 66
Non-custodial sentences 68
Capital punishment 70

CHAPTER 4 – MORALITY, MEDICINE AND THE HUMAN BODY
Use of embryos
An overview 72
Reproductive 1 74
Reproductive 2 76
Therapeutic uses of embryos 78
Research 80
Organ donation
Consent 82
Responses to the moral issues 84
Beating and non beating heart donation 86
Living donors 88
End of life
Assisted dying 1 90
Assisted dying 2 92
Voluntary and non-voluntary euthanasia 1 94
Voluntary and non-voluntary euthanasia 2 96
End-of-life care 1 98
End-of-life care 2 100

CHAPTER 5 – ORIGINS. WAS THE UNIVERSE AND LIFE CREATED?
Religious and scientific approaches 102
Origins of the Universe – the religious approach 104
Origins of the Universe – the scientific approach 106
What are the strengths and weaknesses of the explanations? 108
Origins of life – religious and scientific approaches ... 110
Strengths and weaknesses of religious and scientific approaches 112

CHAPTER 6 – THE EXISTENCE OF GOD
Does God exist? 114
The cosmological argument 1 116
The cosmological argument 2 118
The teleological argument 1 120
The teleological argument 2 122
The teleological argument 3 124
The strengths and weaknesses of the cosmological and teleological arguments 126
Index 128

INTRODUCTION

HIGHER RMPS

THE COURSE

Religious, moral and philosophical studies is one subject, with three distinct, yet overlapping units. As you study you will have the opportunity to explore one world religion, a moral issue and a philosophical question, and as you study you will hopefully come to a greater understanding of how these three areas impact society, our beliefs and our values in Scotland today. Congratulations for choosing one of the best higher qualifications available in Scottish schools today!

ONLINE

Go online to our Digital Zone at www.brightredbooks.net/subjects and click the link to see the full SQA course assessment documents.

COURSE STRUCTURE AND ASSESSMENT

The course assessment is made up of **two components**, both of which are externally assessed: the **exam** and the **assignment**.

The question papers

There are two question papers in the exam and they are worth 80 marks (this is almost 73% of the course) in total. Question **Paper 1** assesses the **world religion** section (30 marks) and the **morality and belief** section (30 marks). The 30 marks in each of these sections is made up of one 10-mark 'analysis question' and one 20-mark 'analysis and evaluation' question.

- 10-mark 'analysis question' – This question has 6 marks available for knowledge and understanding (KU) and 4 marks available for analysis (A). Your analysis skills are very important. If you do not attempt any analysis skills in your answer you can only achieve a maximum of 4 marks, even if you have more KU marks written in your answer.
- 20-mark 'analysis and evaluation question' – This question has 10 marks available for knowledge and understanding (KU), 5 marks available for analysis (A) and 5 marks available for Evaluation (E). In this question analysis and evaluation skills are very important because if you fail to show any of these skills and simply write down your KU your maximum mark is capped at 8 marks.

Question **Paper 2** assesses the **religious and philosophical questions** section (20 marks). This section is made up of one 20-mark 'analysis and evaluation question' and has the same marking structure as the 20-mark question in Paper 1: 10 KU, 5A and 5E.

World religions

Religious ideas have been foundational in shaping the world in which we live, and Scotland today has been heavily influenced by religion – our laws, social structures and even our holidays. **You** will have the opportunity to study **one** world religion from six of the most well-known world religions:

- Buddhism
- Christianity
- Hinduism
- Islam
- Judaism
- Sikhism

This book covers the two most widely studied world religions, which are **Buddhism and Christianity**.

Moral issues

Moral issues impact everyone. Actions and situations that occur result in human beings making choices between what they think is right and wrong. People, however, have many different beliefs, opinions and ideas, so deciding what is right and wrong isn't always straightforward. This course helps us to explore how people have made decisions in the past and how we might make decisions in the future. There are five main areas of morality and belief to choose from in the higher course, and you must study **one** of these:

- Morality and justice
- Morality and relationships
- Morality, environment and global issues
- Morality, medicine and the human body
- Morality and conflict

This book covers the two most widely studied moral issues, which are morality and justice, and morality, medicine and the human body.

Religious, moral and philosophical questions

Philosophy comes from two Greek words: **philo**, which means loving, and **sophos** meaning wisdom, so philosophy quite literally means 'loving wisdom'. We all use philosophy when trying to make sense of the world in which we live. Our thinking and search for wisdom generates questions that help us understand our purpose in this Universe. The **one** philosophical question that you must explore in higher RMPS can come from a choice of four questions:

- Origins – Was the Universe and life created?
- Existence of God – Does God exist?
- The problem of evil and suffering – Who is responsible for evil and suffering?
- Miracles – Are miracles real?

This book covers the **Origins** and **Existence of God** sections of the course.

THE ASSIGNMENT

The assignment is worth 30 marks out of the 110 marks available (27% of the course). For this part of the course, you will have to choose an issue of religious, moral or philosophical significance, and then create a question that you have to answer. For the most part you will be working on your own; however, you are allowed some minimal support from your teacher or lecturer. They will check your progress and make sure you are on the right track, but remember that your work must be your own.

The issue you choose can be from one of the three units that you are currently studying in class; this will give you an opportunity to explore that part of the course in more detail. You can also choose another option from the course that you might be interested in and haven't studied in class. Whichever option you choose, the best advice is to choose an issue that has many different viewpoints available and also has a wide range of accessible sources – this will greatly help you as you research.

The 'write-up' stage happens over 1 hour and 30 minutes and takes place under a high degree of supervision and control. Your final assignment write-up will assess your knowledge and understanding, analysis skills and evaluation skills. Vital during your write-up stage is your 'resource sheet'. This must not have more than 250 words; however, it can contain pictures and mind-maps. It is really important to submit a resource sheet with your assignment. It isn't marked; however, if you don't submit it a penalty of 6 marks can be applied and taken off your final score.

 ## THINGS TO DO AND THINK ABOUT

Being organised is the key to success in any Higher exam. Take some time to think about how your notes and resources are organised. Is it a file or folder with dividers for each section, or a notebook dedicated to each section? Make sure you have these ready to go.

INTRODUCTION

STUDY TECHNIQUES AND THINGS TO DO AND THINK ABOUT

THE TECHNIQUES

As you work your way through the book, the closing Things To Do And Think About features might ask you to use some of the techniques described below. These techniques will help you to understand the contents of the book and help you remember it.

CORNELL NOTES

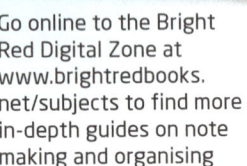

Cornell notes are a system for taking, organising and reviewing notes, created by Prof. Walter Pauk of Cornell University in the 1950s. There are six sections or boxes you create to make a set of Cornell notes. The size of each box or section can vary, but it is more important that the format looks vaguely similar to the example shown to the left.

1. Title (top right)
   This is really important for exam revision to ensure you have covered the entire course.

2. Date (top left)
   The date when you wrote the notes so you can keep them in order chronologically.

3. Main Notes (middle right)
   This is where you put the main thoughts or ideas as you read. Ideally this should be detailed and written in a way that is clearly understood when you are reading it back.

4. Key Points (middle left)
   Just after you write the main notes, pick out the key points and jot them down here as short bullets. The bullets should be easily remembered and might only be one word.

5. Questions (bottom left)
   This section of the notes is extremely useful. These are areas that aren't quite clicking and you need to explore further or may be questions that you think of as you study. Your questions should never go unanswered as they take your learning to a deeper place.

6. Summary (bottom right)
   Ideally, you shouldn't be adding your summary on the same day that the notes were taken. Spend some time later on in the week or even at the beginning of the next week reading through your notes and summarising them in this box.

ONLINE

Go online to the Bright Red Digital Zone at www.brightredbooks.net/subjects to find more in-depth guides on note making and organising your revision.

DON'T FORGET

Make sure your questions are to the point and make sure your answers are in your own words rather than simply copying from the book!

FLASHCARDS

Flashcards are used best when you create them for things you have already learned. If you don't understand a concept, read the chapter in the book again, or watch a video explaining it first. A great habit to get into is creating flashcards 'live' as you are reading through the text in this book. Try placing the format of questions and answers on two sides of a piece of A6 card. Check out this example from Bright Red's very own Revision Card range:

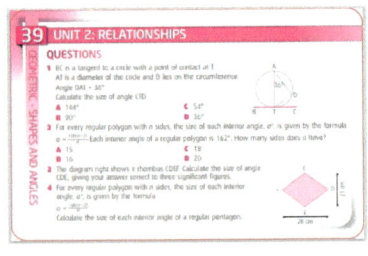
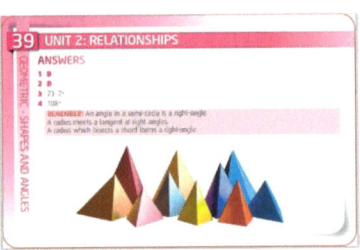

Example questions might be: 'Explain the Buddhist belief Anicca?' Or 'What are the four parts of the Four Noble Truths?' Your answers could be in bullet points or as a piece of text on the reverse of the card, as shown above.

Introduction: Study Techniques and Things To Do and Think About

BRAIN DUMPS

Brain dumps are very useful when learning something new. Pick a topic you want to cover and read it through. Then simply close the book and, using a blank page, write down everything you can remember. That's it.

There are a few further ways in which you can use your finished brain dumps as you study, though. You can look at your brain dump alongside the pages of the book and take note of the things you forgot and go over that material again. You can also do a brain dump on the same topic a day or two later and compare both to see what you are struggling to recall and then revisit that part of the textbook. Both these techniques are putting an emphasis on material that didn't go in the first time.

DON'T FORGET

The process of really focusing on closely reading the topic chosen, and then trying to recall as much as possible right away is what makes the difference.

DUAL CODING

Dual coding is using different ways to represent the information that you are learning. A large proportion of this book is written as text, so useful things that you can do is take chunks of that text and recreate it in a different way; examples are:

- Simple pictures in a mind map
- A cartoon strip
- A diagram
- An infographic
- A table or chart
- A timeline

The science shows that combining text and images as we learn helps our understanding. Creating the images ourselves can also be a very powerful learning technique.

MINI QUIZ

This is another straightforward technique. As you are reading through a chapter in the book, create a mini quiz of five or 10 questions as you go along. Using an A4 piece of paper or opening a Word document, write your questions on one side and your answers on the opposite page. You can complete this at the end of the reading or give yourself a challenge by waiting for a day or two before completing your quiz. An example of mini quizzes in action can be found in the BrightRED Revision Cards or on our online Digital Zone.

THINGS TO DO AND THINK ABOUT

The top five hints and tips for studying:

- Switch between ideas as you study. Don't switch too often, though, as you need to make sure you understand the idea before switching! Revising in a different order will also help you understand the information. The technical term for this is interleaving.
- Just because you read a page from this book once doesn't mean you will always remember it. That's why learning how to recall and retrieve information is possibly more important than reading it for the first time.
- Space out your study and learning. The experts would say that four or five hours spaced over a week is much more beneficial that five hours in one day!
- Linked to the above point, be organised! Know what it is you have to learn and create a timetable for study. It is highly possible for students who are organised and in charge of their learning to jump up a few grades as they know exactly what they need to learn and have created the time and space to learn it.
- Find ways to represent the information for yourself. If there is text in this book you want to remember, then why not turn it into an infographic or a cartoon strip? Similarly, if you see a diagram, you can change it into text or bullet points.

ONLINE

You will find a whole host of supporting material for this book online on our Digital Zone. Go to www.brightredbooks.net/subjects to access the content, links, videos and questions referenced throughout this book.

BUDDHISM

INTRODUCING BUDDHISM

AN OVERVIEW

Buddhism is an incredibly complex world religion, containing many beliefs and practices. Encountering these for the first time can be overwhelming. It can be helpful to compare Buddhism in the Higher course with a classic woven 'friendship bracelet'. When you look at a friendship bracelet it is made up of lots of different coloured threads; all the threads are individual and unique, and yet they all need to come together and weave in and through each other to become the final bracelet.

At Higher level, Buddhism is similar to this. We start by separating each belief and practice into unique parts of the whole, like each individual thread of the bracelet. However, each of these beliefs and practices finds beauty and a complete understanding when they weave in and through each other to give us the final pattern of Buddhism.

We must start somewhere, however, so we have to break Buddhism down. Sometimes this can add to our confusion. For example, we separate the four noble truths as a belief, from the practice of the noble eightfold path, and yet the fourth noble truth is the noble eightfold path! Confused? However, it is important to work through the confusion and keep going. The more of the threads that you understand and begin to weave in and through each other then the more you will begin to see this Buddhism bracelet take shape.

UNIT OVERVIEW

Your teacher or school might approach the areas of Buddhism in a different order than that taken in this book. The main thing is that you understand the course content because that is what you will be assessed on in the final exam. The main areas of the course content are highlighted in bold below.

We will start our journey where the religion begins, with **Beliefs about the Buddha,** who he was and how Buddhism began. We will then consider what the Buddha, and in turn Buddhists, believe about how everything exists in the **Three Marks of Existence**. Next, we consider humanity's place in this existence as we take a closer look at the fundamental beliefs about **The Nature of Human Beings,** Tanha, The Three Root Poisons and Kamma. We then need to develop an understanding of **Samsara,** which is the cycle of birth, life, death and rebirth, before finishing our journey by finally exploring **Nibbana,** the ultimate goal for every Buddhist.

Along the way, there are key practices that a Buddhist must develop and live out to keep them on the right path. These are: **Living According to the Eightfold Path**, the Buddhist basic code of ethics **The Five Precepts,** living in community as part of the **Sangha,** the practice of **Meditation** and the importance of **Devotion,** shown by a Buddhist towards the Buddha.

So, there you have it, you must be aware of:

- Beliefs about the Buddha.
- The Three Marks of Existence: Anicca, Anatta and Dukkha.
- The Nature of Human Beings: Tanha, The Three Root Poisons and Kamma.
- Samsara and Nibbana.
- Living According to the Eightfold Path.
- The Five Precepts and the Sangha.
- Meditation and Devotion.

ONLINE

For a great online resource giving a full overview of the history of Buddhism, go to our Digital Zone and click the link to the History.com website www.brightredbooks.net/subjects

DON'T FORGET

In some way, all of the key beliefs and practices you will study as part of the course are connected and it is very important to keep that in mind.

contd

Buddhism: Introducing Buddhism

One thing that will make a bigger impact on your learning more than anything else is your ability to plan, monitor and evaluate your learning. It is worthwhile making a list of the bulleted beliefs and practices, putting them into a table and then ticking each one off when you feel that you have mastered the content. Take time to go back and review the content and make judgements on how secure you feel you are in each area.

 **ONLINE TEST**

Go online to our Digital Zone to take a quick test on the content of this spread – www.brightredbooks.net/subjects

THINGS TO DO AND THINK ABOUT

Create a simple mind-map with Buddhism in the centre and then all the beliefs and practices as branches coming from the centre. You might want to break further branches off from the each belief or practice with things you already know about these areas from your learning in class.

DON'T FORGET

If you are unsure, ask your teacher because they are there to make sure that you move from a place of not knowing to knowing and so will be keen to help!

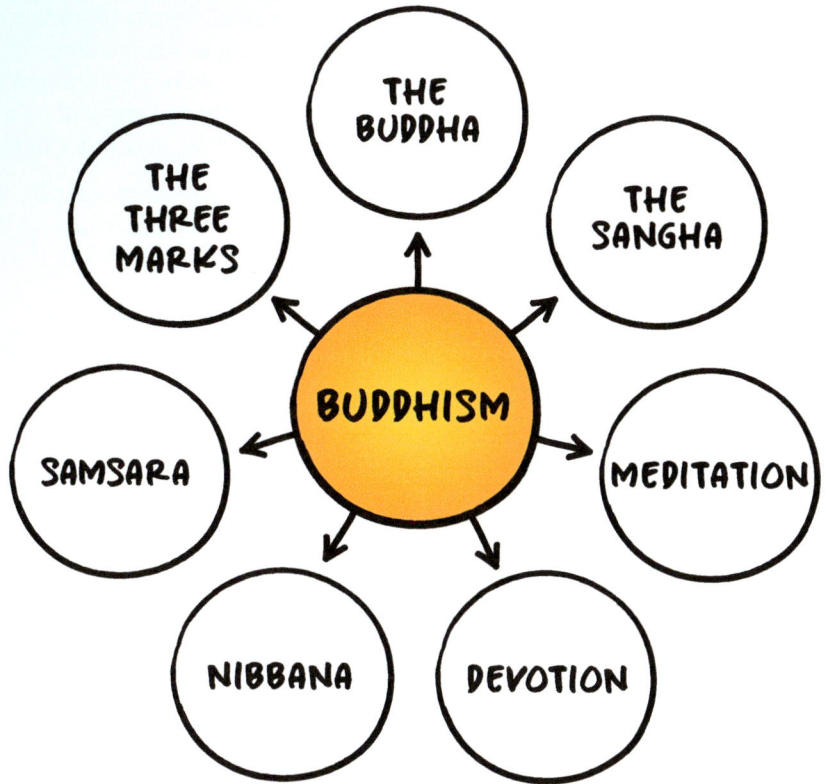

9

BUDDHISM
BELIEFS ABOUT THE BUDDHA 1

SIDDHATTHA GOTAMA

Siddhattha Gotama was born in Lumbini and raised in Kapilvastu at the foot of the Himalayan mountains, on the border between present day India and Nepal. In studying Buddhism there are many spellings of his name; the two most common are the Pali, Siddhattha Gotama and the Sanskrit, Siddhartha Gautama.

You will encounter two languages referred to throughout this Study Guide. Sanskrit is much older than Pali and it was an important language in religion and literature that flourished thousands of years ago. Pali is younger and closely related to Sanskrit. It is a composite language, made up of many different dialects and also the language that Siddhattha (or the Buddha as he was soon to become) used in his teachings. Many scholars consider it to be the simpler of the two languages, which is good for us, as this is the one that we will refer to throughout the book.

Researching Buddha

When using the internet to search for different Buddhist terms, beliefs and practices, you will encounter many websites that use the Pali and many that use the Sanskrit. Usually, the terms look similar in spelling, such as Kamma and Karma, or Nibbana and Nirvana. The information from either source should be relevant as you deepen your understanding of this course; however, be aware that different Buddhist traditions will approach some of the beliefs and practices from slightly different perspectives. Being able to point out these differences is superb analysis. If you become confused or are in doubt, ask your teacher!

ONLINE

To find out a little more about Sanskrit, click the link to the World History website on our Digital Zone - www.brightredbooks.net/subjects

DON'T FORGET

Buddha is not a first name like John or Karen, Buddha is a term that means *enlightened*. It is a special title given to someone who has attained Nibbana or enlightenment.

SIDDHATTHA'S BIRTH

The exact date of Siddhattha's birth is unknown. Buddhist tradition traces it back to sometime between the 6th and 4th centuries BC, while others have tried to be more precise, but it was approximately two and a half thousand years ago. There are many legends surrounding the Buddha's birth, from his mother's vivid dreams of white elephants bringing her son to her, to the wise men prophesying of the greatness of a child that the queen would soon give birth to. This is not uncommon with religious figures or leaders. The other religion this Study Guide covers is Christianity and many of us will be familiar with the story of Mary giving birth to Jesus through immaculate conception.

Whatever legend you choose to believe about Siddhattha's birth, one thing is certain, which is that Siddhattha Gotama and his teachings would become a phenomenon that would change not only the lives of those he would come into contact with, but also the lives of many millions of people thereafter.

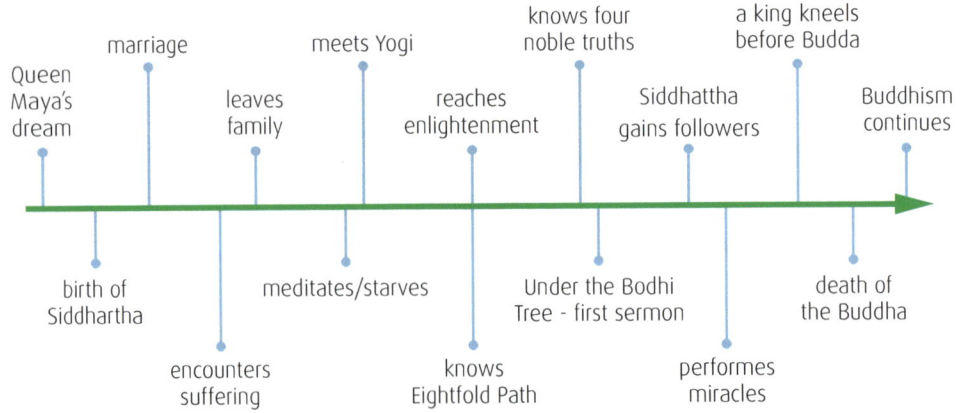

10

Buddhism: Beliefs about the Buddha 1

THE FOUR SIGHTS AND THE GREAT RENUNCIATION

Scholars believe that after a privileged upbringing, in his late twenties, Siddhattha was not satisfied by being contained within the palace walls. His father, the king, had been told that Siddhattha would become either a great ruler or holy man, and he wanted his son to follow in his footsteps, so he kept him close by in the palace throughout Siddhattha's youth and childhood. Siddhattha had a great desire to see the outside world as it really was, and it was on his journeys outside the palace that his spiritual awakening began.

Sources conflict here. Some sources say that one day the Buddha's father granted his wishes to leave the palace, others state that it was without the consent of the king. Some sources say it was one journey, others two and some sources argue that there were four separate journeys. In many ways this information isn't that important for us, and this is a good lesson to learn as we start off on our Higher journey – we must focus on the important and relevant knowledge and information. The important thing here is the fact that the Buddha, along with his loyal friend and royal servant Channa, would embark on a journey (or journeys) that would change his life forever. On these journeys the Buddha would encounter new realities that had been hidden to him throughout his life of luxury within the palace walls; these four encounters would become known as the four sights.

The four sights the Buddha encountered were an old man, a sick man, a dead man and a holy man. After his encounter with the holy man, Siddhattha's life changed forever. He made a decision to give up his life of pleasure in the palace, which included walking away from his family, his wife Yasodhara and his young son Rahula. One night while his wife and son were sleeping, he kissed them both goodbye and ordered his servant Channa to take him out of the city.

THE SIGNIFICANCE OF THE FOUR SIGHTS

The four sights for many are the foundations or building blocks of much of what would come later in the Buddha's teachings. Each of the four sights has strong connections to many other Buddhist beliefs and practices. Have a look at the graphic below, which shows some of these connections and illustrates why the four sights are so important. It is worth noting that you might not have studied all of these beliefs or practices just yet, but don't worry, because as you journey through the unit you will cover them all.

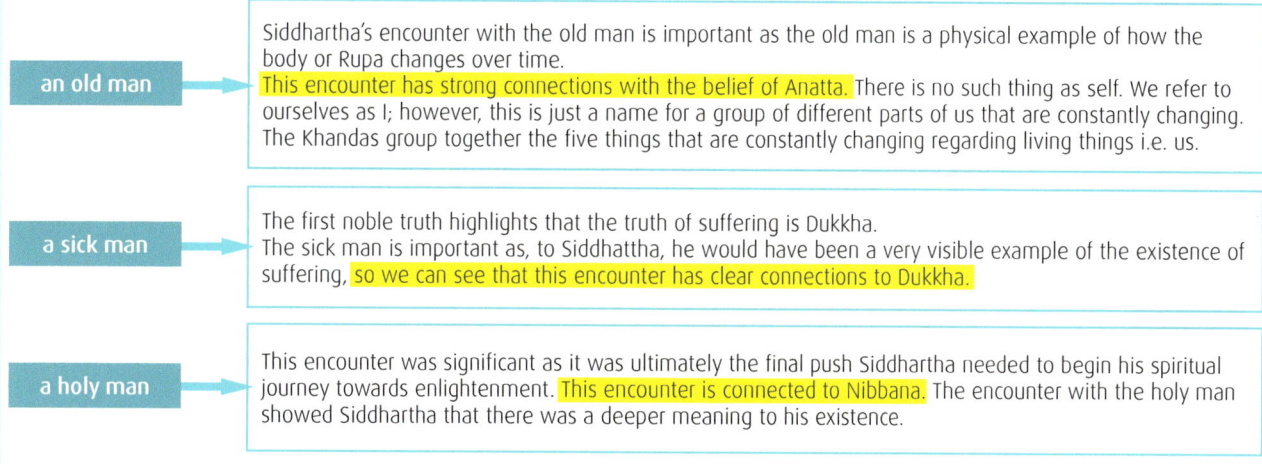

an old man → Siddhartha's encounter with the old man is important as the old man is a physical example of how the body or Rupa changes over time. This encounter has strong connections with the belief of Anatta. There is no such thing as self. We refer to ourselves as I; however, this is just a name for a group of different parts of us that are constantly changing. The Khandas group together the five things that are constantly changing regarding living things i.e. us.

a sick man → The first noble truth highlights that the truth of suffering is Dukkha. The sick man is important as, to Siddhattha, he would have been a very visible example of the existence of suffering, so we can see that this encounter has clear connections to Dukkha.

a holy man → This encounter was significant as it was ultimately the final push Siddhartha needed to begin his spiritual journey towards enlightenment. This encounter is connected to Nibbana. The encounter with the holy man showed Siddhartha that there was a deeper meaning to his existence.

THINGS TO DO AND THINK ABOUT

1. In the significance of the four sights section, the connections are missing from Siddhatha's meeting with the dead man and other Buddhist beliefs and practices. Can you explain these connections in a similar way to those shown?
2. Can you think of any further connections between the four sights and other parts of the Buddhist course you have studied?
3. In what way are beliefs about the Buddha important to Buddhists today?
4. Explain the relationship between beliefs about the Buddha and at least one other belief or practice you have studied. (10 marks)

Remember when answering exam-style questions to always use the question as much as possible in your answer. It is good practice to try and start each developed point like this as this will keep what you are writing relevant and on point. An example of a good opening to an answer can be found on the Digital Zone – www.brightredbooks.net/subjects

 ONLINE TEST

Go online to our Digital Zone to take a quick test on the content of this spread - www.brightredbooks.net/subjects

BUDDHISM
BELIEFS ABOUT THE BUDDHA 2

THE BEGINNING OF SIDDHATTHA'S SPIRITUAL JOURNEY

Siddhattha left the palace and his family behind, beginning a spiritual mission to find the answers to his questions: questions about the nature of reality, what he had uncovered with the four sights and how to reach enlightenment.

The Theravada Buddhist scriptures tell us that Siddhattha's first teacher was Alara Kalama, who was an expert in meditation. He welcomed Siddhattha and taught him how to meditate. However, after mastering the practice Siddhattha realised that meditation alone was only temporary and did not bring eternal peace or end all suffering. Siddhattha's spiritual journey continued. His second teacher was Uddaka Ramaputta, who was also well known for his knowledge and practice of meditation, although, just as before, these meditation techniques and teachings only brought a temporary peace. Siddhattha still hadn't found the answers to his questions, and for the next part of his spiritual journey turned to the extremes of asceticism.

DON'T FORGET

Spiritual journeys weren't unusual in ancient India around the time of the Buddha. Many chose a simple life of poverty to focus their attention on practising a faith or gaining spiritual understanding.

DON'T FORGET

Ascetics tried to gain spiritual enlightenment by living a simple life with strict rules and putting themselves through physically extreme practices.

> "In this way did Alara Kalama, my teacher, place me, his pupil, (Siddhattha), on the same level with himself and pay me great honor. But the thought occurred to me, 'This Dhamma (teaching) leads not to … Unbinding (Nibbana), but only to reappearance in the dimension of nothingness.' So, dissatisfied with that Dhamma, I left."
> Siddhattha Gotama - Maha-Saccaka Sutta

Siddhattha joined a small group of ascetics and stayed with them for more than six years. During this time Siddhattha put himself through physical extremes such as stopping breathing and going without food, but he came to realise that these physical extremes would also fail to bring him enlightenment.

Siddhattha's spiritual journey is important for Buddhists. Siddhattha's spiritual journey allowed him to discover the **middle way**. Not a life devoted to sensual pleasures (such as palace living) or the physical extremes of asceticism (pain and suffering), but a middle way between these extremes. This spiritual journey was also important for Buddhism, as understanding more about the middle way would guide Siddhattha towards establishing one of the most important Buddhist practices, known as the Noble Eightfold Path, which we will explore in detail later.

Not pleasures or riches

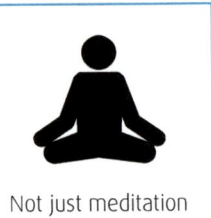

Not just meditation

Not ascetic living

SIDDHATTHA BECOMING THE BUDDHA

There are differing accounts about how Siddhattha and the ascetics parted ways. Most stories tell of a meeting with a milkmaid called Sujata who gave Siddhattha a bowl of milk and rice, but the events surrounding the story are told differently.

One version of the story explains that Siddhattha had made his way to a river to bathe. Because of the physical extremes he had placed himself under, his body was so weak and frail that he couldn't get out of the water. As he struggled, the riverbanks lowered their branches to help him out of the water. At that moment Sujata appeared, offering him the milk and rice. Siddhattha accepted, but the ascetics were disappointed and believed that he had given up on his quest to achieve enlightenment because he had given in to his physical desires and eaten the food.

In another version of the story, we read that Sujata brought the milk and rice and offered them to a rather different, handsome and golden-looking Siddhattha who was deep in meditation. After eating and bathing, Siddhattha took the empty bowl and threw it in the river, whilst declaring that if he is to become Buddha then the bowl would float upstream, which is promptly then did.

Either story brings us to a point where Siddhattha was left alone. With the ascetics gone, Siddhattha returned to meditation. He found a spot underneath a Bodhi

contd

Buddhism: Beliefs about the Buddha 2

Tree and began to meditate. It was underneath this Bodhi Tree that Siddhattha found the answers to his questions, gained enlightenment and became the Buddha.

The Buddha's enlightenment happened in one evening over three stages. The Maha-Saccaka Sutta in the Tipitaka describes these stages as the Three Knowledges:

- On the first watch of the night, the first knowledge Siddhattha attained was the ability to see and understand his many and various past lives.
- On the second watch, the second knowledge Siddhattha attained was detailed visions of the death and rebirth of all types of beings in the Universe and how **Kamma** had an impact on these rebirths.
- On the third watch, the third knowledge Siddhattha attained was how to eliminate ignorance and darkness, attaining **Nibbana** and putting an end to the cycle of **Samsara**.

THE BUDDHA'S FIRST SERMON

This is one of the most significant events in Buddhism's history. Buddha delivered the sermon to a small gathering of five monks at a deer park in Varanasi. His first sermon outlined one of Buddhism's most fundamental beliefs known as **The Four Noble Truths**. These four noble truths are significant as they contain an explanation of the true nature of human reality and how to move from this position to attain enlightenment.

Dukkha - The first noble truth explains that life is full of suffering and un-satisfactoriness. The Buddha gave examples and explained that human experiences such as birth, ageing and death are all causes of our suffering.

Samudaya - The second noble truth explains that Dukkha (suffering and un-satisfactoriness) is caused by craving or by desire. The Pali word used for this craving is Tanha, which literally means to thirst.

Nirodha - The third noble truth explains about the cessation of suffering, in other words there is a way to break free from that suffering.

Magga - The fourth noble truth explains that the way to end suffering is to follow the Noble Eightfold Path.

In the Introduction, we noted that a good example to use when thinking about Buddhism was a friendship bracelet in which each of the threads is individual and unique, yet they come together and weave in and through each other to become the final bracelet. The Four Noble Truths is a prime example of this within Buddhism. It is also full of great analytical points and, when you pick out those **connections**, you will likely notice two things:

- The connections are meaningful. It is hard to properly understand Buddhism without understanding the Four Noble Truths and how fundamental they are to other Buddhist beliefs and practices.
- There are many connections. The four noble truths are linked to The Three Marks of Existence, the nature of human beings, the Noble Eightfold Path, Nibbana and more.

THINGS TO DO AND THINK ABOUT

1. The Life of the Buddha is the perfect question in an exam as it allows you to bring in lots of relevant material from other parts of the course. Draw three graffiti walls showing:
   - Connections to Siddhattha's spiritual journey.
   - Connections to Siddhatha becoming the Buddha.
   - Connections to the Buddha's first sermon.

   You should try to fill as much of your graffiti wall with Buddhist beliefs and practices that are connected. Take it a step further and explain why these things are connected.

2. Just how important do you think beliefs about the Buddha are to Buddhism? This is evaluation and you should try to make a reasoned judgement of your own. Use the sentence stems below to write as many points as you can. This type of task will really support you in your 20-mark questions. Notice how the sentence stems are written from your point of view. Try to make some of your own evaluative points as well.

   In my opinion beliefs about the Buddha are extremely important to Buddhism because…

   From my perspective beliefs about the Buddha are not important to Buddhism because…

   I believe beliefs about the Buddha are important to Buddhism because of the impact his beliefs have on other beliefs and practices such as…

DON'T FORGET

A graffiti wall is basically a blank sheet of A4 paper with a small box somewhere on the sheet containing the name of the wall; the rest of the page is used for writing down things related to the name of the wall.

Beliefs

BUDDHISM

THE THREE MARKS OF EXISTENCE: ANICCA; ANATTA; DUKKHA

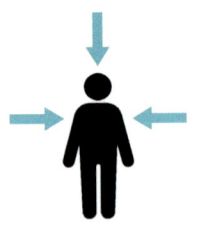

Understanding about self.

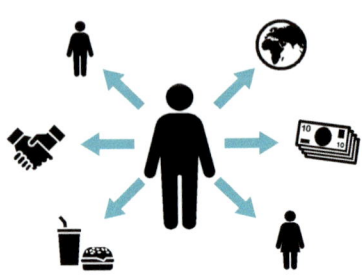

Understanding about how self connects to everything else.

DON'T FORGET

I am what I am now… because of where I have been…and I will be what I will be…because of what I am now. Repeat this sentence a few times and let it sink in. If you can understand this sentence then you have taken an important step on the road to understanding *dependent origination*.

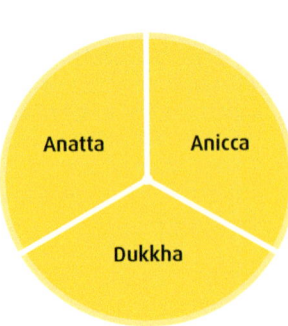

WHAT DOES IT MEAN TO EXIST?

This section of the course deals with an important question for a Buddhist: *What does it mean to exist?* What are the fundamental things Buddhists understand about themselves and how does a Buddhist's understanding of self connect with everything else around them?

The three marks of existence are:

- Anicca: Impermanence; everything changes.
- Anatta: Soullessness or no self.
- Dukkha: Un-satisfactoriness or suffering.

The word exist means to be alive, or to experience some sort of reality. Buddhists believe that everything that exists in this Universe, everything that is alive or experiences some sort of reality, is connected. Nothing in our Universe can exist independently, everything that is alive or exists is dependent upon other things – the Buddhist term for this is *dependent origination*: a network of causes and effects that are woven together.

A Buddhist also believes that *all living beings* will bear three marks or *will have three distinguishing features*. These three features help to explain why existence is made up of a network of causes and effects that are woven together. Furthermore, these three features help a Buddhist to understand what it means to exist and how their existence connects with everything else around them. To a Buddhist, these three distinguishing features are known as the *three marks of existence*: Anicca, Anatta and Dukkha.

ANICCA, WHAT IS IT?

The Pali word Anicca translates as impermanence. Impermanence means that everything in our Universe, the living things and the non-living things, are constantly changing and will never stay the same. This is easy to understand, from the most obvious changes to our animate (living being) selves, like our nails growing longer, hair changing colour and skin ageing or wrinkling. There are sometimes less obvious changes to inanimate (non-living) things, such as paint fading or metal rusting on cars.

Why is Anicca important?

Anicca is important to a Buddhist because there is nothing that impermanence doesn't apply to. It tells us that everything in our Universe, all the living and non-living things, are constantly changing. The Buddhist can do nothing to change this. They must instead try to understand it and accept it. When a Buddhist understands and accepts that everything changes, they have a solid foundation for living out their beliefs and practices.

Essentially, this means that a Buddhist will have a greater chance of reaching their ultimate goal, Nibbana or enlightenment (something we will learn a little more about later). More immediately, however, Anicca is important to a Buddhist because knowing that things will change and not stay the same should encourage a deeper appreciation of the here and now. As time moves on, things will change or cease to be, so enjoy them while they last.

ANATTA, WHAT IS IT?

Anatta literally translates as 'no self' or 'no soul'. This belief put forward by the Buddha was very countercultural, as many of the religious thinkers alive at that time in northern India believed that every individual had a permanent, unchanging and intelligent soul. Vedic and Upanishadic teaching put forward that all beings contained a part of the body that then moved on at the time of death. They called this Atta. The Buddha however disagreed: he suggested that there is no self or no 'you'; therefore, there can be no soul going

contd

Buddhism: The Three Marks of Existence: Anicca; Anatta; Dukkha

beyond our physical death. The Buddha believed that all living beings are constantly changing, that there is not one thing about us that will remain the same over time. The Buddha grouped these changing elements together and they are known as the five Aggregates or five Khandas.

Anatta and the five Aggregates/Khandas

Buddhists believe that each human being is composed of five Khandas. These Khandas are the five building blocks that make up human existence and they are constantly changing. Over time, one group of Khandas will be replaced by another group of Khandas. This Buddhist belief suggests that each part of you is continually changing. This is why a Buddhist believes in Anatta. There is no such thing as self: what appears to be a person is in fact an ever-changing group of the five Khandas, and these are listed below:

- The physical body
- Physical sensation
- Sensory perception
- Habitual tendencies
- Consciousness

ANATTA AND THE QUESTIONS OF KING MILINDA

The Buddhist story that tries to explain this belief of Anatta or 'no self' comes from an ancient Buddhist text known as *Milindapanha* or *'Milinda's questions'*. It is a dialogue between King Milinda and a Buddhist monk known as Nagasena. King Milinda began questioning Nagasena regarding the nature of self. Milinda wondered how there could be, as the Buddha had suggested, no such thing as self. Nagasena replies using this example of a chariot to try and prove his point and explain what the Buddha meant. It's a great example for you to use to explain the belief.

The story makes it clear just how difficult it is to define the term self. Just like the chariot, we can use it to label a concept; however, it is a label that is very much dependent on an ever-changing group of different parts, which we have identified as the Khandas. So, the self of today is going to be a different self tomorrow.

DUKKHA

The Pali word Dukkha is translated as un-satisfactoriness or suffering: It is the **First Noble Truth** that we will explore in a later section. The Buddha explained that many of our human experiences, such as birth, old age, death and disease, can all bring suffering and that suffering is everywhere. In his writings, the Buddha highlighted three distinct types of Dukkha or suffering:

- Suffering caused by pain: this type of suffering is the result of unpleasant physical or mental experiences.
- Suffering caused by conditioned existence: this simply means that because we exist, suffering exists. Suffering is therefore universal.
- Suffering caused by change or impermanence: changes in our lives can be pleasant and unpleasant experiences; both, however, can bring suffering. When we are enjoying our lives, we desire for these pleasant changes to continue. The issue is that pleasant experiences don't last forever, but we desire them to, and in doing so we cause ourselves to suffer. The Buddhist belief of **Anicca** described above explained that everything is impermanent and everything changes. This is strongly connected to this type of **Dukkha**.

ONLINE

Go online to our Digital Zone to read Buddhist stories about Anatta and Dukkha at - www.brightredbooks.net/subjects

THE IMPACT AND IMPORTANCE OF THE THREE MARKS OF EXISTENCE

After exploring this core belief, you may think that Buddhism seems quite negative: that everything changes, there is no you and life is inevitably unsatisfactory and full of suffering. However, many would argue that it is exactly the opposite. Understanding the three marks of existence is hugely important for a Buddhist, because when you understand that this is how life works, you become better prepared to deal with the present.

ONLINE TEST

Go online to our Digital Zone to take a quick test on the content of this spread - www.brightredbooks.net/subjects

THINGS TO DO AND THINK ABOUT

We encountered Cornell notes on page 6 and they are an effective way to make organised notes and a super way to revise. Follow the guidance on page 6 to make your own Cornell notes for each of the Three Marks of Existence.

BUDDHISM

THE NATURE OF HUMAN BEINGS: TANHA; THREE ROOT POISONS; KAMMA

ONLINE

To find out more about The Fire Sermon, click the link at our Digital Zone – www.brightredbooks.net/subjects

TANHA

Tanha means to crave, although sometimes the word thirst or desire is used. In the Second Noble Truth (Samudaya), the Buddha taught that Tanha is the cause of Dukkha (suffering). The concept is that, as human beings, we are never truly satisfied. We become attached to things all around us. There are certain things that we seem to crave. We might crave material things such as money, electronics goods, houses and cars, but we may also crave experiences, feelings and relationships.

In a famous sermon known as 'The Fire Sermon' the Buddha explained to some ascetics (Jatilas), or holy men, the truth of Tanha through a metaphor. The Buddha's teaching in The Fire Sermon explains that if a fire keeps feeding on flammable things it will never burn out. Similarly, human suffering will never be extinguished if it is continually fuelled by human cravings or desires.

THREE TYPES OF TANHA

There are three types of **Tanha or craving** in Buddhism:

Kama-Tanha

Craving pleasures through your senses. An example of this is tasting something good and then wanting more.

Bhava-Tanha

A craving for existence, for life or for self. This craving stops us from accepting that everything is impermanent and always changing.

Vibhava-Tanha

A craving to get rid of the defilements or negative things in our lives such as anger, jealousy and hatred.

ARE ALL DESIRES WRONG?

Although cravings tied to the Three Root Poisons are supposed to lead to suffering, desiring things that come from good roots may not. This type of craving or desire is not known as **Tanha** but as **Chanda** (Dhammachanda).

Chanda isn't craving, but is the desire to act in a wise and virtuous way. A good example of this would be the Buddha's desire to end suffering through the act of meditating.

THE THREE ROOT POISONS

In Buddhism, there are three bad roots or root poisons, which are sometimes known as **Akusala** (the three good roots are known as **Kusala**). These three bad roots or root poisons are **greed, hatred and ignorance or delusion.**

Greed

Greed is a craving for things that we think will bring satisfaction. Greed might cause us to crave objects and status or pursue material ambitions. We think that when we attain these things we will be satisfied, but quickly find out that this isn't the case, and further greed and craving arise. A consequence of greed is that it means you are so consumed by making yourself greater that you do not show compassion or generosity towards others. The opposite good root to greed is *generosity*.

Hatred

The Pali term used for this root poison is *Dosa*, which means hatred, anger or aversion. Hatred and anger mean to intensely dislike or to show hostility towards something or someone. Aversion means to avoid, and things you might choose to avoid are unpleasant emotions, bad situations or unfriendly relationships. Rather than avoid these things, Buddhism teaches us to embrace them with compassion and kindness. The opposite good root to hatred is *benevolence* (love and kindness).

contd

Buddhism: The nature of human beings: Tanha; Three Root Poisons; Kamma

Ignorance/delusion

This means a lack of knowledge or understanding. The way in which you see the world around you and understand your part in it is misunderstood. It's almost as if you are being tricked – tricked into believing things are permanent and there is such a thing as self. The true nature of reality is how it is explained in the Four Noble Truths. The opposite good root to ignorance is *wisdom*.

THE THREE ROOT POISONS AND THEIR CONNECTIONS.

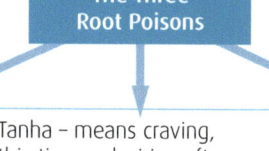

Kamma – one of the things which determines whether Kamma is positive or negative are the intentions behind the action. The Buddha taught that if an action is based on one of the good roots, it will likely lead to generating a positive Kamma. If it is based on one of the root poisons then it would more likely lead to negative Kamma.

Tanha – means craving, thirsting or desiring after things. This is almost inseparable from the root poison of greed. The root poison of greed is the fuel for the craving in our lives.

Samsara – is the belief of birth, death and rebirth. In Buddhism, Samsara is often represented by a wheel; and at the centre of this wheel you will notice a chicken, a pig and a snake biting each others tails. These three animals represent the Three Root Poisons of greed, hatred and ignorance. It is these three poisons that keep the wheel in motion.

KAMMA

The word Kamma translates into the word action, and the belief is most easily understood as the sum or total of a person's moral actions, both in this life and through previous lives. Buddhists describe Kamma as being a natural law, which means that each individual being is in charge of generating their own positive or negative Kamma. It is not something that is decided or handed out by a supreme power like a God or deity. You are in control of your actions; there are reasons why you act in a particular way and these moral actions will generate positive or negative outcomes. Think of it like the ripple effect of throwing a stone into a pool or a puddle; the action is throwing the stone and the ripples that will inevitably result are the consequences.

SKILFUL ACTIONS AND CONSEQUENCES

Kamma is not the same as good or bad luck. Kamma is considered to be a skilful or an unskilful action. A skill is something that you can practise and work at to improve, and Kamma can be considered in the same way.

A Buddhist will try to make sure that all their moral actions have intentions that come from the three good roots (Kusala). This is a deliberate choice and takes an element of skill, effort and determination and this is why Kamma can be a skilful action. Skilful actions *will more likely lead* to generating positive Kamma. Not thinking about your actions, being lazy or intentionally basing your moral actions on the Three Root Poisons would be an unskilful action and *is more likely to lead* to negative Kamma. The reason for this is that as well as the **intention** and the **action**, there are also **consequences**.

The consequences of our actions are difficult to know. We can predict what the consequences might be; however, those predictions don't always come true. Kamma can also progress through different lifetimes, so a Buddhist believes that the consequences for actions carried out in this lifetime might only be realised in lifetimes to come. For moral actions to be skilful and generate positive Kamma, a Buddhist would predict the consequences of their actions to be positive and in line with other Buddhist beliefs and practices.

 THINGS TO DO AND THINK ABOUT

Use **dual coding** (page 7) to remember the key points for Tanha, the Three Root Poisons and Kamma.

 **DON'T FORGET**

When talking about generating positive or negative Kamma through skilful or unskilful actions, you can never completely guarantee whether the Kamma generated will be positive or negative, which is why the words *more likely to* are used.

 **DON'T FORGET**

Kamma is complex! To generate positive Kamma, Buddhists consider two things before any moral action. They will ensure that the intention of the action comes from the three good roots and they will try to predict the consequences of their actions, making sure that they are positive and in line with other Buddhist beliefs and practices.

 ONLINE

Go online to our Digital Zone to read about Kamma and Dhammapada – www.brightredbooks.net/subjects

 ONLINE TEST

Go online to our Digital Zone to try some questions on this spread – www.brightredbooks.net/subjects

BUDDHISM
SAMSARA

THE CYCLE OF BIRTH, LIFE, DEATH AND REBIRTH

The word Samsara translates into English as the phrase 'continuous flow' or 'endless wandering'. It is the Buddhist belief that there is a repeated process of birth, life, death and rebirth. This is an endless cycle that can only be broken by attaining Nibbana.

SAMSARA AS A PICTURE

Samsara is often represented as a picture. The picture, known as the Bhavacakka (displayed below) shows Yama, the Lord of Death, holding or turning a wheel containing many images significant to how a Buddhist understands the process of birth, life, death and rebirth. Depending on the artist the picture may vary, but there is a group of images that usually appear. Outside the wheel, as well as Yama, there is a picture of the Buddha, often pointing towards the moon: this is a symbol of hope showing that liberation from the wheel of life is possible and that Nibbana can be obtained, just as he has shown.

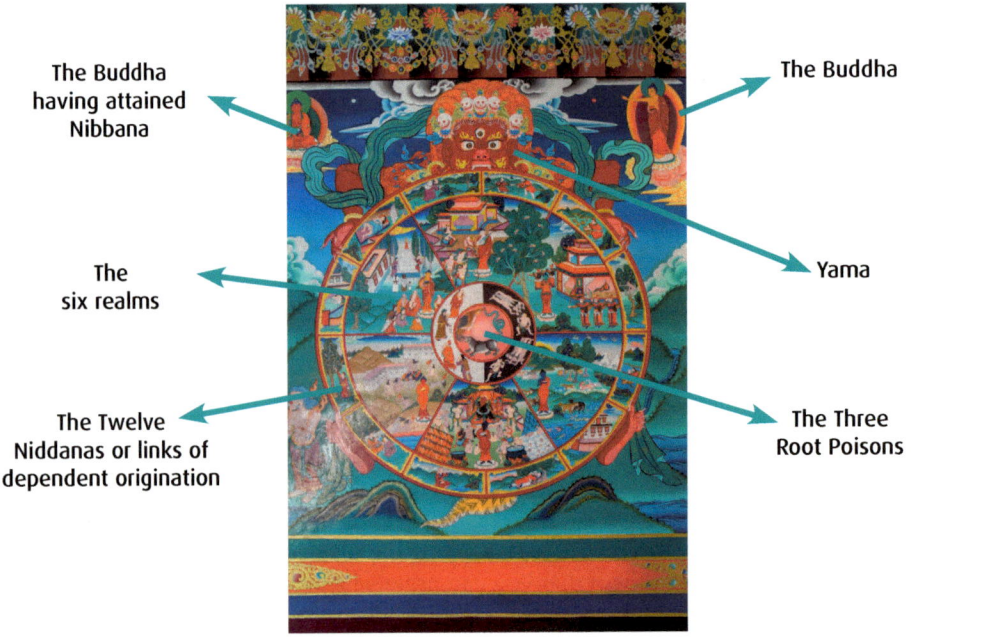

- The Buddha having attained Nibbana
- The six realms
- The Twelve Niddanas or links of dependent origination
- The Buddha
- Yama
- The Three Root Poisons

THE THREE ROOT POISONS

Greed, hatred and ignorance are represented by a chicken, a pig and a snake. The picture shows each animal biting one another's tails at the centre of the wheel, continually feeding off each other. It is these Three Root Poisons that keep the wheel and the cycle of Samsara continually in motion. If you think of how a car wheel works, the axel goes through the centre or hub of the wheel and it is this central part of the wheel that makes it spin, which is similar to how the Three Root Poisons operate within the wheel of birth, life, death and rebirth – keeping the cycle continually in motion.

THE SIX REALMS

Just beyond the Three Root Poisons, moving outwards on the wheel we find the six realms. These realms are interpreted differently within the Buddhist tradition: some Buddhists interpret the realms literally and believe they are actual stages of life and rebirth that you can travel through on the journey towards enlightenment. Others interpret

contd

> **DON'T FORGET**
>
> We explored the Three Root Poisons in detail earlier in this chapter and looked at how these root poisons are linked to Samsara.

the realms metaphorically, with each realm representing a stage of life that they currently find themselves in. For example, the realm of the Pretas (hungry ghosts) might represent a stage in your life where you are giving in to greed. The six realms are outlined below.

The realm of the devas (gods)

Notice that the word 'gods' here has a small 'g'. Buddhists do not believe in an all-knowing, all-powerful God that we find in Christian, Jewish and Muslim traditions. These gods in this realm are spiritual beings who live a luxurious life with no needs or wants. For many Buddhists the gods represent **pride**, as they have a confidence that they are higher beings, they have no motivation to try and escape Samsara, but even they will suffer and die.

The realm of the asuras (demi-gods)

For many Buddhists the asuras represent **jealousy** as these demi-gods would like to take the place of the devas. They are highly competitive and do everything for their own selfish desires.

The realm of the pretas (hungry ghosts)

The hungry ghosts are never satisfied and are always wanting more. They represent **greed**.

The realm of the hells

This realm is often depicted with imagery of fire and ice. The beings stuck in ice are in a place of pain and suffering. Those in the fire are angry and abusive. The realm represents **evil and wickedness**.

The animal realm

The imagery here shows the Buddha carrying a book or a scroll that animals can't read or understand and are guilty of a lack of knowledge and understanding. The animal realm represents **ignorance**.

The human realm

The human realm represents **selfishness**. The teaching of the Buddha is available to all; however, for many the default position is to follow your own selfish desires and thirst after things that in the end will only bring suffering.

THE TWELVE NIDANAS

The Twelve Nidanas are pictured as the outside circle on the wheel of life. These images show the 12 stages of this continuous cycle of birth, life, death and rebirth. We are not going to look at each individual stage as what is useful for us to know is why they are important to a Buddhist. The stages are also known as the 12 links of dependent origination. This means that each of the links has an impact on the next and they depend on each other: it is a pattern of cause and effect. These links of dependent origination are important as they symbolise that all the parts of birth, life, death and rebirth are connected. The event that is beginning for you now is dependent on what has happened before and will have an impact on what has yet to happen.

ONLINE

Research the Twelve Nidanas further by clicking the links on our Digital Zone at www.brightredbooks.net/subjects.

SAMSARA IN THE DHAMMAPADA

One of the most well-known verses in the Buddhist scriptures about Samsara is found in verse 153 of the Dhammapada.

'Through many a birth in samsara have I wandered in vain, seeking in the builder of this house (of life). Repeated birth is indeed suffering!'

Scholars believe that this verse was spoken by the Buddha just as he had attained enlightenment. In this verse the Buddha explains what his life was like before reaching Nibbana, describing how he went through a cycle of many rebirths, which caused him to suffer. This verse is important to Buddhists because it explains that this current life is a cycle of rebirth that will bring suffering, so suffering can be expected. In the verse that follows (verse 154) however, the Buddha explains that this cycle can be stopped by attaining enlightenment, just as he demonstrated through his own life.

THINGS TO DO AND THINK ABOUT

1   Create some **flashcards** to retrieve some of the main details you have learned about Samsara. As prompts use:
    - A basic definition of Samsara.
    - What is the Bhavacakka?
    - How is Samsara connected to the Three Root Poisons?
    - Explain three of the six realms.
    - What are the Twelve Nidanas?
    - Dhammapada verse 153.

BUDDHISM
NIBBANA

WHAT IS NIBBANA?

Nibbana is the ultimate goal for a Buddhist. It literally means to 'blow out' or to extinguish, in the same way that you might think of blowing out a candle. It doesn't mean to blow out or extinguish life, but rather to blow out the Three Root Poisons of greed, hatred and ignorance. Once these poisons have been extinguished, suffering will cease and the Buddhist will reach enlightenment.

Nibbana is hard to define, because the ordinary person can't comprehend it or understand it through reason, in fact many Buddhist scholars would say that Nibbana can only really be understood when it is experienced.

DON'T FORGET

Remember that Nibbana is also referred to as Nirvana in Sanskrit.

IS NIBBANA A PLACE?

Nibbana is not a physical place. Unlike other world religions such as Christianity or Islam, this end goal for a Buddhist is not a physical place such as heaven or paradise, rather, it is a state of mind. The life of the Buddha gives us an insight into two important distinctions we must consider when trying to understand what attaining Nibbana means. First, there is the Nibbana that is attained during life. The Buddha showed that it was possible to become and live as an enlightened being. Second, there is the final Nibbana, or Nibbana without remainder. Final Nibbana is attained when an enlightened being passes away. They will no longer be reborn as they are completely free from the Samsaric cycle of birth, life, death and rebirth.

THE BUDDHA'S TEACHING ON NIBBANA

It was common within early Buddhist sources to have Nibbana described as what it was not or by using negative terms, such as a place where the root poisons are **blown out**, or a place **absent** of desire and a place **without** craving. It is evident that the Buddha in his teaching discouraged his followers from asking or wondering about what Nibbana was and taught that you should be more interested in striving to attain it. One well known story that highlights this is the Buddha's story of the poisoned arrow.

'Suppose someone was hit by a poisoned arrow and his friends and relatives found a doctor able to remove the arrow. If this man were to say, 'I will not have this arrow taken out until I know whether the person who had shot it was a priest, a prince or a merchant, his name and his family. I will not have it taken out until I know what kind of bow was used and whether the arrowhead was an ordinary one or an iron one.' That person would die before all these things are ever known to him.'

Buddhanet.net – Buddhas wisdom and compassion

The parable clearly explains the Buddha's thinking on what is important and what is not. The Buddha believed it was much more important to attain Nibbana than to figure out the mysteries of its nature.

HOW DOES A BUDDHIST ATTAIN NIBBANA?

Within Theravada Buddhism (which is the focus of the SQA course), the fourth Noble Truth explains that the way to end suffering and reach enlightenment is to follow the Noble Eightfold Path. A Buddhist who has attained enlightenment by following the teachings of the Noble Eightfold Path is known as an Arhat. On becoming an Arhat, a Buddhist has extinguished the Three Root Poisons, and will have broken free from the cycle of Samsara and attained Nibbana.

While most of our learning has focused on the Theravada tradition within Buddhism, it is only one of the many different traditions within Buddhism. However, most scholars would agree that although there are many traditions within Buddhism, there are two main branches of the religion: Theravada is one and the other is known as Mahayana Buddhism. Typically, the Mahayana tradition is introduced in the Nibbana section as Mahayana Buddhists approach Nibbana in a somewhat different way, so it gives some good content for analysis.

The aim of a Mahayana Buddhist is not to become an Arhat but to become what is known as a Bodhisattva. Mahayana Buddhists still follow the teachings of the Buddha; however, to become a Bodhisattva they must achieve the six perfections. They attain the six perfections by becoming perfect in six specific areas of their life: patience, morality, generosity, energy, wisdom and meditation. The major difference between Mahayana and Theravada Buddhists is that once they reach these positions the Arhats have gained freedom from the cycle of Samsara; however, the Bodhisattva may choose to stay in the cycle of Samsara so that they can show others the path to enlightenment, which is seen as a very compassionate act.

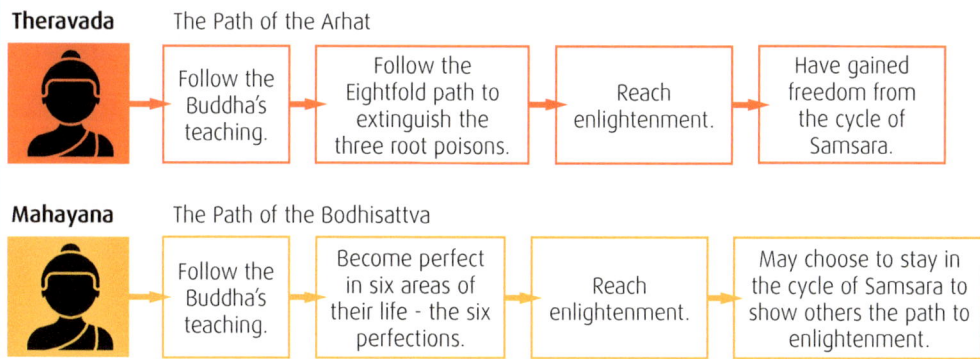

DON'T FORGET

By Buddhist teachings, an enlightened person enjoys a state of supreme joy that comes from being entirely free from cravings and attachments.

THINGS TO DO AND THINK ABOUT

1. Nibbana is connected to many other beliefs within Buddhism that we have covered earlier in this chapter. Take some time to explain how Nibbana is connected to Dukkha, Tanha, the Three Root Poisons and Samsara.

2. Analysis! Use the diagram of the paths of the Arhat and Bodhisattva to explain how a Buddhist reaches Nibbana. The skill of analysis is important in both 10- and 20-mark questions, so it needs to be mastered. In your explanation try to make as many points of analysis as you can. Try and use the words 'connect', 'compare', 'similarity', 'difference' and 'consequence'.

3. Because Nibbana is hard to comprehend, some have asked the question: 'Is Nibbana nothingness?' A favourite story that gives an answer to this question is the story of the turtle and the fish. Have an internet search for this story and use it to explain why Nibbana is not nothing!

ONLINE

Go to the Digital Zone at www.brightredbooks.net/subjects and click the links to read the story to find out more about the turtle and the fish.

ONLINE TEST

To take a test on this topic, go to our Digital Zone at www.brightredbooks.net/subjects.

Practices

BUDDHISM

THE NOBLE EIGHTFOLD PATH

WHAT IS THE NOBLE EIGHTFOLD PATH?

The Eightfold Path is a set of eight guiding principles that the Buddha outlined in his first sermon at the deer park in Varanasi. The Buddha taught and showed through his own life that practising the Eightfold Path is how you navigate that Middle Way between a life of pleasure and a life of physical extremes.

The eight guiding principles are Right View, Right Intention, Right Action, Right Speech, Right Livelihood, Right Mindfulness, Right Effort and Right Concentration. These eight principles are often further categorised into what is known as the threefold way. These three sections are Wisdom, Morality and Meditation. Buddhists understand that the eight stages of the Noble Eightfold path aren't set out as levels to complete in order. You don't master stage one before moving onto stage two. Rather the guidelines are to be used as a way to shape your whole life and live in a way that is modelled on the practice of the Buddha, in order to reach enlightenment and break free from Samsara – just as he did.

DON'T FORGET

Earlier in this chapter, when exploring the four Noble Truths, we learned that the Eightfold Path is central to the fourth Noble Truth and that following this path is the only way to bring an end to suffering.

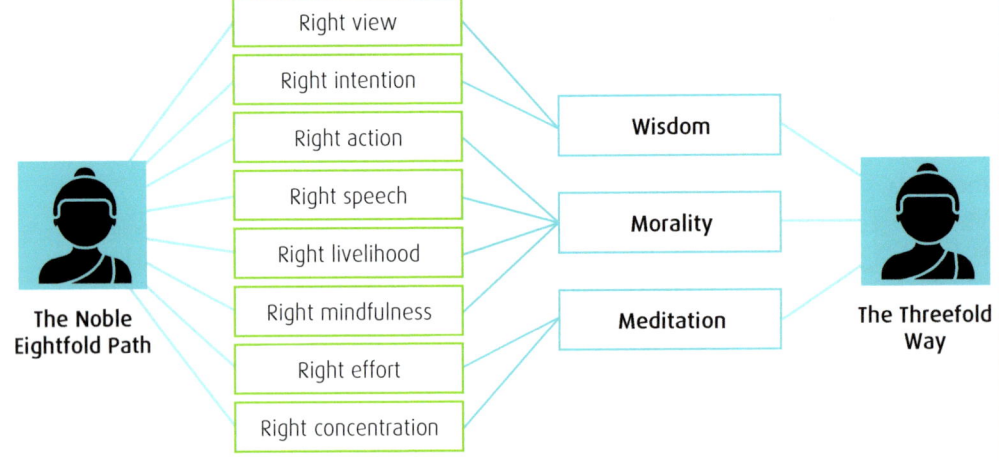

THE BUDDHA'S TEACHING ON THE NOBLE EIGHTFOLD PATH

There is a well-known passage in the Dhammapada that highlights the importance of following the Eightfold Path. The Buddha was very clear that if you want to end suffering there is only one path that will lead to that outcome, the Eightfold Path.

273 Of all the paths the Eightfold Path is the best; of all the truths the Four Noble Truths are the best; of all things passionlessness is the best: of men the Seeing One (the Buddha) is the best.

274 This is the only path; there is none other for the purification of insight. Tread this path, and you will bewilder Mara.

275 Walking upon this path you will make an end of suffering. Having discovered how to pull out the thorn of lust, I make known the path.

276 You yourselves must strive; the Buddhas only point the way. Those meditative ones who tread the path are released from the bonds of Mara.

Dhammapada 273 to 276

ONLINE

For another overview of the Eightfold Path, click the link to the Buddhist Review article on our Digital Zone - www.brightredbooks.net/subjects

The final verse of this passage is also very significant for a Buddhist in understanding the Eightfold Path. When translated into English, verse 276 uses the word strive, which helps a Buddhist to understand that while the guidelines have been explained there is work to be done and it will require effort.

A CLOSER LOOK AT THE EIGHT GUIDING PRINCIPLES

Right View (Understanding)

Right view or understanding means more than learning about and understanding the Buddha's teachings, it means knowing these teachings by experience so that your view is built upon them. Buddhist teaching about the word understanding helps to highlight this.

In the English language, the word understanding means to comprehend something by knowing; however, in Buddhism, there are two types of understanding. These are known as *Anubodha* and *Pativedha*. *Anubodha* is not unlike our definition of the word understanding, using intellect to comprehend or know something. While this intellectual grasp of things is important, it is a deeper understanding, *Pativedha*, which consists of seeing things in their true nature and knowing them by experience that is important. This type of understanding is only acquired through meditation and shows the importance of practising all other parts of the Eightfold Path collectively, as Right View cannot exist without the other parts of the path.

Right Intention (Thought)

A famous phrase in English is 'What were your intentions?' This means, before an action took place, what did you think might happen, or plan for? Your intentions are the reasons behind why you do what you do. For a Buddhist, these reasons are believed to come from either good roots or bad roots: we explored these terms earlier and know them as Kusala and Akusala. Following this guideline means that any Buddhist intentions, thoughts and action should come from good roots, and be established on understanding, benevolence (love and kindness) and generosity.

Right Action

Often called right conduct, in following this guideline a Buddhist would seek to develop a lifestyle where they conduct themselves in the right way. To conduct themselves in the right way they would follow the five precepts. These are:

- Refrain from taking life.
- Refrain from taking what is not given.
- Refrain from misuse of the senses.
- Refrain from wrong speech.
- Refrain from intoxicants that cloud the mind.

Right Speech

Right speech is one of the eight guiding principles of the path and it is also one of the five precepts. Buddhists should seek to speak the truth and to abstain from harmful speech. The Buddha taught that you can do this by not telling lies, not talking in ways that cause others to fall out with each other, not using speech that is malicious or abusive towards others and by not gossiping.

Right Livelihood

Right livelihood is related to your job. Buddhists should try to work in a way that follows the teachings of the Buddha. The Buddha was quite clear in the five types of job that a Buddhist should avoid. These are the business of weapons, business in human beings, business in intoxicants and business in poison.

Right Mindfulness

Right mindfulness means to have an awareness of all that is going on, both inside and outside your body. The Buddha taught that cultivating right mindfulness was the key to avoiding suffering and embracing happiness.

'If with a pure mind a person speaks or acts, happiness follows him.'

The Buddha – Dhammapada verse 2

The Buddha taught that fully developed mindfulness takes in four categories, the body, feelings, the mind and phenomena (or mental objects). We will explore meditation as a separate topic later in the chapter.

Right Effort

This guiding principle teaches a Buddhist about the effort required in developing mindfulness. Having mental discipline requires determination and motivation. It requires effort to prevent poisonous states of the mind and to embrace positive states of mind.

Right Concentration

Right concentration is keeping the mind focused during meditation. Right concentration works alongside effort and mindfulness to develop the mind, helping a Buddhist move towards enlightenment.

THINGS TO DO AND THINK ABOUT

1. Go online to our Digital Zone (www.brighredbooks.net/subjects) to use the 'Making the most of a quote' diagram to develop the two quotes from the Buddha from Right Livelihood and Right Mindfulness above.

2. Read over the notes on the Noble Eightfold Path and do a brain dump fill by following the instructions on our Digital Zone. Make sure you take the time to explore any of the ideas you think you need to relearn rather than review! It might be worthwhile discussing some of these with a teacher if possible.

BUDDHISM
SILA AND THE FIVE PRECEPTS

ONLINE

Go to our Digital Zone at www.brightredbooks.net/subjects and click the link to the Madhyamaka website to access a great list of Buddhist terms and explanations.

SILA, MEANING MORALITY OR MORAL CONDUCT

Sila can be translated as morality or moral conduct. At the start of this chapter, we considered that Buddhism was a little like a friendship bracelet with lots of individual strands that are interweaved to make the complete picture. Sila is one of those strands that does a lot of interweaving. **Sila** has a big part to play in the **Noble Eightfold Path** and **Punna**, which we encountered when we examined the Noble Eightfold path and explored it in detail. We haven't seen the term **Punna** before, but it is a Buddhist term that translates into our English word **merit**; this merit helps a Buddhist gain **positive Kamma** and achieve a better rebirth and **is obtained** by giving, meditating and **correct moral conduct** or Sila.

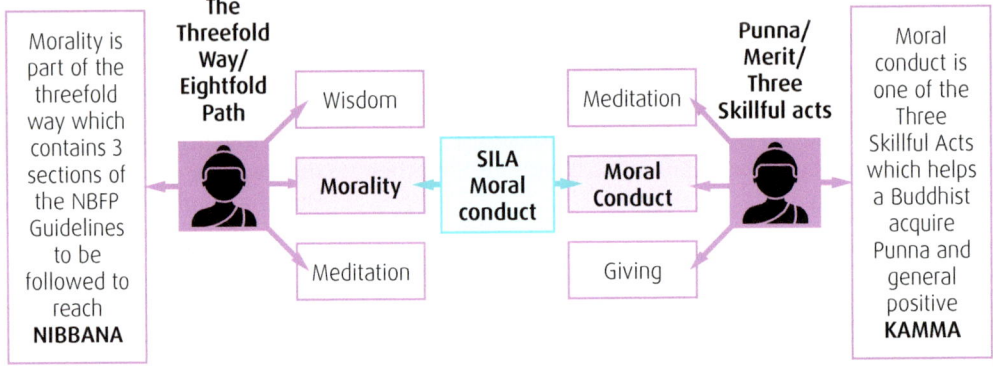

This helps highlight just how **important** the **five precepts** are, because for a Buddhist to achieve proper moral conduct or morality that is in line with the Buddha's teaching, they have to follow the five precepts.

WHAT ARE THE FIVE PRECEPTS?

The **five precepts** are part of a set of 10 larger instructions, known as the **ten precepts** that are used to define the correct moral code for a Buddhist. A **lay Buddhist** must follow the five precepts, while a Buddhist monk or a nun would follow all 10 precepts as part of their disciplined life within the **Sangha**. A fully ordained monk (Bhikkhu) or nun (Bhikkhuni) would follow hundreds more guidelines or instructions. The five precepts any Buddhist should follow are outlined on the next page.

contd

Buddhism: Sila and the Five Precepts

Refrain from taking life

This means Buddhists should not kill any other living or sentient being. This includes animals as well as humans. The Buddhist belief of Ahimsa, not causing harm to any living thing, is closely linked to this precept.

Refrain from taking what is not given

This precept explains that a Buddhist should not steal. Some understand this precept as not only stealing, but refraining from taking things that are not freely given, and can teach a Buddhist how they should respond to other global issues such as slavery.

Refrain from misuse of the senses

Buddhists should refrain from any overindulgence in sensual pleasure. This can be understood as gluttony, which is overindulgence or greediness regarding food and drink, or misconduct of a sexual nature.

Refrain from wrong speech

Just as explored in the Noble Eightfold Path, the Buddha taught that you should not tell lies, nor talk in ways that cause others to fall out with each other, nor use speech that is malicious or abusive towards others and nor gossip.

Refrain from intoxicants that cloud the mind

Buddhists should avoid taking drugs or consuming alcohol as these can have an impact on how the mind works, causing you to think less clearly.

The 10 precepts. Buddhists must refrain from...

- ... taking life
- ... taking what is not given
- ... misuse of the senses
- ... wrong speech
- ... intoxicants that cloud the mind
- ... eating after midday
- ... participating in worldly amusements
- ... adorning the body with ornaments and perfume
- ... sleeping on high or luxurious beds
- ... accepting gold or silver

(Buddhist monks and nuns follow all 10; Lay Buddhists follow the first 5.)

THINGS TO DO AND THINK ABOUT

This section began by looking at Sila (moral conduct) and explained that the Five Precepts are important to a Buddhist today because a way to ensure correct moral conduct is to follow the five precepts. So, use what you have learned in this chapter (including the diagram on Sila) to answer this 10-mark analysis exam-style question:

Analyse the importance of following the Five Precepts. (10 marks)

ONLINE TEST

To take a test on this topic, go to our Digital Zone at www.brightredbooks.net/subjects.

BUDDHISM
THE SANGHA

WHAT IS THE SANGHA?

The Sangha is often understood as the community of Buddhist monks and nuns. Some schools of Buddhism would argue that the Sanghat is a term that encompasses all followers of **the Dhamma** (the Dhamma is the teachings of the Buddha or Buddhist doctrine). This includes laymen and laywomen as well (those not ordained as monks or nuns). You may also see this referred to as the **Lay Sangha**.

The monastic Sangha, however, refers to the monastic communities of monks and nuns that live in monasteries known as **Viharas**. During the time of the Buddha, he and his followers had a somewhat nomadic lifestyle, moving from one location to the next. As time moved on, the Buddha and his followers were given buildings to use as meeting places and these would eventually become permanent monasteries where they would live.

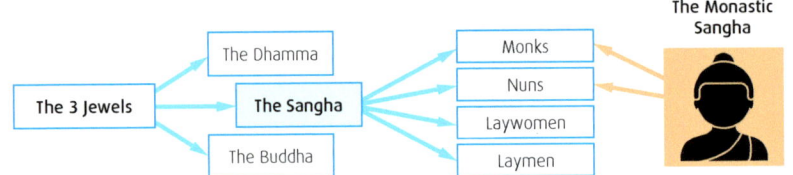

LIFE AS A MONK OR NUN

Monks/Bhikkhus and nuns/Bhikkhunis who take up permanent residency inside the monastic Sangha do so to remove themselves from a worldly lifestyle that is often a source of desire, attachment and suffering. Living in the Vihara gives Buddhist monks and nuns a supportive environment in which to practise the teachings of the Buddha in an effort to develop spiritually in their journeys towards enlightenment.

Bhikkus have few or no possessions. There are, however, a small number of items that they own or that are provided to them from the monastery. These will usually include:

contd

- **An alms bowl** – The word Bhikku literally means someone who depends on alms (donations of food and money). Those who set themselves apart living a monastic lifestyle rely heavily on lay Buddhists to contribute to alms giving. This is something that many lay Buddhists see as a positive action, remembering that giving is one way to acquire Punna and generate positive Kamma.
- **A set of robes** – These are often yellow, orange or brown in colour; in ancient India or Vedic traditions yellow was a colour associated with renunciation, which means leaving your old life behind.
- **A needle and thread** – These are used to mend the robes.
- **A water strainer** – Buddhists monks use the water strainer to make sure that they are not swallowing any living things unknowingly. Remember that Buddhist teaching explains that a Buddhist must show compassion and respect to all living things.
- **A razor** – A Buddhist monk or nun will have a shaved head. Hair is associated with vanity and it takes time to look after your appearance if you have longer hair. A Buddhist doesn't see this as important in their pursuit of enlightenment so it is easier to remove it and keep it removed, hence the need for the razor.

A DAY IN THE LIFE OF A BUDDHIST MONK

There are differences in what a typical day in the life of a Buddhist monk might look like, it will depend on where the monastery is in the world and some of the cultural differences that might also be present. The following is taken from a documentary, where the creators spent a day with a Buddhist monk, Manapo, from the Forest Hermitage monastery in Lower Fulbrook in England.

5:30 am – A bell is rung as a sign to get up.

6:00 am – Morning Puja, this involves chanting followed by meditation.

7:30 am – One hour of chores, these are an important discipline in a monastery, making sure the place where you live is looked after and well kept.

8:30 am – An hour of personal time.

11:00 am – One main meal of the day. The food is received or given to the monks, who are dependent on the generosity of others to provide, and this must be eaten before midday.

Late afternoon – More personal time that might include walking meditation, reading or studying Buddhist teachings.

8:00 pm – Evening Puja, this is similar to morning Puja but involves different chanting. This is followed by further personal time.

11:00 pm – Bedtime.

ONLINE

Go to the Bright Red Digital Zone at www.brightredbooks.net/subjects to click the link and watch a documentary on a day in the life of a Buddhist monk.

THINGS TO DO AND THINK ABOUT

The possessions of a monk or a nun all signify something important. Take some time to dual code the section of text – 'Life as a monk or a nun'. Remember dual coding is turning the text into pictures or diagrams and is explored in the study skills section on page 7.

BUDDHISM
MEDITATION

WHAT IS MEDITATION?

Meditation (Samadhi) is an extremely important practice within Buddhism. When examining the life of the Buddha we learned that it was through the practice of meditation that he reached enlightenment. We have also explored the Noble Eightfold Path and seen that the practice of meditation makes up three of the eight guiding principles of the path. Through the right effort and right concentration, a Buddhist will practise meditation with the goal of becoming fully aware of themselves, paying attention to their own mind and body, gaining proper insight into reality – with the ultimate aim of reaching enlightenment.

DON'T FORGET

Meditation can be defined as transforming your mind or your state of consciousness in a controlled way.

Meditation is not an easy practice because our minds constantly wander and throw up distractions. Many Buddhist sources and texts liken the mind to a monkey swinging through trees from branch to branch or use the analogy of taming a wild elephant. Getting your body and posture in the right position is also important. Although meditation can be carried out in any position, the traditional sitting posture for meditation is often used as it allows you to remain relaxed, healthy and comfortable for a long period of time. It is known as the seven-point posture of Vairocana and means sitting with a straight spine, shoulders back, hands in your lap or on your knees, legs crossed, chin tucked in, eyes relaxed but preferably open and your lips slightly open while breathing through your nose.

The Theravada Buddhist tradition highlights two main types of meditation, Samatha (calming) meditation and Vipassana (insight) meditation, both of which are important in reaching enlightenment. Samatha meditation calms and focuses the mind in order for Vipassana meditation to take place.

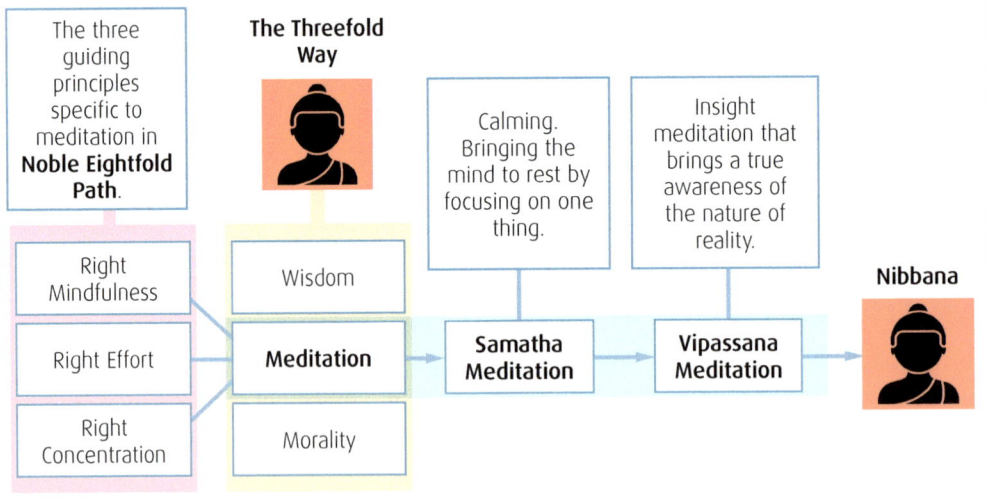

SAMATHA AND VIPASSANA MEDITATION

Samatha meditation

Samatha meditation attempts to calm the mind by concentrating on a single object. A Buddhist will bring themselves to a calm state by mindful concentration on one thing, which allows them to focus more deeply. The Buddha taught that using a visual object known as a Kasina was also a helpful way to focus the mind. There are 10 Kasina in total

contd

that are listed in the Pali scriptures and these are often represented in the form of a coloured disc that a Buddhist will set in front of them to focus and concentrate on. A Buddhist might also choose to focus their mind on their breathing - this practice is known as anapanasati meditation. Once the mind is calmed and focused it will be in a better place to start insight meditation, which is known as vipassana meditation.

Vipassana meditation

Vipassana or insight meditation is meditation that helps a Buddhist understand the true nature of reality and eventually leads to liberation from Samsara and enlightenment. Buddhist teachers explain that this takes time and plenty of practice. Vipassana meditation retrains the mind in a way where one who is meditating reaches a deeper sense of awareness of who they are and the nature of the reality around them. This type of meditation is often initiated with a teacher because it strips back the layers of life so that you come to a new awareness and understanding of what reality is and your place in it.

It is interesting to note that some Buddhist traditions view Samatha and Vipassana meditation as less of a process where Samatha leads to Vipassana, but rather as two inseparable concepts that go hand in hand, both leading to the other happening simultaneously. The Theravada tradition mostly alludes to the mind having to be calmed and focussed before deeper insight meditation takes place.

> **DON'T FORGET**
>
> Various denominations or schools within Buddhism use meditation in many ways with different techniques.

THE BRAHMA VIHARAS

There is no doubt that the ultimate aim for a Buddhist who devotes their life to meditation is enlightenment. However, the Brahma Viharas (or four wholesome states of mind) highlight another important purpose of meditation, which is the immediate practical impact that meditation can have on the meditator and those who they encounter.

The Buddha taught that by cultivating these states of mind through meditation and then practising them throughout your daily life, the meditator would live a peaceful life that benefited others. The meditation and practical conduct have a very important relationship, as the more you meditate on these wholesome things the more you are inclined to react in a wholesome way in practical everyday conduct. In turn, the more you conduct yourself in a wholesome way, the more concentrated the mind becomes regarding these wholesome qualities.

THINGS TO DO AND THINK ABOUT

1. Meditation is connected to many other beliefs and practices we have looked at within Buddhism. Start by creating a mind-map, with meditation in the centre and make as many connections with other beliefs and practices as you can, then attempt this 20-mark question (remember to include analysis and evaluation; for hints and tips look at the answering exam style questions section).

   Of all the Buddhist practices, meditation has the most impact.

   To what extent do you agree? (20 marks)

BUDDHISM
DEVOTION

WHAT IS DEVOTION?

To show Devotion means to show reverence, deep respect or adoration. In the context of Buddhism, it is the reverence, deep respect or adoration that Buddhist followers show towards the Buddha. In many books and sources, you may see the word worship used in place of devotion or used interchangeably. Some scholars would argue that worship is a term that is used whenever the follower of the religion is showing devotion towards a deity or God. The Buddha, however, was an ordinary man who became enlightened and was not a God, so many opt instead for the term devotion.

It could be argued that devotion towards the Buddha can be shown in many ways, spending time understanding his teachings, developing Buddhist beliefs or keeping Buddhist practices might all equate to devotion towards the Buddha. In this segment we will look at four specific things that have the main intention of showing reverence, respect or adoration towards the Buddha: Puja, Buddhanussati (Buddha mindfulness), festivals and retreats.

Devotion

Buddhist **devotion** is the **respect or reverence** that Buddhists show **towards the Buddha**. They can do this in a **number of different ways**.

→ Puja
→ Buddhanussati
→ Festivals
→ Retreats

PUJA

Puja is a word that originated long before the Buddha, coming from the Vedic traditions that shaped Hinduism and the world that Siddhattha Gotama was born into. In Theravada Buddhism, the word Puja refers to the ceremonial devotional practice that Buddhists take part in to show their devotion towards the Buddha. Puja can take place in various settings, the Vihara (temple), a stupa (a dome-like structure containing Buddhist artifacts), or it can take place at home. These ceremonies can also vary depending on the country you are in. Typically, the ceremonial practice of worship includes:

- Chanting and mantras – this is the repeating or singing of religious phrases or quotations from the Dhammapada. This includes the Three Refuges (Tisarana) and the Five Precepts (Pansil).
- Offerings – offerings will often be in the form of flowers, incense, candles and food and will be offered in front of an image or statue of the Buddha.
- Teaching – teaching may come in the form of sermons; Bhikkus may give guidance and help bring understanding to the Buddha's teachings.
- Meditation.

DON'T FORGET

Understanding these qualities and using them in meditation will allow the Buddhist to gain a deeper knowledge of the Buddha and help to show him reverence and respect as they remember him.

BUDDHANUSSATI

Buddhanussati is defined as Buddha Mindfulness or mindfulness on the Buddha's virtues. This type of meditation encourages the Buddhist to focus their concentration on the Buddha's qualities or virtues during meditation. There are nine Pali words or phrases that make up the nine qualities or virtues of the Buddha; feel free to research all nine if you wish but recalling one or two will be sufficient for any exam-style question. One of the qualities of the Buddha that is used during Buddha mindfulness is **Sugato**, which means 'a great speaker' or the one who has the right words to say at the right time. Another quality is **Buddho**, which translates as the one who knows the Four Noble Truths.

Buddhism: Devotion

FESTIVALS

There are often cultural differences that impact how different countries celebrate the Buddha during festivals; however, there are a few festivals that globally have a lot in common, and these specific times of the year allow Buddhists to come together to show reverence and deep respect to the Buddha.

Buddhist New Year

The Theravada new year festival is celebrated over three days and begins on the first full moon in April. The festival allows Buddhists to spend a few days remembering how fortunate they are to have been born in the human realm and follow the Buddha's teachings and way of life. The festival is a symbol of new life and new beginnings, with the Buddhist belief of Kamma playing a central role. Sand sculptures are often constructed on riverbanks, with the grains of sand linked to wrongdoing; when the river washes the sand away it is symbolic of wrongdoing and the bad Kamma associated with it being washed away. Water is also seen as a sign of newness and new beginnings: images of the Buddha will be washed with clean water, but many will also take to the streets and splash water on each other, in what usually turns into a massive water fight.

Vesakha

Vesakha or Wesak is the most important of the Theravada Buddhist festivals and is a time to remember the birth, enlightenment and death (entry into final Nibbana) of the Buddha. Light is used symbolically to remember these stages of the Buddha's life, with people carrying lanterns through the street and hanging them outside houses. In many south-east Asian countries, lay Buddhists will go to the temple to worship with the monks and nuns. The lay believers may take on the extra five precepts during the festival as well as give alms or food to the monks and nuns.

RETREATS

During the rainy season, the Buddha encouraged his followers to stay in one place and meditate more intensely. In southeast Asian Buddhist communities today, many still observe **Vassa**, the monastic retreat during the 3-month monsoon period. In Thailand many Buddhist males will use **Vassa** as a time when they can temporarily experience the life of a monk. Retreats are a meaningful time for a Buddhist and are important to lay Buddhists living in the UK. It is an opportunity to spend more concentrated time on meditation and reading the Dhammapada, and many will go to monasteries and retreat centres around the UK and spend anywhere from a few days to a month exploring their faith more intensely.

Amaravati

Amaravati is a Theravada Buddhist monastery near London. It hosts a programme of short and long retreats, which are mostly in groups and held in silence. The routine on the retreats emphasises formal meditation instruction and practice. Each retreat has a slightly different approach but they all generally focus on the Buddha's teachings in the Theravada tradition. This includes different forms of meditation (including guided, silent and walking) and reflections on aspects of Buddha's teachings. There is also an opportunity for questions and answers with the teacher.

> **DON'T FORGET**
>
> In many Buddhist countries lay believers will set captive fish and birds free. This compassionate act gains the Buddhist merit and generates positive Kamma.

> **DON'T FORGET**
>
> Vesakha gets its name from the second month of the lunar calendar, and the festival is celebrated on the first full moon day of this month.

> **ONLINE**
>
> There are many Buddhist retreats in Scotland. Click the links on our Digital Zone to see where they are and the approach they take.
> www.brightredbooks.net/subjects

THINGS TO DO AND THINK ABOUT

1. Write an explanation of the word devotion.
2. Four ways that we have explored the Buddhist practice of devotion is through Puja, Buddhanusatti, festivals and retreats. Create four flashcards with each of these terms as a prompt and the appropriate response explaining each of the four ways on the back of the flashcard and use them until you are secure in your explanation of each.

CHRISTIANITY

INTRODUCING CHRISTIANITY

Christianity as a world religion takes its name from the person of Jesus Christ. However, to truly understand the beliefs and practices in this course, we must look backwards into the Old Testament and move forward through the life and work of the Church.

OLD TESTAMENT BEGINNINGS

Christians believe that the Old Testament of the Bible starts with an account of the creation of the Universe and human life, and documents the journey of God's chosen people, the Israelites. It contains important guidance about the Christian faith and, alongside the New Testament, provides instruction on how a Christian should live their life.

It is through the Old Testament that we become aware of the very close links that Christianity has with Judaism. The Jewish scriptures and the Christian Old Testament are very similar, and it is important to note that when Jesus refers to 'the Scriptures' in the Gospels, as a Jew, it is these Jewish scriptures that he is referring to. In the SQA course the Old Testament is very important as we explore the **beliefs** section of the course, specifically **beliefs about God** and **the nature of human beings**.

DON'T FORGET

In some way, all of the key beliefs and practices you will study as part of the course are connected and it is very important to keep that in mind.

ONLINE

For a great online resource giving a full overview of the history of Christianity, go to our Digital Zone at: www.brightredbooks.net/subjects

DIFFERENCES IN THE CHURCH

Jesus' first followers, his disciples and apostles, were responsible for forming the Christian Church after his death and resurrection, and the Church has been on a significant journey ever since. Throughout the last 2000 years or so there have been different opinions on how the Bible should be interpreted, how beliefs have been formed and how the faith has been practised. This is important for us as we study the religion, as many of the different denominations within Christianity have their own interpretations of the beliefs and practices we will study.

The **Eucharist**, which is also known as **Holy Communion**, is a good example of this. Many Churches differ on their views regarding the bread and wine, what takes place during a service and the frequency of when services should take place, all of which are explored later.

Christianity: Introducing Christianity

UNIT OVERVIEW

The beliefs and practices you will study throughout the Christianity unit are outlined below.

Beliefs

- beliefs about God
- the nature of human beings: free will; sin; stewards
- beliefs about Jesus
- judgement; Heaven and Hell

Practices

- living according to the Gospels
- Christian action; the Christian community
- worship: prayer; Eucharist

 ## THINGS TO DO AND THINK ABOUT

One thing that will have a bigger impact on your learning than anything else is your ability to plan, monitor and evaluate your learning. Take control! Use the list of beliefs and practices above, put them into a table and tick them off when you feel you have mastered them. Take time to go back and review the content, thinking about how confident you feel you are in each area. How are you going to address your areas for improvement? Make a plan and stick to it.

Confident	Work to do!

If you are unsure about something then ask your teacher, who will help you move from a place of not knowing to knowing! You must use them as one of the best resources you have.

Beliefs

CHRISTIANITY

BELIEFS ABOUT GOD

Although religions differ from each other in terms of tradition, belief and practices, there are some core beliefs and values that may be similar. When we investigate a religious belief or the concept of a higher power, in some ways we find more similarities, and in others we find even more stark differences.

GOD OF ABRAHAM

Judaism, Christianity and Islam are all **monotheistic** religions, which centre on the belief that there is one supreme being. These three religions are referred to as 'Abrahamic' religions. The most important thing to understand is that the Jews believed in one God, who revealed himself to Abraham. Although the Abrahamic religions differ in terms of key beliefs and practices, they can trace their heritage back to the covenant God made with Abraham. The key beliefs of the Abrahamic faith are the existence of one eternal God (without beginning or end); that God is all powerful (omnipotent); that God is all knowing (omniscient); and that God is all loving (omnibenevolent).

The Jews believed that it was the God of Abraham and Moses who had created the cosmos, the Earth and human beings, and not these strange gods that other people believed in. To ensure that they kept these beliefs, they wrote down their own creation account to express their faith in the one God and creator of all that there is. It is within the book of Genesis that we find these creation stories.

DON'T FORGET

The pagan cultures surrounding the early Jews at the time had their own religion and creation stories. They believed that the Sun and the Moon were gods and that there were gods everywhere.

GOD AS CREATOR

A central Christian belief about God is that God is the **Creator** of the Universe and everything contained within it. The idea of God as a creator is first found in the book of Genesis in the Bible and is an important part of Christian teaching. Christians believe that God created the Universe out of nothing (*ex nihilo*). This links to the characteristic of God being omnipotent (all powerful).

> *In the beginning God created the heavens and the earth. Now the earth was formless and empty, darkness was over the surface of the deep, and the Spirit of God was hovering over the waters. And God said, "Let there be light," and there was light. God saw that the light was good, and he separated the light from the darkness. God called the light "day," and the darkness he called "night." And there was evening, and there was morning—the first day.*
>
> (Genesis 1: 1–50)

ONLINE

To understand more about other cultures surrounding the early Jews, go to our Digital Zone at www.brightredbooks.net/subjects.

THE CHARACTERISTICS OF GOD

To understand the nature of God in Christianity, you need to understand the many characteristics of God. The following table lists the attributes most often associated with the Christian God.

Omnipotent	God is all powerful and this is shown in scripture many times, often as the all-powerful **Creator**.
Omniscient	God perfectly and eternally knows all things that can be known, past, present and future. In wisdom He creates all things and orders the Universe. God's wisdom is unlimited.
Omnipresent	God fills the Universe in all its parts and is present everywhere at once. This is true of all three members of the Holy Trinity who are of one substance; where there is one, the others are also there.

contd

Christianity: Beliefs about God

Transcendent	This literally means 'to go beyond' and describes how God surpasses the Universe. God created the Universe but is not dependent upon it. God transcends or stands apart from the Universe.
Eternal	This refers to God's endless past, His unending future and His present experience of all time. God has no beginning as we understand it, nor does He have an end.
Immanent	This literally means 'to remain within' and is used to describe how God never goes beyond Himself, nor does He leave Himself when he comes to us. God is closer to us than we are to ourselves.
Omnibenevolent	God is all loving. His love has no limits or bounds. He loves humanity unconditionally and offers forgiveness for all sins.

TRINITY

We know that Christians are monotheistic and believe in one God, but they also believe he exists in three parts or persons: the Father, the Son and the Holy Spirit, known collectively as the Trinity.

God the Father

Christians believe that God is the creator of everything and that, like a good parent, wants to protect his creation. God as the Father can be explored more by looking at the attributes such as omnibenevolent and transcendent.

God the Son

Christians understand the omnibenevolent nature of God further through the incarnation of Jesus. For Christians, the incarnation shows that Jesus was fully God and fully human. It is an essential part of belief in the Trinity. Through the incarnation of Jesus, humans were able to start repairing their damaged relationship with God.

God the Holy Spirit

This is the power of God at work on the Earth. In the scriptures it is often depicted as wind, fire or in the form of a dove. It is through the power and workings of the Holy Spirit that God is known today, and how Christians can know what God wants them to do.

THE CREED

Key Christian beliefs are highlighted in the Creed, including beliefs about the nature of God. The Creed consists of 12 articles that affirm the **core doctrines of Christianity**, such as the Trinity, the incarnation of Jesus, the crucifixion, resurrection and the ascension of Jesus Christ, the work of the Holy Spirit, sin and salvation, judgement and the world to come.

THINGS TO DO AND THINK ABOUT

1. Sketchnoting as a mind-map is a great way of remembering key knowledge and understanding. It is a mixture of drawings, doodles and text. Create a mind-map of the Trinity; however, instead of just simply writing on the mind-map, sketchnote with some text, drawings and doodles.
2. What do Christians believe about the Nature of God? (10 marks)
3. Explain the relationship between beliefs about the Nature of God and at least one other belief or practice you have studied. (10 marks)

 **DON'T FORGET**

Remember what was said in the answering exam-style questions section. Always use the question as much as possible in your answer. It is good practice to try and start each developed point like this as it will keep what you are writing relevant.

 ONLINE

Go to our Digital Zone at www.brightredbooks.net/subjects when tackling question two in the Things to Do and Think About section to see a version of how a good response starts!

CHRISTIANITY

THE NATURE OF HUMAN BEINGS

HUMANS AS THE IMAGE OF GOD

Christians believes that human beings are the pinnacle of God's creation. Genesis 1: 27 states that mankind was made in the image and likeness of God. This is reflected in **humanity's ability to think, reason and make moral decisions, create, and form relationships.** The image of God is often referred to as *'Imago Dei'*. It sets humanity apart from all other living things and many Christians believe, therefore, that every human person is valued and possesses the dignity of person.

DON'T FORGET

Some Christians believe it is the voice of God guiding them to do the right thing. Christians can develop their conscience by studying the Bible, learning about the teachings of the Church, and following the example of Jesus.

FREE WILL

Christians believe that intellect and free will are gifts from God at the time of creation. This means that people can think for themselves and make decisions using those thoughts. Humans can therefore weigh up decisions as well as evaluate outcomes to make good moral choices. St. Augustine believed that God knew everything, including future events, but humanity still had the freedom to choose which path or direction they were to take. Humans are not robots programmed to act in a certain way, but free persons able to make their own decisions, both good and bad. Christians believe that their moral conscience helps them to make those decisions and that it develops through age, experience, knowledge and understanding what God wants for them.

DON'T FORGET

Christians believe that God sent Jesus to give them the ultimate example of how to have good relationships with each other and with God.

STEWARDS OF CREATION

Stewardship reminds humans that creation does not belong to them, but that humans are responsible for caring for the world. The concept of stewardship provides a framework in which human responsibility for our planet can be understood. In biblical times a steward was the highest-ranking servant, the person who managed the possessions of his master. Stewardship contrasts with human ownership of the world. The stewardship concept reminds Christians that they are the caretakers of God's Earth and it is not for them to corrupt or destroy it.

What does it mean to be a steward of creation?

For Christians, humans have responsibility to care for God's creation but they do not own it. They have been given dominion, which means they are the dominant species, but the world belongs to God.

DON'T FORGET

Find out for yourself what the Bible says about stewardship in these two verses: Genesis 1:28; 2:15.

How might Christians be responsible stewards?

Christians may behave as responsible stewards by showing their concern about global warming. They could be against nuclear weapons and other weapons of mass destruction because of the devasting effect they can have on the planet. They may donate money to a group such as Christian Aid that helps to bring relief to disaster areas of the world.

How might Christians misuse their position of stewardship?

Some Christians might think that having dominion allows them to do what they want with the planet. The Earth's resources are there purely for human consumption. This view justifies exploiting the Earth's resources and justifies harmful behaviour.

SIN

If we consider the nature of human beings as described above, we can see that Christians believe human beings were granted intelligence and decision-making capabilities by God.

contd

Christianity: The Nature of Human Beings

They also believe that humans possess a moral conscience and have free will to choose between good and evil. Christians therefore believe that they were created by God with the ability to obey or disobey. This disobedience is often described as sin.

Genesis 3

Genesis 3 is an account of how sin and death entered the world. Adam and Eve, as the first humans, lost their lives in paradise because of their disobedience of God's commands. God is deemed to have given Adam and Eve all the good things of creation to enjoy. They were given one command by God: not to touch the Tree of the Knowledge of Good and Evil. However, the serpent (Satan) tempts Adam and Eve by telling them they are being denied by God and that they should seek knowledge by eating an apple from the tree. Rather than doing what God has commanded them to do, Adam and Eve exercise their free will by choosing to believe the serpent and eat the fruit.

 **DON'T FORGET**

According to the Oxford English Dictionary, sin is *'an immoral act considered to be a transgression against divine law'*. According to St Augustine, *'sin is any word or deed or thought against the eternal law'*.

Readings of this passage led Christian thinkers to believe that the sin of Adam and Eve meant humanity also lost perfection and innocence. It brought suffering and decay into God's creation. Others have seen the account as a way of explaining disorder and evil in the world because of human failure. The world as we know it, with disease and death, was not the world that God created or intended. This is often referred to as The Fall.

Short-term consequences	Long-term consequences
The serpent had to crawl on its belly.	Suffering and evil entered the world.
Eve experienced pain in childbirth.	Alienation from each other. Adam tries to blame Eve, then blames the serpent. Humans are set against each other and all of creation.
Adam had to work the land.	Alienation from creation.
	The Fall also separates humans from their perfect world. This new, harsh world is clearly in opposition to the perfect environment of Eden created by God.
Adam and Eve were banished from the Garden of Eden.	Alienation from God.
	Being banished from the Garden of Eden meant Adam and Eve became strangers from God. They could only hope for reconciliation brought about by God. Without that move, humanity could not fulfil their purpose to be in relationship with God.

ORIGINAL SIN

Original sin refers to the sin that Adam and Eve committed. Different Church denominations understand original sin differently. Augustine thought that humanity was originally perfect, immortal and blessed with many talents, but then Adam and Eve disobeyed God, and introduced sin and death to the world (Genesis 3:19). Adam had sinned and **all of humanity** had to deal with the consequences. Human beings have thus inherited sin, like a disease, from Adam. The Protestant theologian, John Calvin (1509–64), **agreed** with Augustine. He believed that humanity's unbelief and disobedience had so fundamentally changed humans that little, if anything, of God was left.

 **DON'T FORGET**

The story tells us that this changed human beings so that they were no longer what God made them to be. Their sudden awareness of their nakedness and loss of innocence causes them to try and hide their shame.

Whether Christians believe the historical account of the Genesis story or not, the story of The Fall does serve to provide some Christians with a framework to try and understand human free choice and the connection of all humanity with sin. The root of sin, suffering and death is humanity's wrong moral choices and disobedience. In the New Testament, Christians are shown how the relationship with God was restored. The life and the resurrection of Jesus strengthens the Christian belief that good has overcome evil. The suffering and death of Jesus atoned for this act of original sin and provided the means for recovery from the fallen state.

 **DON'T FORGET**

For many Christians, the root of sin, suffering and death is humanity's wrong moral choices and disobedience.

 THINGS TO DO AND THINK ABOUT

Read Genesis 1 and think about which of the following statements (a) apply to God and (b) apply to humanity, or (c) both:

- Creates the Universe and sees it is good
- Care for the Universe
- Is creative and knowledgeable
- Finds fulfilment in relationship
- Provides for creation
- Is unique
- Has moral conscience
- Has free will

CHRISTIANITY
BELIEFS ABOUT JESUS

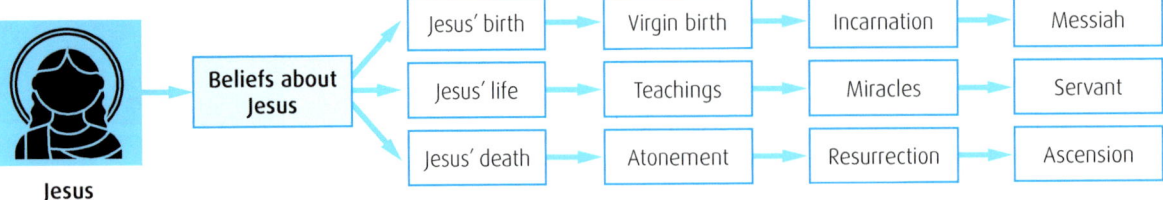

JESUS' BIRTH

The Bible tells us that Jesus was born during the reign of Herod the Great, so rather than the 0 BC that many might assume, it was probably a few years earlier, most likely on or before 4 BC. At that time the Jews were under the rule of the Romans and had to take part in a census, so Mary (the mother of Jesus) and Joseph (his father) travelled from Nazareth to Bethlehem to register their names. When they arrived in Bethlehem there was nowhere for them to stay so they ended up in with the animals and this is where the pregnant Mary gave birth to Jesus. Jesus' birth is a significant event for Christians and we are going to explore a few important beliefs associated with this event: the **Virgin Birth, the Incarnation** and the **Messiah.**

The Virgin Birth

The Virgin Birth is significant as it shows the role that God had to play in Jesus' birth. Christians believe that Jesus was conceived supernaturally, without a human father and only through the miraculous work of the Holy Spirit. This is important as it shows that **the Messiah** (the saviour of all humanity) can only come through God, not humans. Many Christians also believe the Virgin Birth is important because, as Jesus did not have a human father, he did not descend from Adam in the same way the rest of humanity did – so was not affected by **original sin.** Some Christians believe in what is known as the **immaculate conception**, which takes this idea of Jesus being born sinless a little further, explaining that Mary, Jesus' mother, was conceived without sin and therefore her conception was immaculate, so could pass on no sin to Jesus during his birth.

The Incarnation

The Incarnation was explored earlier in this chapter as we developed an understanding of the Holy Trinity. The word incarnate means 'in human form', so Christians understand that although Jesus was born as a human, he was also fully God. This is important as it means Jesus is truly God and truly man. Many Christians believe this to be one of, if not the most amazing miracle in the Bible, that an omnipotent, omniscient God could become a man.

Messiah

Christians believe that Jesus was the Messiah as many of the prophecies or predictions of the Messiah were fulfilled through his birth. One of the most famous comes from the book of Isaiah in the Old Testament: 'Therefore the Lord himself will give you a sign: The virgin will conceive and give birth to a son, and will call him Immanuel' (Isaiah 7: 14). Jesus as **Messiah** is important because he is not only the saviour of the nation of Israel, but the saviour of all humanity as the one who will restore the relationship between humanity and God. Jesus' closest followers also gave him the title of Messiah, a title that Jesus accepted, but asked his followers not to share with others.

JESUS' LIFE

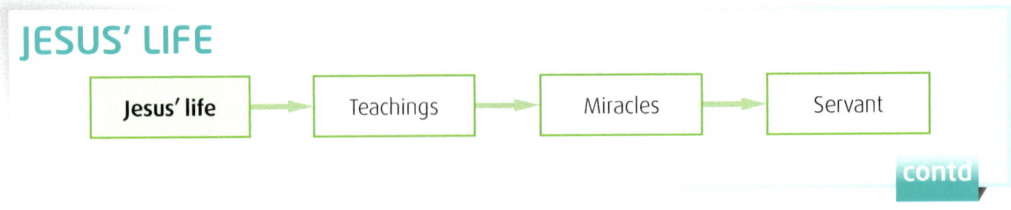

DON'T FORGET

Have a read of Luke 2 verses 1 to 21 for a deeper dive into the story.

DON'T FORGET

The word **Messiah** comes from the Hebrew word 'mashiah'. In Judaism, the idea of the Messiah was a future king who would be the saviour and deliver the nation of Israel from its oppressors.

contd

Christianity: Beliefs about Jesus

Little is known about Jesus between his birth and his adult years. One story in Luke 2 tells of how a 12-year-old Jesus was found in the temple in Jerusalem. Jesus was sitting with the teachers, listening to them and asking them questions. Everyone who heard Jesus speak was amazed at his understanding of the scriptures. This was an early glimpse into the teacher he would become. Most of what the Bible tells us about Jesus' life comes from his adult ministry when he was in his thirties.

Teachings

The **teachings** of Jesus come in different forms, many of which are found in the Gospels. Jesus interpreted Old Testament scriptures, gave summaries, told stories, asked questions and used parables. Jesus' teachings are important because not only did they carry **authority** for their original listeners, but they also do for Christians today. Following Jesus' teachings also has significance for Christians regarding the afterlife and entry to heaven.

Miracles

During Jesus' lifetime he carried out many **miracles**. Christians believe miracles are extraordinary events that cannot be explained by natural means or scientific evidence, but supernatural events that are the work of God. Miracles are important as they reinforce that Jesus was divine and fully God in human form. The Gospels record more than 30 miracles performed by Jesus. Many of these miracles show Jesus healing people, and this is important for Christians today as highlights the importance of showing **compassion** towards others.

Servant

A final belief Christians have about the life of Jesus was how he lived as a **servant**. Jesus explains the importance of this himself in the Gospel of Matthew: 'whoever wants to become great among you must be your servant, and whoever wants to be first must be your slave, just as the Son of Man did not come to be served, but to serve, and to give his life as a ransom for many' (Matthew 20: 26–28). This belief about Jesus is important for Christians as **it is a revolutionary concept**. Greatness is often associated with importance, power and wealth, yet Jesus' life seems to turn this idea on its head as he taught that true greatness comes from a willingness to serve and care for others.

> **DON'T FORGET**
>
> Christians today believe that Jesus' teaching is a **moral guide**, which provides instructions on how they should treat others and engage with the world around them.

THINGS TO DO AND THINK ABOUT

Beliefs about Jesus spotlight – part one. There are nine key beliefs about Jesus highlighted in this topic and the next. In this topic there are three beliefs about his birth and three beliefs about his life. Take a page of A4 paper and put one belief in the middle of the page. Then, starting around the outside of the page, create five large boxes. Move clockwise around the boxes, answering these tasks:

- Write a definition of the belief.
- Use the belief in a sentence.
- Draw a picture to illustrate the belief.
- List other words or beliefs connected to yours.
- Write a question where your key belief is the answer.

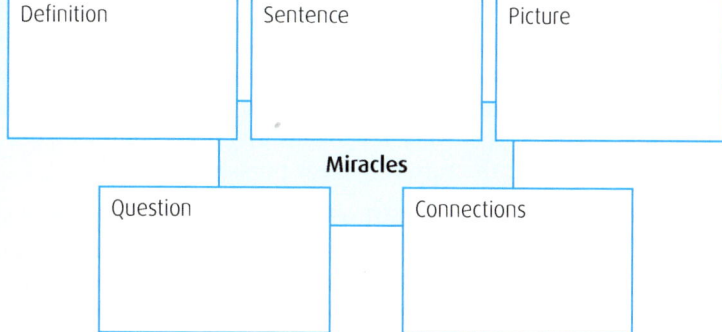

Repeat this for each of the beliefs on this spread.

CHRISTIANITY
JESUS' DEATH

THE ULTIMATE SACRIFICE

Jesus' death → Atonement → Resurrection → Ascension

Jesus' ultimate act of service for his followers was shown through his death. Christians remember the events surrounding Jesus' death during Holy Week. The significant events in the week leading up to Easter Sunday are

- Jesus' entry into Jerusalem during Palm Sunday (Luke 19: 28–40).
- the Passover meal and Jesus washing the disciples' feet (John 13).
- Jesus is betrayed and arrested in Gethsemane (Matthew 26: 36–56).
- Jesus is tried before Pilate (Matthew 27: 11–26).
- Jesus is crucified (Luke 23: 26–43).
- Jesus dies and is buried on what is known as Good Friday (Luke 23: 44–56).

ATONEMENT

One belief surrounding the death of Jesus is that of **atonement**. The term atonement comes from the phrase 'at one' and means to make amends, to reconcile or restore things to how they should be. It is an important belief for Christians as it highlights the connection between Jesus' death and the ability to be at one with God.

There are, however, many different theories regarding atonement. Many Christians, specifically those from reformed or Protestant denominations, believe in the **penal substitution view of atonement**. This explains that humans deserve God's wrath because of their sin, but Jesus died on the cross as a sacrifice for humans, taking the punishment and paying for or 'atoning' for the sins that separate humans from God.

This penal substitution view of atonement is a development and slightly different view of atonement than that which is held by the Catholic Church. Catholic theology argues for the **satisfaction theory of atonement**; it is somewhat similar to the penal substitution view, but the major difference is that while it explains that Jesus suffers on our behalf, it does not go on to elaborate that the suffering is for punishment.

Another view on atonement is **the moral influence theory**, which explains that the death of Jesus showed God's love for human beings, and as humans respond by loving God, we become forgiven. The big difference with this view compared with the other two is that it does not propose that Jesus died to remove humans from God's wrath, rather that humans are forgiven by loving God.

Christianity: Jesus' death

RESURRECTION

The **Resurrection** of Jesus is the belief that after his death and burial Jesus rose from the dead. Early on the Sunday morning after Jesus' death a group of women visited the tomb. When they arrived, they found the stone that covered the grave had been rolled away and the tomb was empty. Two men appeared in shining white clothes and explained to the women that Jesus had risen from the dead. The resurrection of Jesus is important to Christians as **it is a sign of God's power**. The resurrection of Jesus shows that sin and death have been defeated. Jesus' resurrection ensures a future hope for humanity, as the apostle Peter explains in his writings in the New Testament, 'we have been given new birth into a living hope through the resurrection of Jesus Christ from the dead' (1 Peter 1: 3).

ASCENSION

Christians also believe in Jesus' **ascension**. Forty days after Jesus' resurrection he ascended to heaven in front of his followers. The ascension is important to Christians as Jesus now returns to heaven, to sit at the right hand of God the Father after completing his mission on Earth. Jesus' ascension gives Christians hope of their future ascension to heaven, as he promised that he would one day return to bring them to heaven. John 14: 2–3 state: 'My Father's house has many rooms; if that were not so, would I have told you that I am going there to prepare a place for you? And if I go and prepare a place for you, I will come back and take you to be with me, that you also may be where I am.'

 ## THINGS TO DO AND THINK ABOUT

Beliefs about Jesus spotlight – part two. There are three key beliefs about Jesus highlighted about the death of Jesus in this topic. Take a page of A4 paper and put one belief in the middle of the page, then starting around the outside of the page create five large boxes, then move clockwise answering these tasks in the boxes.

- Write a definition of the belief.
- Use the belief in a sentence.
- Draw a picture to illustrate the belief.
- List other words or beliefs connected to yours.
- Write a question where your key belief is the answer.

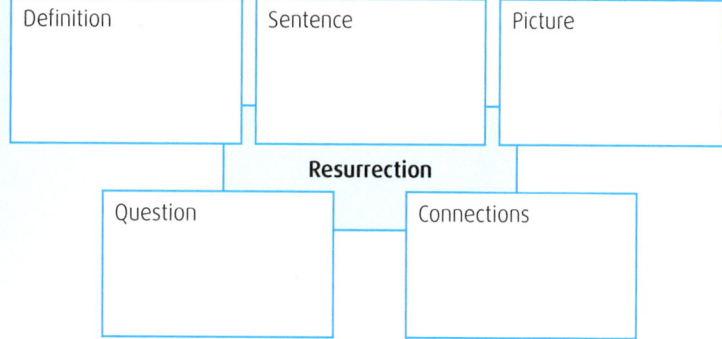

Repeat this for each of the beliefs.

41

CHRISTIANITY

JUDGEMENT: HEAVEN AND HELL

WHAT IS JUDGEMENT?

Christians believe that everyone will at some point face a final judgement. The Bible tells us that both God and Jesus (remember the concept of the Holy Trinity here) will act as the judge during this process, which will involve rewarding those who have obeyed God's laws and punishing those who have disobeyed God's laws. The Bible describes this final judgement in the Book of Revelation: 'And I saw the dead, great and small, standing before the throne, and books were opened. Another book was opened, which is the book of life. The dead were judged according to what they had done as recorded in the books.' (Revelation 20: 11–15).

WHY JUDGEMENT IS IMPORTANT FOR CHRISTIANS

Christians believe that the final judgement is important for a number of reasons.

Justice will take place

You may have heard the saying 'Life is not fair'. The Bible, however, paints a different picture, and with the idea of the final judgement shows a Universe that is fair as God is in control and will, in the end, judge those who have done wrong, as the apostle Paul states in Colossians 3: 25: 'Anyone who does wrong will be repaid for their wrongs, and there is no favouritism'.

Incentive for morally good behaviour

Christians believe that one day God will judge their actions. If they want an eternal reward for their actions they will want to be judged favourably by God, so will want to live a morally good and righteous life. Jesus explains the importance of 'storing up for yourselves treasures in heaven' in Matthew 6: 20.

Makes it easier to forgive others

Many Christians believe that because God or Jesus will assume the position of judge, then they do not have to. There is no need to take revenge for someone's wrongdoing because God will judge them for their actions. The book of Romans in the Bible explains this, as it says 'Do not take revenge, my dear friends, but leave room for God's wrath, for it is written: "It is mine to avenge; I will repay," says the Lord.'

Motivation for sharing their faith

We will explore Heaven and Hell later in this chapter but Christians believe that those who are judged favourably by God will spend eternity with him in Heaven. Those, however, who are judged unfavourably will perish in Hell. This means that Christians will want to share their faith with others so that their eternal destiny is in Heaven with God.

HEAVEN AND HELL

Christians believe in the afterlife. This means that whenever someone dies on Earth, the physical body will decay but the soul (the non-physical, spiritual part of a human) will live on for eternity. As explained earlier in the chapter, God will act as the judge and His decision will determine whether that eternity is spent in Heaven or Hell.

Heaven

The Bible defines the word Heaven in three different ways:

1. The literal sky above our heads.
2. The place where God lives.
3. The place where those who obey God and follow Jesus will spend eternity.

contd

Christianity: Judgement: Heaven and Hell

Heaven is the ultimate goal for all Christians, where they will be reunited with God and Jesus after death. There is debate among Christians as to whether Heaven is a place or a state of mind. The lack of empirical evidence has been a reason for many to doubt that it is an actual place.

There are passages in the Bible that suggest **it is a place**. We have already looked at Jesus' ascension, which explains that 40 days after Jesus' resurrection, Jesus was lifted up while in the presence of his followers and a cloud took him out of their sight to Heaven. One of the most famous prayers in the Bible, The Lord's Prayer, starts with the line, 'Our Father, who art in heaven', signifying that Heaven is the place where God lives. In the Gospel of John, Jesus is quite clear that Heaven is a place, as he says to his disciples: 'My Father's house has many rooms; if that were not so, would I have told you that I am going there to prepare a place for you?' (John 14: 3). The first verses in the Bible in the book of Genesis also appear to suggest it is a place, as it explains 'In the beginning God created the heaven and the earth'. (Genesis 1).

Quite recently, however, Pope Benedict explained that Heaven **was not a place** in the Universe, but rather a concept that as humans we would struggle to define; he said, 'by the term "Heaven" we are not referring to somewhere in the Universe, to a star or such like; no. We mean something far greater and far more difficult to define with our limited human conceptions.' (Holy Mass on the solemnity of the assumption of the blessed Virgin Mary; Castel Gandolfo, 2010.)

DON'T FORGET

Some Christians have a different understanding and believe that there are **two different Heavens**. There is the present Heaven, an intermediate state, where a Christian goes when they die. Then there will be 'the new heavens and the new earth' (Revelation 21) that will come into being after the final judgement when Jesus comes to Earth again, in what some Christians call the second coming.

Hell

The most common understanding of Hell is a place of eternal suffering, darkness and death, which is often associated with an image of fire. The teachings of Jesus in the Gospels regularly refer to Hell as a place of punishment and separation from God.

There are **two parables** in the Bible that give some more insight into Heaven and Hell: the **Parable of the Sheep and the Goats** and the **Parable of the Rich Man and Lazarus**.

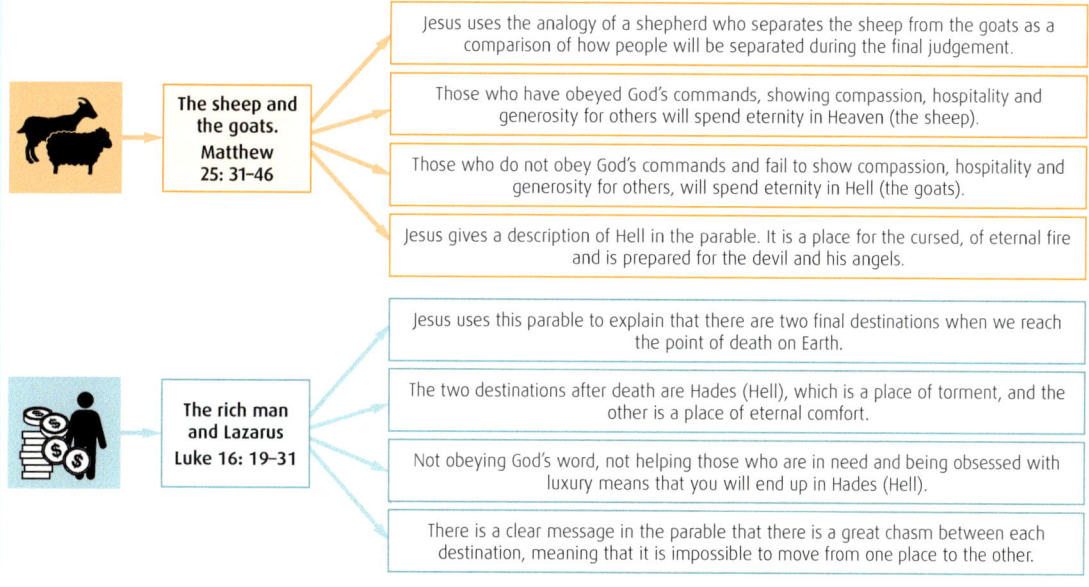

THINGS TO DO AND THINK ABOUT

1. Exam-style questions:
   - 'Analyse the importance of Christian beliefs about judgement' (10 marks)
   - 'Evaluate the significance of Christian beliefs about Heaven and Hell' (20 marks)

2. Have a closer look at the two parables above, the Parable of the Sheep and the Goats and the Parable of the Rich Man and Lazarus. Read the stories from the Bible then use a six-grid storyboard to describe each story. Leave your storyboards for a day, then come back to them, and on a separate page:
   - Use your storyboards to write a summary of each parable.
   - Use your written summary to explain what the parables teach about Heaven and Hell.

Practices

CHRISTIANITY
LIVING ACCORDING TO THE GOSPELS

The Gospels are the first four books of the New Testament in the Bible: Matthew, Mark, Luke and John. These four books record almost everything that is known about Jesus and include his teachings that Christians follow to live a life that is pleasing to God. The word 'gospel' translates as good news: the good news about Jesus Christ. The central message of Jesus' teaching in the Gospels is **the Kingdom of God**. This kingdom should not be understood as a physical realm, but as a time when God's power and authority became visible through Jesus' life and ministry, and his teachings showing how kingdom citizens should live their lives.

PARABLES

Parables were one of the teaching methods that Jesus used in the Gospels. They are short simple stories that need interpretation and are used to teach important moral or spiritual lessons. Parables were used by Jesus to engage, challenge and instruct his listeners. Let us take a closer look at a few parables and what they say about how people should live.

The Parable of the Good Samaritan

This parable can be found in Luke 10: 25–37. A short summary of the parable goes like this: a Jewish man was travelling between Jerusalem and Jericho and was robbed and badly beaten up on the way. A priest and then a Levite (a priest's assistant) walked by and left him. A Samaritan (Samaritans and Jews are seen as enemies) saw the Jew, bandaged him up, helped him to an inn, paid for his stay and looked after him. Jesus told this parable so his followers would:
- Show compassion towards everyone.
- Love their enemies.
- Show generosity to others.
- Treat others the way you would want to be treated.

The Parable of the Lost Sheep

This parable can be found in Luke 15: 4–7. A short summary of the parable goes like this: someone has 100 sheep; he loses one of them, then leaves the other 99 sheep to go and look for it. He finds the lost sheep and rejoices with all his friends and neighbours. Jesus told this parable so his followers would:
- Understand Jesus' love and compassion for them.
- Realise everyone was important to Jesus.
- Know that God forgives and rejoices when humans choose to be forgiven.

The Parable of the Rich Fool

This parable can be found in Luke 12: 16–21. A short summary of the parable goes like this: a rich man had an exceptionally large harvest. He wanted to keep all his crops so he tore down his barns and built bigger ones. He thought he was set up for many years, that he would be able to take life easy, eat, drink and be merry. But that very night he lost his life and so he did not get to enjoy everything that he kept for himself. Jesus told this parable so his followers would:
- Beware of being greedy.
- Understand generosity.

THE SERMON ON THE MOUNT

For many Christians the Sermon on the Mount is Jesus' most influential section of teaching in the Gospels. It is found in chapters 5, 6 and 7 of Matthew's Gospel. Saint Augustine, one of the most significant early Church fathers, said 'I think that he will find in it, so far as regards the highest morals, a perfect standard of the Christian life' (Augustine, On the Sermon on the Mount).

contd

Christianity: Living according to the Gospels

The Beatitudes

The Beatitudes are sayings of Jesus that introduce the Sermon on the Mount, and they highlight how Jesus' followers should engage with others and the world they live in. Let us explore a selection of these:

- **Blessed are the meek** – The word meek can be seen here as gentle or submissive. This complements Jesus' example of being a servant and submitting to the will of others; Jesus also calls his followers to serve others.
- **Blessed are the merciful** – Treating others with mercy means showing them compassion whenever they are in suffering or distress. Jesus expects his suffers to show compassion and love to all humanity.
- **Blessed are the peacemakers** – Christians are called by Jesus to be peacemakers, to actively resolve conflict.

KEY TEACHINGS FROM THE SERMON ON THE MOUNT

Be Salt and Light

Jesus said you are the 'You are the Salt of the earth' (Matthew 5: v. 13). It might seem like a strange thing for Jesus to say, but two of salt's properties are to preserve and enhance the flavour of the food it comes into contact with. Many Christians interpret this passage to mean that they are called by Jesus to preserve the good in the world so that it does not spoil or become corrupted by evil, as well as to enhance the lives of others. Jesus also said, 'You are the Light of the world' (Matthew 5: v. 14). Many Christians interpret this to mean that, as Jesus' followers, they should bring light to the darkness and light the way for others.

Bring Peace

Jesus said that 'anyone who is angry with a brother or sister will be subject to judgement' (Matthew 5: v. 22). In this part of the Sermon on the Mount, Jesus was explaining that in the Old Testament it teaches that if you 'take someone's life' you would be subject to judgement. He goes a step further in these verses and says even **being angry is enough to face God's judgement**; instead, Christians are called to bring peace.

Show Forgiveness

Again, Jesus explains a familiar Old Testament teaching, which states 'an eye for an eye and a tooth for a tooth'. This is interpreted as people should be punished in the same way that they offended, or that if someone wrongs you then you seek revenge. Jesus contradicts this teaching by saying 'If anyone slaps you on the right cheek, turn to them the other cheek also'. (Matthew 5: v. 39). **Instead of seeking revenge a Christian should show forgiveness.**

Love your Enemies

This one is straightforward. Jesus said, 'You have heard that it was said, "Love your neighbour and hate your enemy". But I tell you, **love your enemies** and pray for those who persecute you, that you may be children of your Father in heaven.' (Matthew 5: 43–45)

DON'T FORGET

It is worthwhile taking time to read through all three chapters of the Sermon on the Mount in Matthew's Gospel. They conntain a few of the key messages that can be chosen regarding how a Christian should live their life.

THINGS TO DO AND THINK ABOUT

1. This chapter highlights some key messages from the Sermon on the Mount regarding how Jesus instructs Christians to live. Read through Matthew chapters 5, 6 and 7 and create a mind-map of all the different ways Jesus highlights for Christians to live.

2. Answer these exam-style questions:
   'Analyse the purpose of living according to the Gospels' (10 marks)
   'Evaluate the significance of living according to the Gospels' (20 marks)

3. This chapter has explored how Jesus teaches his followers to live by looking at parables and the Sermon on the Mount. Jesus also taught others how to live by his actions. Read the following passages and pick out the key messages or teachings from Jesus on how to live as a Christian.
   - John 8: 1–11
   - John 13: 1–17

CHRISTIANITY

CHRISTIAN ACTION: THE CHRISTIAN COMMUNITY

WHAT IS CHRISTIAN ACTION?

Christian action is living the life of a Christian. A simple definition is **doing** something when the intentions (the **why** you do it) come from Christian beliefs, values or example. A very simple definition is **doing what Jesus did or what God has told you to do**.

EXAMPLES OF CHRISTIAN ACTION

We have learnt about who Jesus was and what he taught. Two of the major themes that have been identified are Jesus' **'service to others'** and his teachings around **'love and compassion'**. Let us explore some examples of how the Church and Christians try to follow this example and teaching today through Christian action.

Challenging inequality

Genesis 1: 27 states 'So God created mankind in his own image, in the image of God he created them; male and female he created them'. The New Testament of the Bible also says 'There is neither Jew nor Gentile, neither slave nor free, nor is there male and female, for you are all one in Christ Jesus' (Galatians 3: 28). Many Christians believe that humanity has been created in the image of God, and all are equal through God; therefore, all humanity should be treated equally. The world however is full of **inequality** and this **needs to be challenged**.

Christian Aid is a Christian organisation that challenges inequality. One area of their work is to work alongside governments and influence policy. In 2015, Christian Aid worked alongside the vice president of Zambia to produce and enact the Gender Equity and Equality Act of 2015. They also work in many countries supporting women to be treated equally, giving them greater influence in their homes and communities.

Ensuring Justice

In Matthew 11: 42, Jesus challenges the Pharisees for 'neglecting the love and justice of God'. Jesus challenges his followers to make sure that people are treated fairly, so Christians fight against injustice in the world. **The Catholic Agency For Overseas Development (CAFOD)** is one Christian organisation that campaigns for a fairer world. A recent campaign run by **CAFOD** is to help fix the global food system; they believe the food system is broken and smaller farmers are being treated unfairly. CAFOD are campaigning to protect the rights of farmers and challenging laws that could threaten their ability to provide for their families and communities.

Tackling Poverty

Giving to the poor is a theme that runs throughout the Old Testament scriptures and is something that is important to Jesus in the New Testament. In the Sermon on the Mount in Matthew 6, Jesus gives a clear message to his followers to give to the needy. Jesus also spoke these words when talking to the Pharisees in Luke's Gospel: 'when you give a banquet, invite the poor, the crippled, the lame, the blind, and you will be blessed. Although they cannot repay you, you will be repaid at the resurrection of the righteous.' (Luke 14: 13–14). **Tearfund** is a Christian charity that works alongside partners and churches to address the issue of poverty in more thanr 50 countries. Tearfund tackles poverty during disasters and conflict, they engage in community development and also advocate and influence on issues of poverty and injustice at a local, national and global levels. Many Christians will **volunteer and give of their time** for Tearfund and other organisations doing similar work.

ONLINE

You can read more about their projects and how Christians can challenge inequality by clicking the link to their website on the Digital Zone, www.brightredbooks.net

ONLINE

This is just one example of how Christians attempt to ensure justice in our world; you can find out more by clicking the link on our Digital Zone, www.brightredbooks.net

DON'T FORGET

This type of volunteering, often known as short-term mission, allows Christians who have regular jobs opportunities to act as Jesus did or in the way that God has instructed.

Christianity: Christian action: the Christian community

Praying

Many Christians believe that prayer is a way in which they can communicate with God and ask Him to intervene. This specific type of prayer that focuses on the needs of others is known as intercessory prayer and is a type of Christian action.

Giving/donating

We have explored a number of Christian organisations in this chapter but to support these charities and ensure that their work can be carried out, many Christians donate to them financially. This also allows Christians who may not be able to act physically to still play their part in serving and loving others.

CHRISTIAN COMMUNITY

Churches across Scotland and across the world have many expressions of Christian community as part of their offer of 'being' or 'doing' church. The church service itself allows Christians to gather together, but we will explore this further in the next chapter when we look at corporate worship. Churches also run many activities during the week that bring people together. These include community cafes, toddler groups, youth groups, warm spaces, choirs, music groups and language classes.

Young people in Scotland can take part in Christian organisations that meet weekly or frequently. The **Boys Brigade** and **Girls Brigade** are two good examples. Both of these Christian organisations value and seek to build community, organising activities and opening up spaces that have a focus on building friendships and developing relationships. Many of these groups also provide other opportunities to create community, such as sports teams, residential weekends away and summer camps

The Iona Community has centres on the islands of Iona and Mull that offer spaces to be part of a Christian community. When visiting these centres, time is spent exploring faith, taking part in creative activities and having discussions over meals. Community is also expressed through communal living.

Taize is a **monastic fraternity** (a brotherhood for men who live separately in a community to focus on spiritual development) based in Burgundy in France. It is also an **ecumenical** community, which means that it attempts to bring all denominations of Christian churches together. While many brothers (monks) live on site, thousands of Christians from across the world visit to experience Christian community each year.

The New Testament of the Bible uses a specific word to help us understand Christian community and it is the Greek word 'koinonia' - or in English, 'fellowship'. Fellowship can be understood as relationships among Christians based on their shared beliefs and actions; these relationships are fostered by spending time together or meeting up with each other.

Summer and Easter are busy times for Taize meetings; these meetings are usually week-long events where Christians (predominantly aged 17-35 years) gather to deepen their Christian faith through community prayer, singing, meditation and sharing with others.

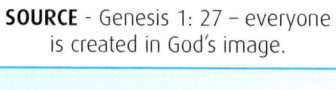 THINGS TO DO AND THINK ABOUT

1. Looking at examples of Christian action, take the text and turn it into a diagram that highlights the **source, belief and action**. The first one has been started as an example.

   SOURCE - Genesis 1: 27 – everyone is created in God's image.

   SOURCE - Galatians 2: 28 – all are one in Jesus Christ.

   BELIEF - Christians should challenge inequality.

   ACTION - Organisations like Christian Aid work alongside governments to influence policies so people are treated as equals.

2. Explore some other organisations that work alongside the Church to serve others and show care and compassion. What does each believe, where do their beliefs come from, and what type of Christian action is each involved in?
   - Scottish Catholic International Aid Fund (SCIAF)
   - CrossReach
   - AMOR Ministries
   - Eagles Wings Dundee
   - Caritas Social Action Network

3. Acts 2: 42–47 is one of the first expressions of the Christian Church as a community. Create a mind-map that illustrates some of the things they did that helped build that Christian community.

CHRISTIANITY

WORSHIP: PRAYER AND THE EUCHARIST

Christian worship is defined as the devotion that is given to God (or the Holy Trinity). **Individual worship** is carried out by the worshipper on their own and **community worship** occurs when two or more Christians gather. Christian worship can involve many different activities, such as singing songs of praise, meditation, prayer and the Eucharist. The two types of worship we will examine in detail as part of the Higher course are prayer and the Eucharist.

PRAYER

Prayer comes in many different forms; you can **pray individually** or you can **pray in a group** (community). Prayers can take seconds or last for hours. Some Christians pray with their eyes open, some close their eyes to avoid distraction, others read prayers out loud and some write prayers down. Despite all of the different forms that prayers can take, all types of prayer have one thing in common: **it is a time for Christians to talk and listen as they communicate and develop their relationship with God**.

The Lord's prayer

In the Gospels (Luke 11: 1–13) we read that the disciples had been watching Jesus as he prayed. After Jesus had finished, one of his disciples came to him and asked him how *they* should pray. What Jesus taught them has since become known as 'the Lord's Prayer'. There are two accounts in the Gospels found in Matthew 6 and Luke 11. The Lord's prayer is recited by Christians all over the world. **It is significant for Christians** as **they can meditate on the words and teachings of Jesus** as they read and speak it. It is also useful as it **gives Christians a pattern to follow** as they pray.

 DON'T FORGET

The Lord's Prayer
Our Father in heaven,
hallowed be your name,
your kingdom come,
your will be done,
on earth as in heaven.
Give us today our daily bread.
Forgive us our sins
as we forgive those who sin against us.
Lead us not into temptation
but deliver us from evil.
For the kingdom, the power, and the glory are yours
now and for ever.
Amen.

(Contemporary version, Church of England)

WHY IS PRAYER IMPORTANT?

We learned earlier that prayer is important for Christians because it allows them to communicate and develop their relationship with God. Let us explore some elements of prayer that highlight how important this practice is for Christians. These four elements make up the acronym ACTS and is a popular model of prayer that has been around for some time.

A – Adoration: Adoration is praising God for who He is – note the difference between this and thanking God for what he has done (Thanksgiving). Giving adoration in prayer allows Christians the opportunity to remember that God's divine nature is wonderful in itself. God deserves his followers' love and respect, simply for who He is and they should recognise that as they pray.

C – Confession: Confession in prayer is a Christian admitting to God that they have sinned against him and they require his forgiveness. The Bible says in John 1: 9, 'If we confess our sins, he is faithful and just and will forgive us our sins and purify us from all unrighteousness'. There is a slight doctrinal difference here between some denominations of the Christian Church as while some believe they can ask God directly to forgive their sins through Jesus, others such as the Catholic Church may express sorrow for sin through prayer (**contrition rather than confession**), then would use the sacrament of confession to ask for God's forgiveness in the presence of a priest.

T – Thanksgiving: Prayer allows Christians to give thanks to God for the things that He has done in their lives.

S – Supplication: Supplication means asking for things, either for yourself or for others. Prayer allows Christians to ask God to meet their needs and to meet the needs of others. This ties in with Christian action, praying for those in poverty, war, and those who are ill.

 **DON'T FORGET**

This is sometimes known as 'intercessory prayer'.

Christianity: Worship: Prayer and the Eucharist

EUCHARIST

The word Eucharist comes from the Greek word 'Eucharistia', which translates as 'thanksgiving', and is an event that takes place in most Christian churches allowing followers to give thanks for the death of Jesus Christ. It is known by different names across different denominations and is sometimes referred to as Communion, Holy Communion and the Lord's Supper.

There are some Christian churches that do not celebrate Communion. Quakers believe all of life is a sacrament and should not be limited to a specific time or event throughout the week. The Salvation Army also do not practise communion as traditionally wine is used and the Salvation Army believe this could be counterproductive for any alcoholics in their congregations. They also acknowledge the disagreements between other denominations regarding the Eucharist so choose not to practise it themselves. There are also variances in how often Eucharist/Communion takes place. In some Roman Catholic churches it can be daily; Anglican churches such as the Scottish Episcopal Church and many Baptist churches celebrate it weekly; the Church of Scotland celebrate it three or four times a year.

WHAT IS THE EUCHARIST?

The biblical basis for the Eucharist comes from the Last Supper, a meal that Jesus had with his disciples on Passover (a very significant Jewish festival) in the week before his death. The three synoptic Gospels (Matthew, Mark and Luke) all record the event. Jesus met with his disciples, took bread and wine and he blessed it, explaining that the bread was his body and the wine was the blood of the covenant, which would be poured out for the forgiveness of sins. Jesus told the disciples to eat and drink in remembrance of him. The next day Jesus was taken and crucified.

In churches today, Eucharist/Communion services differ depending on the denomination; however, there will often be prayers, scripture reading and songs or music. The bread and wine often sit front and centre of the church on a table and are usually handed out by the Priest or Minister (and in some churches also Elders and Deacons).

WHY IS THE EUCHARIST IMPORTANT?

For many Christians taking part in the Eucharist/Communion, this is their most important act of worship. What is remembered during this act is the new covenant Jesus spoke of during the last supper, and it is very significant, as it is the promise that God makes with humanity, explaining that **He will forgive sin** for those that believe in his Son Jesus Christ. The elements taken during a Eucharist or Communion service remind Christians of **the sacrifice that Jesus made for humanity**. The bread is symbolic of Jesus' body broken on the cross and the wine is symbolic of Jesus' blood, which will wash away the sins of those who believe in him, and in turn **restore the relationship** between a Christian and God.

The Eucharist/Communion is also important for Christians as it reminds congregations of their shared identity as God's people. It reminds Christians that they are part of a community – communion is taken with others and some denominations drink the wine at the same moment together, while others drink from the same cup to symbolise this.

 ## THINGS TO DO AND THINK ABOUT

1. Read through the Lord's Prayer as printed in this chapter. What type of things are being prayed for? How could this prayer be used as a pattern for Christians to create other prayers? (Asking for forgiveness, etc.).
2. Attempt these two exam-style questions:
   - Evaluate the importance of prayer (20 marks)
   - Evaluate the significance of the Eucharist (20 marks)

MORALITY AND JUSTICE

UNDERSTANDING MORAL ISSUES

USING THE CRAVE FRAMEWORK TO EXPLORE MORAL ISSUES.

Higher RMPS allows schools and pupils to choose one moral issues topic from five different topics. Regardless of the topic you choose there are four key things that will help you to be successful:

- A solid knowledge and understanding of the **topics**.
- In-depth knowledge and understanding of **the moral issues raised by those topics**.
- Being able to **analyse the religious and non-religious responses** to those moral issues.
- Being able to **evaluate the religious and non-religious responses** to those moral issues.

This chapter and the next will give you the knowledge and understanding needed for the *Morality and justice* and *Morality, medicine and the human body* topics. Once you have a solid grasp of the topics you explore the moral issues raised by them. The CRAVE framework (let's just call it CRAVE) will help support you to explore the moral issues encountered.

One of the reasons RMPS is so valuable as a subject is because life is ever changing. As we interact with the world around us, one of the most difficult challenges we face is deciding what is right and wrong. RMPS helps us to explore that.

This is where CRAVE comes in. A way to remember it is by asking the question: 'Can I CRAVE to make the right decision?' Each of the letters acts as a filter to help you explore moral issues raised by the topics and decide what might be right and what might be wrong. Have a look at the flow diagram below and see if you can follow the process.

C - Consequences **R** - Rights **A** - Autonomy **V** - Virtue **E** - Everyone else	If we determined the impact of these five filters on the actions or situations, we can begin to suggest or define moral issues that might be raised.

The E for 'everyone else' comes in twice when using the CRAVE framework. For an issue to be considered a moral issue, it must generate different beliefs or opinions after the issues that arise go through the CRAVE filter. Thus they are moral issues, not just matters that arise. If different beliefs or opinions don't arise, then it's just an issue, not a moral issue.

Actions or situations are areas that create moral issues for consideration. Examples would be war, IVF, the environment, etc.

An important issue or subject that arises from an action or situation. Moral issues bring about a discussion or argument because different beliefs or opinions arise.

An Example of a Moral Issue - Rights of the child

If the action or situation is 'saviour siblings' and we put it through the CRAVE framework focusing on R - rights, we can suggest that a moral issue is the rights of the child being born as a Saviour Sibling. We can confirm the issue as a moral issue with contrasting viewpoints (E). A Utilitarian might agree that the rights of the saviour sibling might be compromised as it is for the greater good for all concerned, whereas some Christians (those without issue in the IVF process to even get this far) might argue that as all life is made in God's image it deserves to be treated equally and fairly and not as a commodity which takes away rights.

A CLOSER LOOK AT THE FIVE CRAVE FILTERS

C: Consequences

A consequence is an effect or result that might happen because of a particular action or situation. As an example, if we think about In Vitro Fertilisation (IVF), a consequence of the procedure is that there will be leftover embryos. There are different views regarding these embryos, which allows us to reason that this consequence is actually a moral issue.

R: Rights

Human rights are highly relevant when it comes to deciding on moral issues. Read through the Universal Declaration of Human Rights and familiarise yourself with them (there are 30 in total). Throughout the topics, rights relevant to that area are picked out. These rights try to promote a common good; however, there are often conflicts of opinion regarding certain rights or the *consequences* of upholding certain rights.

contd

Morality and Justice: Understanding moral issues

A: Autonomy

The word autonomy comes from two Greek words, *auto* meaning self and *nomos* meaning rule. Having autonomy is the ability to control your own decisions. Any action that is going to be taken is decided by yourself.

V: Virtue

The word virtue means morally good. In certain situations you may do what you think is the morally good thing and assume that this is the best action to take. However, when weighed up against consequences, rules or laws this may not always be the case, and so a moral issue will follow.

E: Everyone else

This is possibly the most straightforward way of determining moral issues. If there is a conflict in opinion between how everyone else might approach a particular action or situation, then this issue is a moral issue. Everyone else might include religious viewpoints, non-religious viewpoints, the law and other systems of ethics.

EXPLORING DIFFERENT RELIGIOUS VIEWPOINTS

When it comes to religious viewpoints, moral values are constructed upon religious beliefs and many of those religious beliefs come from sacred writings or sacred texts. Religious viewpoints can be complex. Many sacred scriptures were originally written in ancient languages, which means that they need to be translated in order to be understood. There may also be different interpretations of the texts, different teachings of religious leaders, or different cultures and traditions. This can mean that there are many similarities, but also differences of opinion within religious viewpoints. When using religious viewpoints at Higher RMPS level it is good to start thinking about these similarities and differences. Saying all Christians or Buddhists is usually quite inaccurate, and it is important to say many or some. It is even better if you can talk about the tradition or denomination a viewpoint comes from such as Theravada Buddhists or The Roman Catholic Church.

NON-RELIGIOUS VIEWPOINTS

In non-religious viewpoints, sometimes known as secular viewpoints, moral values are usually constructed upon reason, concern for others and scientific thinking.

Utilitarianism – a philosophical principle that can help us explore making moral decisions based on consequences. The main thinking behind Utilitarianism is what we call *the principle of utility*, which states that actions are right if they promote happiness or pleasure and wrong if they produce unhappiness or pain. Utilitarians believe that when making moral decisions, we should do what brings the greatest happiness to the greatest number of people.

Kantian ethics – in order to consider whether something is right you have to use reason and consideration for others. Actions are morally right or wrong based on a set of rules or principles and not their consequences. Kant used categorical imperatives which are commands that you have to follow regardless of your desires. They are moral obligations and are based on reason. In simple terms a morally good act is one that can become a universal law.

THINGS TO DO AND THINK ABOUT

1. Use the CRAVE framework to identify moral issues for the topics you are studying.
2. Using Dual Coding, which we explored in our study techniques section, create:
    - a diagram that shows how a religious person might make a moral decision;
    - a diagram that illustrates how a non-religious person might reach a moral decision.

DON'T FORGET

In Vitro Fertilisation is a medical procedure whereby an egg is fertilized by sperm in a test tube or elsewhere outside the body.

DON'T FORGET

CRAVE is there as a guide; there may be other things that help pick out moral issues from actions or situations, but it is a good place to start.

DON'T FORGET

Some of the CRAVE filters can work together. This is highlighted in the section on Rights, where it is noted that the moral issue might come about because of the consequences of upholding certain rights. Have a closer look at the framework and see if you can pick out some moral issues for the topic you are studying at Higher level.

DON'T FORGET

Another thing to remember about the distinction between an issue and a moral issue is that a moral issue generates different opinions or viewpoints about the issue, which is why the 'E' appears twice in the CRAVE framework.

DON'T FORGET

To explore the Utilitarian viewpoint in more detail have a look at the differences between Act, Rule and Preference Utilitarianism.

Causes of crime

MORALITY AND JUSTICE

ENVIRONMENTAL INFLUENCES

In Higher RMPS, the causes of crime are referred to as either environmental influences or psychological factors. Some examples of **environmental** causes of crime are:

1. Poverty
2. Upbringing and Adverse Childhood Experiences (ACEs)
3. Peer pressure

POVERTY

Poverty on its own is unlikely to lead to criminal behaviour; rather, it is usually a combination of factors. In association with other factors, individuals may be propelled towards crime. Those who live in poverty have far fewer options open to them in life. People living in an impoverished area with a low income may also be more likely to have fewer qualifications, which leads to fewer job opportunities. Entrenched poverty results in high levels of inequality, which has links not only to property crime, but also to violent crime.

Those most likely to be affected by crime are the poorest in society. The University of Edinburgh's School of Law found that those living in deprived communities are most likely to be affected by crime, despite the overall drop in crime over the last 10 years. They found that half of the communities with the highest crime rates are in the top 20% of areas with the highest level of chronic health issues. In addition, one-third of the communities with the highest rates of crime are in the top 20% of areas with the highest levels of unemployment. This reinforces the idea that the causes of crime can be complex and contributing factors are rarely isolated.

What are the moral issues raised by poverty as a cause of crime?

Inequality in society – research by the University of Edinburgh's School of Law suggests that poverty which leads to criminality points to inequalities in society. It could be argued that those who commit crime out of need rather than greed should be supported and treated with compassion, rather than judged and condemned. Others may argue that because not all poor people resort to crime, then criminality is very much still a choice. They may go further and argue that communities where crime is higher, should take responsibility for this and work to improve their area.

Broken systems – many would argue that a society where poor people are more likely to commit crimes shows that the systems are not working as they should be. They might argue that there should be a redistribution of wealth through taxes and spending to end poverty once and for all. As part of this, there might be a fairer benefits system for those who are unable to work or who work in low-income employment. Making those changes should ensure that fewer people turn to crime and live happier, more fulfilled lives as a result. However, others might argue that raising taxes is unfair on those who have worked hard to get a well-paid job and live a comfortable life. They may argue that it is not the responsibility of the wealthier sections of society to pay for the poor, that the poor must be willing to work hard to climb out of poverty.

DON'T FORGET

Because the victims of crime are far more likely to live in impoverished areas, it might suggest that not enough is being done for all members of society, which impacts unfairly on their health and life opportunities.

UPBRINGING AND ADVERSE CHILDHOOD EXPERIENCES

One environmental cause of crime is upbringing, in particular Adverse Childhood Experiences (ACEs). This is where your upbringing and experiences influence the choices you make, particularly in relation to crime. An ACE can be any one of several things, such as domestic violence, a parent with a mental health problem, parental abandonment through separation or divorce, a parent in prison, being the victim of abuse (emotional, physical or sexual), a parent with substance abuse issues and being the victim of neglect (physical or emotional).

Determinists believe that we are less governed by free will and are more influenced by the internal and external factors we are exposed to. This argument is supported by data that shows 25% of the prison population are care experienced, with 53% of young men who

ONLINE

A great resource for researching ACEs is the Public Health Scotland website. Click the link on our Digital Zone - www.brightredbooks.net/subjects - to find out more.

contd

Morality and Justice: Environmental Influences

are in prison having been permanently excluded from school. This suggests that those who have adverse childhood experiences are more likely to commit criminal acts and face custodial sentences.

The Welsh ACEs Study (Public Health Wales, 2015) found that those with 4+ ACEs were 15 times more likely to be a perpetrator of violence in the previous 12 months and 20 times more likely to face a custodial sentence in their lives. This is caused by prolonged exposure to stress in childhood, which affects healthy brain development. This can cause behavioural problems and risk taking in childhood and criminal behaviours in adulthood.

What are the moral issues raised by upbringing/ACEs as a cause of crime?

Not all people who experience a poor upbringing commit crime – it is true to say that while statistically those who face multiple ACEs are more likely to commit crime, most do not. Some might deduce from this that a poor upbringing/ACEs is merely an excuse for those who make a choice to commit acts of crime. They may argue that they fail to take responsibility for their actions, but rather blame events in their past – looking backwards rather than forwards. However, those who disagree with this view would argue that the link between ACEs and criminality is well known and that we need a more compassionate and trauma-informed approach towards children, young people and adults affected by those experiences.

A need for compassion – Scotland is well on its way to becoming an ACE Aware Nation. This means taking a trauma-informed approach, where instead of asking a vulnerable individual, 'What's wrong with you?', instead we ask, 'What happened to you?' Many would argue that, by taking a more compassionate approach, public services can work together to identify what protective factors can buffer the effects of childhood trauma. In doing so, this will enable those children to reach their true potential and live more fulfilled lives, and in turn reduce crime and victimisation. However, there are many who see this as a soft-touch approach that removes personal accountability and excuses criminal behaviour.

PEER PRESSURE

Another environmental cause of crime is peer pressure. This is when the people a person socialises with have a direct impact on the way they behave. Young people may find themselves drawn into gang culture as a means of helping them carve out their own identity, or perhaps just to survive in the community they live in.

What are the moral issues raised by peer pressure as a cause of crime?

Many might say that no one really makes you do anything, you make that choice for yourself. Some might argue that being able to stand up to your peers is an important part of becoming an adult. However, there are many who would point out that not all children and young people have the self-esteem and self-belief to have the confidence to stand out from their peer group. For some, this may be the only group they feel accepted and included in. There may also be an element of 'grooming' behaviour by older peers in the group, where young people are groomed into criminal behaviours to benefit the leaders of the gang.

Lack of opportunities for young people mean many would argue that it's hardly any wonder young people are peer pressured into crime when so few opportunities for achievement exist for them. These opportunities may be in the form of extracurricular activities, which are inaccessible by some young people because of their cost and the level of parental commitment required. The subsequent feelings of exclusion, some would argue, make young people more susceptible to peer pressure and gang culture. However, there are others who would disagree and argue that all young people have opportunities through education, both in the classroom and through extracurricular activities.

THINGS TO DO AND THINK ABOUT

Summarise what you have learned about environmental causes of crime. It might be helpful to use headings to organise your notes, e.g., description of cause; moral issues; responses. How has what you learned made you feel about environmental causes of crime? What would you share with someone else about the discussion?

DON'T FORGET

This source highlights that once we know the links between ACEs, stress responses and behaviours, not only can we plan to target support towards families who need it the most, but we can encourage public services to work collaboratively to build protective factors for children and young people suffering from trauma.

DON'T FORGET

Some might also express concern about the costs associated with those types of approach in a climate where budgets to public services are being cut. They might question any type of investment in terms of the impact it has on children and young people who are not experiencing ACEs, but who still need opportunities to fulfil their potential.

DON'T FORGET

The brain development of a teenager means they are prone to risk-taking behaviour, and potentially poor judgement which can lead to criminality. Peer pressure on its own is unlikely to lead to serious crime, but combined with other factors, it may lead to violent crime and subsequently a prison sentence.

DON'T FORGET

The Pupil Equity Fund and Scottish Attainment Challenge are publicly funded initiatives in education designed to close the attainment gap between the least and the most economically disadvantaged. As a part of these initiatives, resources are targeted at the most economically disadvantaged young people to improve their educational outcomes and increase inclusion, weakening the first line of argument.

MORALITY AND JUSTICE
RELIGIOUS AND NON-RELIGIOUS RESPONSES

Many religions show concern about the moral issues identified by the different aspects of environmental causes of crime. We will explore some Christian responses here.

POVERTY

Source 1
'Give justice to the weak and fatherless; maintain the right of the afflicted and destitute.'
Psalm 82:3

Meaning: Humans have an innate sense of right and wrong gifted by God, and our desire for justice is synonymous to being Christian. It is the duty of every Christian to fight for, and protect, the vulnerable in our society.

Source 2
'When the obsession with possessing and dominating excludes millions of people from primary goods; when economic and technological inequality is such as to tear the social fabric; and when addiction to unlimited material progress threatens the common home, then we cannot stand by...'
Pope Francis

Meaning: We live in a materialistic, consumerist world where possessions are valued above all else, and our desire to continually gain more blinds us to the plight of those who go without. This obsession divides us, taking away our humanity; it is the duty of Christians to make a stand against it.

Give justice to the weak - Source 1

For most Christians, belief in social justice is at the very core of their religious values. Many Christians see **inequality in society** as a call to action to work to address the unfairness in society and redress the balance, which would in turn reduce crime. This comes from their belief in human dignity, belief in the sanctity of life and belief that all people deserve opportunities to prosper. Other Christians might respond to say criminality is always immoral and is representative of people who have chosen to misuse the free will gifted to them by God. They might argue that we must shift our focus to the victims of crime, who are vulnerable and in need of support.

DON'T FORGET

Social justice is a belief that all people should have equal opportunity to wealth, health, privileges and opportunities.

We cannot stand by - Source 2

Many Christians believe that we should all work together to ensure that the systems in society work for the benefit of all, in particular the vulnerable and needy. Where **systems are broken,** it becomes their social responsibility to take actions to fix them. By using their voices and taking action, Christians embody what it is to be made in God's image. Some other Christians may not support this. This may be because they aren't Catholic, and don't hold the Pope as a moral authority, or it may be because they believe we should trust our democratically elected leaders to fund and operate public services as they see fit, perhaps believing that the state and church should not mix.

UPBRINGING AND ADVERSE CHILDHOOD EXPERIENCES

DON'T FORGET

Christians might also be concerned and feel compassion for the victims of crime as well, and would not want them to be forgotten about.

Source 1
'Behold, children are a gift of the Lord, the fruit of the womb is a reward.'
Psalm 127:3

Meaning: Children are a gift from God and should be treated with dignity and respect. They should not be treated as an inconvenience but treated with the compassion afforded to them as God's creation.

Source 2
'Compassion allows you to see reality; compassion is like the lens of the heart: it allows us to take in and understand the true dimensions. In the Gospels, Jesus is often moved by compassion. And compassion is also the language of God...'
Pope Francis

contd

Morality and Justice: Religious and non-Religious Responses

Meaning: Compassion is the language of God, while indifference is the language of man. It is part of the human struggle to be able to see the world through the lens of compassion, but it is only then that true understanding is achieved.

Children are a gift from God – Source 1

Most Christians view children as a gift from God. That children would endure trauma is a moral concern for Christians and there are many examples of Christian charities who campaign to bring about equity and social justice for children. Most Christians wouldn't want to be drawn into discussions that **not all people who experience a poor upbringing commit crime** as it generalises and doesn't take account of individual circumstances.

Pope Francis on compassion – Source 2

Many Christians would want compassion to be a cornerstone of any decision-making by policymakers and would support a more compassionate approach to people who have experienced ACEs. By adopting compassion, they grow into their relationship with God and understand more fully their God-given purpose to make a positive difference in the world.

DON'T FORGET

The YMCA provides a mentoring service working with young people on the verge of entering the criminal justice system and it has successfully reduced reoffending rates.

PEER PRESSURE

Source 1

'The YMCA is an inclusive Christian youth organisation, open to people of all faiths and none. We work to transform the lives of children and young people, empowering them to create positive change in their lives and communities.' www.ymca.scot

Meaning: In the mission statement of the YMCA, the inclusive nature of their work is highlighted. In addition to this, it is emphasised that the charity doesn't fix the problems of young people, but gives them the tools to become more resilient.

ONLINE

To investigate humanism more, click the link on our Digital Zone at www.brightredbooks.net/subjects

ONLINE

You can find out more about RORI by clinking the link on our Digital Zone – www.brightredbooks.net/subjects

YMCA – Source 1

Many Christians acknowledge the pressures young people face to conform and belong.
The YMCA sees those pressures and actively seeks solutions to support young people in making better choices. They create opportunities for young people to be successful, improving their self-esteem and confidence. They are committed to broadening the horizons of young people and giving them a safe space where their voices can be heard.

NON-RELIGIOUS RESPONSES

Humanists believe that understanding the causes of crime is important because once we know what they are, we can begin to work together to address them. Humanists don't believe in an intrinsically good or bad 'human nature', but rather that our behaviour is shaped by biological and social factors. There's evidence that more crime is committed in very unequal societies by disadvantaged groups who are discriminated against. These include people who suffer from mental illness, addiction and poverty. Most criminals are young men from the lower socio-economic groups, and many are unemployed. Of course, most people from deprived backgrounds are law-abiding, and privileged individuals have caused some of the most damaging crimes to society. But overall, the evidence shows that societies with a strong healthcare and support system have less crime. A Humanist would suggest that we look at what we can do to improve the quality of life of people who feel they have little to lose by committing a crime.

Reducing Offending, Reducing Inequality (RORI)

Public Health Scotland's 'Reducing Offending, Reducing Inequality' (RORI) promotes a collaborative and cohesive approach between health and justice. RORI identifies and influences effective practice for better outcomes for vulnerable groups of society, such as those affected by poverty and ACEs. RORI believes that the solution to addressing the causes of crime is to take an early-intervention approach, that is trauma-informed and compassionate.

THINGS TO DO AND THINK ABOUT

Go online and watch the Panorama documentary *How Scotland Cut Violent Crime*. Make some notes on:

- What are some of the main responses to tackling the causes of crime in Scotland?
- How effective do you think those responses are? Give reasons for your viewpoint.
- Do you think this would be an effective approach to crime if applied nationwide across the UK? Explain your answer.

MORALITY AND JUSTICE

PSYCHOLOGICAL FACTORS

Psychological factors can be split into two aspects:
1. Addiction
2. Mental Health

ADDICTION

There are different types of addiction, some of which may increase the likelihood of criminality. Those who are addicted to alcohol are more likely to be prone to violent behaviours. Alcohol Focus Scotland found that 42% of violent crime was alcohol-related, while the Prisoner Survey found that two in five prisoners reported being drunk at the time of their offence. While it is not clear if those individuals had an alcohol addiction, it suggests an unhealthy relationship with alcohol and its misuse, leading to violent crime. In Scotland, alcohol misuse is recognised as a public health problem, with clear cost implications for health and justice.

Addiction to drugs can often lead to crime. Drugs impair the ability to think logically and act rationally, sometimes leading to criminality. Drug possession is in itself an offence. However, those addicted to drugs are prone to other crimes, such as stealing. Sociologist Colin Bell commented that drug abuse is 'above all, a deeply entrenched social problem with serious consequences for public health and justice.'

What are the moral issues raised by addiction as a cause of crime?

Addiction is often symptomatic of trauma

Many of those who experience addiction have experienced adverse childhood experiences or trauma in their adult lives. Where the feelings associated with the traumatic event are not processed, they may self-medicate with alcohol or drugs. Trauma expert Suzanne Zeedyk says, 'Drug use comes from addiction, and addiction comes out of trying to meet the needs of a body to self-soothe… Rather than recommending immediate fixes, we need to get fiercely curious.' This source suggests that drugs are used by adults who cannot self-regulate their emotions, nor manage their mental pain.

It is still a choice

There are many who would argue that substance abuse fundamentally remains a choice. Some may even go so far as to say that those choices are based on selfish impulses and a failure to put family before their own personal gain.

ONLINE

You can find out a lot more about Mind at their website. Click the link on our Digital Zone – www.brightredbooks/net/subjects – to explore more.

MENTAL HEALTH

There has been a great deal of research exploring links between mental health and crime. Victim Support and the charity Mind found that those with mental health conditions, rather than being the perpetrators of crime, are five times more likely than the general population to be the victims of assault (this increases 10-fold for females).

There are, however, some links between more serious mental illnesses and violent crime. One forensic psychiatrist, Dr Das, speaks of his experience of working in secure psychiatric hospitals. He says, 'Sufferers of schizophrenia typically experience paranoid delusions; common forms include the unshakeable belief that others are watching, following, laughing at or even wishing to kill the sufferer. If you were trapped on a psychiatric ward and genuinely believed your life was in danger, pre-emptive violence might arguably be a very sane choice.' This source suggests that symptoms of illnesses like schizophrenia may cause the sufferer to become violent out of fear for their own safety.

What are the moral issues raised by mental health as a cause of crime?

Underfunding of mental health services

Many would argue that mental illness should never lead to crime as those suffering should receive treatment. Following a Freedom of Information Request, the party leader of the Liberal Democrats revealed that one young person in NHS Grampian waited almost seven years for their treatment to begin with Child and Adolescent Mental Health Services (CAMHs). This raises questions about the escalation of mental health issues among children and young people, especially when they are left untreated for so long.

DON'T FORGET

It is generally accepted that mental health is inextricably tangled up with other drivers of crime, such as substance abuse and trauma, and so can be difficult to identify as a cause of crime all on its own.

contd

Furthermore, because poor mental health often arises as a result of other factors, such as trauma and adversity, funding needs to be carefully allocated considering all the factors, taking a holistic approach whenever possible.

Failures to support those with mental health issues in the justice system

The Criminal Justice Joint Inspection for England and Wales reported that thousands of people come into the justice system each year but with their needs missed at every stage. It reported failings in the sharing of information between agencies, meaning that offenders were not given the support they needed. People with mental health conditions are over-represented in the prison system.

RELIGIOUS RESPONSES

Many religions show concern about the moral issues identified by the different aspects of psychological causes of crime. We will explore some Christian responses below.

Addiction

Source
'Do not get drunk on wine.'   Ephesians 5:18
Meaning: Alcohol can lead to recklessness and poor decision-making; anything with the power to harm or control an individual needs to be handled with care.

Mental health

Source
The Church teaches that every human life is sacrosanct, and while we are each a unique individual, our shared likeness in the image of God shows that we also have bonds of reciprocity which spur us to strive for a common humanity. In the same way, our mental health is both an individual and a shared issue.   catholicsocialthought.org.uk

Meaning: Every life is meaningful and has inherent value. As we are made in the image of God, we have a responsibility to respond positively to others and develop our sense of humanity. Mental health issues are a burden that should not be borne alone but shared.

While Christians are conscious of the impact that substance use may have on behaviour and morality, many would also be sympathetic towards those experiencing addiction. Many Christians recognise the impact of adversity and trauma and the relationship this has with addiction, poor mental health and criminality.

NON-RELIGIOUS RESPONSES

One non-religious response to the moral issues arising from psychological causes of crime comes from the Scottish Government's Justice in Scotland: Vision and Priorities.

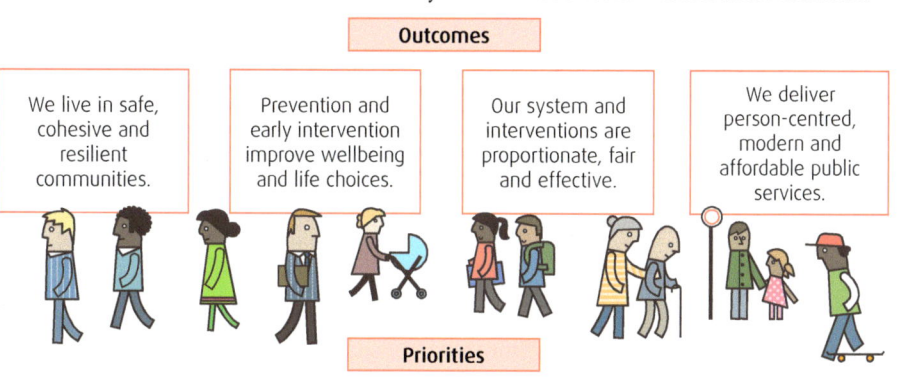

ONLINE

You can read more about this response on our Digital Zone at www.brightredbooks.net/subjects

Part of the vision for Scotland's justice system is to 'work with others to improve health and wellbeing in justice settings, focusing on mental health and substance use'. This proposes a more cohesive approach with better collaboration and information sharing with other agencies. It is indicative of a move in justice approaches to focus on intervention and creating a fairer and more resilient society that benefits everybody.

THINGS TO DO AND THINK ABOUT

1. Working with a classmate, create a chart in your jotter split into two columns – the first headed *Confident* and the second *Work to do*

Confident	Work to do!

Complete the list and consider how are you going to address your areas for improvement? Make a plan and stick to it.

Purposes of Punishment

MORALITY AND JUSTICE

REFORMATION

There are four main purposes of punishment that we will look at one by one in the following pages:

1. Reformation
2. Retribution
3. Protection
4. Deterrence

ONLINE

You can read more about the work of Turning Point by clicking the link on our Digital Zone - www.brightredbooks.net/subjects.

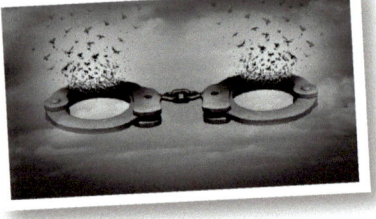

DON'T FORGET

Others may argue that a focus on reformation provides opportunities for offenders to truly change and be afforded opportunities that they may previously have missed out on.

REFORMATION

Reformation is one purpose of punishment that seeks to show the offender the error of their ways and offer them opportunities to change. This could be through counselling, or even restorative meetings with their victim, or the family of their victim. Restorative justice would allow the offender to hear first-hand the impact of their crime, take responsibility and repair the harm caused by their crime. An evaluation of Glasgow's youth restorative justice services found that 56% of those contacted took part in a restorative process and levels of satisfaction among those who participated were high. Reformative punishment may involve a programme of rehabilitation, which allows the offender to learn new skills, broadening their horizons and providing opportunities to survive which don't involve crime. This could be part of a prison sentence, or a community sentence like a Community Payback Order.

An example of a partnership between the justice system and a charity, with a focus on reformation, is Turning Point Scotland, who take a person-centred approach to all areas of social justice. In relation to offending, they 'have worked in partnership with NHSGGC, Glasgow courts, criminal justice teams, community addiction teams and voluntary sector organisations to break the cycle of offending which results in the "revolving door" syndrome of people maintaining their involvement in the justice system and prison service'.

WHAT ARE THE MORAL ISSUES RAISED BY REFORMATION AS A PURPOSE OF PUNISHMENT?

Too soft an approach

Some might argue that reformation is not punitive enough and goes too softly on the offender. In turn, this could mean that the victim, or the family of the victim, feel that justice has not been served, which could cause them to lose faith in the justice system. Furthermore, if the offender is not punished severely enough, it may lead to them committing further crimes as there is no real deterrent in place. A consequence of this is a much less safe society for us all to live in.

It is expensive

The Howard League estimates the cost of reformation, with 14% (£60.8 million) being spent on rehabilitation and 16% (£66.7 million) being spent on reintegration services to support prisoners moving back into the community. There are many who would argue that this is a high cost in the face of reoffending levels, which the Scottish Government in 2020 estimated to be at 26.3% for the 2017–2018 offender cohort. However, while this appears to be a high number of individuals reoffending, the Scottish Government reports this to be at an all-time low, suggesting that there is some merit in rehabilitation.

RELIGIOUS VIEWS ON MORAL ISSUES ARISING FROM REFORMATION

Source

'If a person foolishly does me wrong, I will return to him the protection of my boundless love. The more evil that comes from him the more good will go from me. I will always give off only the fragrance of goodness.'

The Buddha

Morality and Justice: Reformation

Meaning: If considered in the context of reformation, this source could be interpreted to mean that hateful acts should be met with compassion and love. Forgiveness should be sought and given at all costs. This suggests that reformation should be pursued and that no individual should be punished excessively with no way back.

Buddhists believe that extreme or inhumane punishment of an offender does not achieve anything and the most morally acceptable of all purposes of punishment is reformation, and so would not agree that reformation is *too soft an approach*. Buddhists would not support more punitive approaches as they believe punishment should only be enough to allow the offender to make right their wrongs. Furthermore, they would be less concerned with the *cost* as they believe that rehabilitation, both within their sentence and back into society, must be a priority. Buddhists believe that anyone can change; this can be exemplified by Siddhattha himself transforming from a partying prince to a devout holy man.

NON-RELIGIOUS VIEWS ON MORAL ISSUES ARISING FROM REFORMATION

Utilitarians would likely favour reformation because it saves one more person from becoming a criminal and transforms them into a productive law-abiding citizen. Rehabilitation means an individual has gone through a process where they no longer want to commit or be involved in crime. While Utilitarians favour deterrence as a purpose of punishment, reformation is preferable to individual deterrence as this means a criminal is simply afraid to commit the crime(s) again.

In relation to the belief that reformation is *too soft an option*, Utilitarians might disagree. Jeremy Bentham said that punishment could not be justified when its costs outweighed its benefits. The costs of punishment include the evil of coercion, restraint, apprehension (the pain of the person) and sympathy (the pain others experience out of concern for the one punished). These costs must be weighed against the benefits of punishment, and include the degree of the offence, the number of offences, the likelihood of repeat offences (or of deterring future offences) and the displeasure of the people who are aware of the crime. Where reformation reduces repeat offences or minimises suffering, Utilitarians would favour this and be satisfied with the nature of the punishment with rehabilitation at its centre.

In relation to the belief that reformation is *too expensive an option*, Utilitarians would perhaps draw on the principle of utility: that the moral thing to do is whatever brings about the greatest happiness and least amount of suffering for the greatest number of people. If investment into punishments with reformation as their focus meant cuts to other public services, Utilitarians might disagree with their use. For example, where this impacted on health and education, the cost would need to be offset and weighed up to determine its efficacy.

> **DON'T FORGET**
>
> Utilitarianism is a belief that actions are right if they are useful for the benefit of a majority.

> **DON'T FORGET**
>
> Utilitarians would also want to consider the long-term consequences; if investment into rehabilitation meant a safer and more crime-free society, they would very much support this cost.

THINGS TO DO AND THINK ABOUT

Create a revision bookmark or know-it-all sheet like the examples below that you can use to help consolidate your learning on reformation as a purpose of punishment.

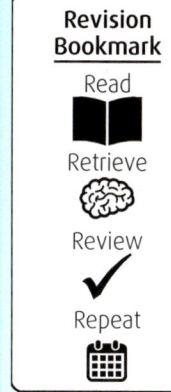
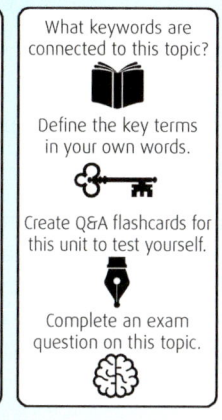
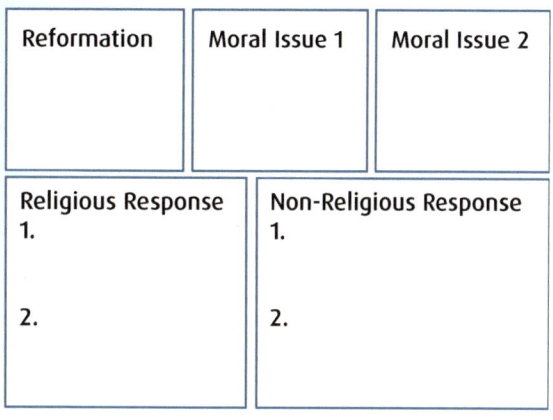

MORALITY AND JUSTICE
RETRIBUTION

WHAT IS RETRIBUTION?

Retribution as a purpose of punishment can be understood as exercising a punishment that makes the offender pay for what they have done wrong. There will inevitably be suffering for the individual being punished, with the punishment being proportionate to the crime. Those who favour retribution believe that it meets the needs of victims and gives assurances to wider society that adequate punishment will be given to those who break the law. This can restore faith and trust in the justice system and its efficacy.

While it could be argued that some types of sentences in Scotland have an element of retribution, Scotland's justice system is not retributive in nature. The Scottish Government has committed to ensuring consistent, quality restorative justice is available across Scotland by 2023. They are led by research around the world that evidences lower rates of reoffending for offenders who engage in this process and higher rates of satisfaction among victims.

DON'T FORGET

An example of a retributive punishment is the death penalty, where someone is executed for taking the life of another. Some argue that this restores balance and brings comfort to the family of the victim.

ONLINE

Go online to our Digital Zone at www.brightredbooks.net/subjects to view a map of the world showing countries that apply the death penalty.

WHAT ARE THE MORAL ISSUES RAISED BY RETRIBUTION AS A PURPOSE OF PUNISHMENT?

Retribution is unsophisticated and uncivilised

Many would argue that retributive punishment holds no place in a civilised society. They might say that it is reactive and takes no account of the underlying factors that drive individuals to crime. A factor like poverty may be beyond a person's control, and therefore further punishing someone who has faced adversity or suffered from a loss of opportunity can be viewed as cruel and disproportionate. A consequence of this may be that the punishment leads to an unequal and inequitable society, which is divisive and resentful.

It offers little opportunity for reformation

With a strong focus on punishment that might be harsh and disproportionate to the crime, many would argue that there is no room for reformation. By nature, retributive punishments do not build on opportunities for reformation. For example, capital punishment is the most retributive of all punishments. In condemning the offender to death, there are no second chances; no possibility of learning new skills to rehabilitate to a crime-free life after release. Many would argue that this marks a society lacking in compassion and regressive in outlook. A consequence of this is that it rubs off on individuals, with people believing that some lives are disposable, with some people mattering and others not. Others would disagree, arguing that punishment can be retributive and still offer opportunities for reformation.

DON'T FORGET

There are some who would argue that rather than being unsophisticated and uncivilised, retribution sends a clear message that serious crimes will be dealt with seriously. Justice is therefore served to victims and their families and may empower them, bringing back the value taken at the point of crime.

DON'T FORGET

In Scotland, those given the longest of life sentences would still have opportunities to participate in rehabilitative programmes – even when their sentence means never returning to outside society.

RELIGIOUS RESPONSES TO THE MORAL ISSUES RAISED BY RETRIBUTION

Source

'Eye for eye, tooth for tooth, hand for hand, foot for foot, burning for burning, wound for wound...'

Exodus 21:24

Meaning: Many Christians interpret this source to justify retributive punishments, that one act deserves a punishment of an equivalent measure. Other Christians might look at the context of the society in which it was originally written. At that time, society was violent and could even be lawless. Some theologians believe the source could be intended to act as a deterrent to would-be criminals, rather than as a guide for punishment.

contd

Morality and Justice: Retribution

Christians might respond to the idea that retribution is unsophisticated and uncivilised in different ways. If they interpreted the Exodus source literally then they would disagree. They could argue that the Bible is inspired by God's word and if it is written in the Bible then it must be taken with reverence and followed accordingly. They may argue that this sends a clear message concerning the sanctity of life and that God believes those who commit the most serious crime of murder should have retribution exacted upon them with a matching punishment.

There are other Christians who would look at this source then remind people that Jesus himself said, 'You have heard that it was said, "Eye for eye, and tooth for tooth". But I tell you, do not resist an evil person. If anyone slaps you on the right cheek, turn to them the other cheek also.' (Matthew 5:38-39) This source could be interpreted to suggest that injury should not be met with injury. This may be considered in the context of Jesus's teachings on forgiveness; that we are all better than our worst acts and deserve second chances.

In terms of retribution offering little opportunity for reformation, Christians may show concern. Jesus taught that we are all capable of change and that even the worst of sinners can transform their lives. This is evident through the work of many Christian organisations that work with offenders and ex-offenders. Prison Fellowship Scotland work in prisons offering hope to inmates. They believe that 'nobody is beyond redemption, believing in transformation' and work with offenders in many ways. One way in which they demonstrate their Christian values is through their restorative justice initiative, The Sycamore Tree. This encourages accountability for actions and encourages offenders to see the impact of their crime on the victims.

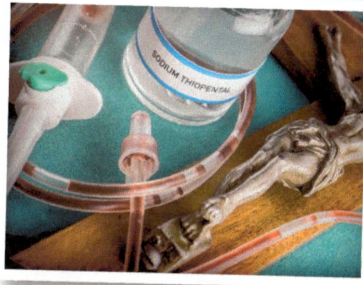

NON-RELIGIOUS RESPONSES TO THE MORAL ISSUES ARISING FROM RETRIBUTION

Humanists generally would disagree with retributive punishment and would be concerned with the moral issues raised by it.

Many Humanists would feel that revenge would not be likely to lead to a better outcome for all parties apart from perhaps the temporary satisfaction for the victim. They would note that not all crimes committed are meant and not every criminal is entirely responsible for their actions or crimes. They would point to the role of social factors too and that these should be taken into account when punishment or retribution is being considered.

With this in mind, it is probable that Humanists would be concerned about the type of society we would become if we only sought retributive punishments. Humanists understand that offenders are influenced by environmental and psychological factors that can pull them towards crime, reducing their culpability, which, in turn, should impact on the type of punishment we give.

> **DON'T FORGET**
>
> Many Christians believe that Jesus's death means there is always a way back to God with true repentance and faith.

> **ONLINE**
>
> For more on the Humanist approach to punishment, click the link on our Digital Zone at www.brightredbooks.net/subjects

> **DON'T FORGET**
>
> Humanists favour reformation and would be concerned where a punishment was overly harsh, with retribution as its goal, leaving little opportunity for rehabilitation.

THINGS TO DO AND THINK ABOUT

Create a mind map like the one below using the sub-headers to guide you.

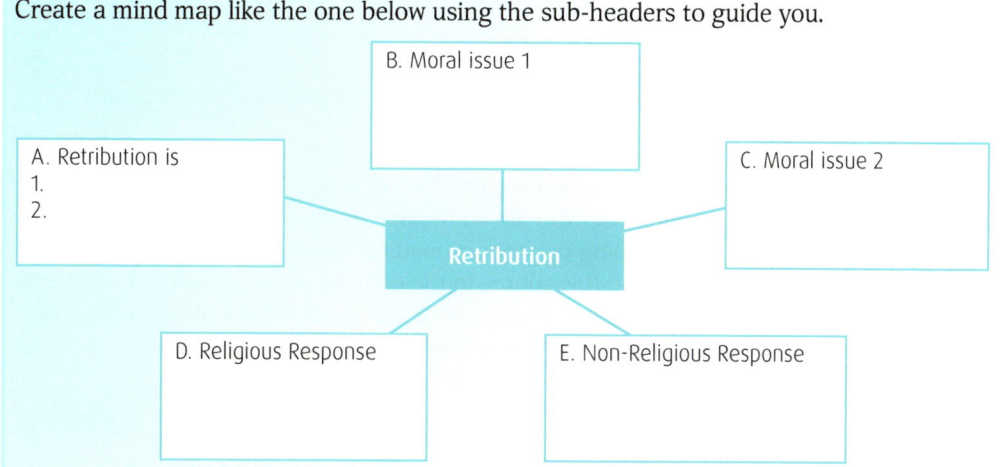

MORALITY AND JUSTICE
PROTECTION

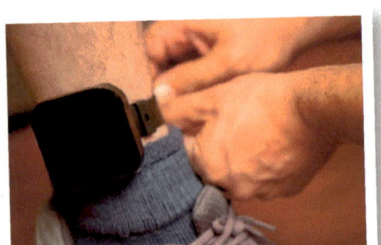

PROTECTION OF WHOM?

When sentences are passed for the purpose of protecting society, they aim to keep order and ensure that citizens are safe. One example of this is a custodial sentence. When the offender is confined to prison, wider society is protected from their criminal behaviours. This protection may extend to the offender himself who, when incarcerated, cannot offend, hurting themselves or others in the process.

Most sentences in Scotland carry an element of protection. An example of this is electronic tagging. Electronic tagging ensures that society is protected by enforcing a curfew on the offender to restrict when they can be out. Tagging sometimes also places restrictions on those areas where an offender is allowed to be. This is especially true in the case of domestic violence offenders, making sure the victim of the crime is protected from being approached or contacted.

WHAT ARE THE MORAL ISSUES RAISED BY PROTECTION AS A PURPOSE OF PUNISHMENT?

Protection only lasts for as long as the sentence

One moral issue arising from protection is that it is only effective for as long as the sentence lasts. When the offender is released, society may be at risk again. This is supported by the high recidivism rates in Scotland, where one in four offenders reoffends after their release from prison. This might suggest that protection is only effective when combined with investment in rehabilitation. If the cause of the crime has not been targeted, the protective benefits of prison become negligible.

DON'T FORGET

Recidivism is a word used to describe the tendency of a convicted criminal to reoffend.

Protection of the offender

One moral issue arising from protection is that prisons can be dangerous places with prisoners being subject to attack and harm. This is particularly true for those committing the most heinous of crimes, such as the murder of children; those offenders are repeatedly targeted and often left with life-changing and life-threatening injuries. Society has been protected from any potential future crimes they may have committed, but they themselves are not protected from the violent intent of other prisoners. However, many would argue that this is not an issue in itself. Offenders who come under attack are simply living with the consequences of their actions. Some might argue that this is little more than they deserve after the crimes they have committed and the harm they have inflicted.

RELIGIOUS RESPONSES TO THE MORAL ISSUES ARISING FROM PROTECTION

Source

'Defend the weak and the fatherless; uphold the cause of the poor and oppressed.'

Psalm 82:3

Meaning: Christians may interpret this source in different ways. They would certainly be concerned about protecting those who are vulnerable in society, and this extends to the victims of crime, the victims being disproportionately from disadvantaged groups. However, they may also understand this source in the context of the causes of crime: that those who commit crime are often poor, oppressed and disenfranchised. Christians may understand the teachings to indicate that the offenders also need protection.

contd

Morality and Justice: Protection

Christians believe that humanity was given the duty of stewardship, which means looking after all of God's creation. This might mean that even the worst of offenders should be protected and, consequently, most Christians would want to ensure that offenders were given opportunities to become a better version of themselves, even if their punishment involved protecting society for their offences and the offender from themself. They would be concerned if a sentence only achieved protection of society for the length of the sentence itself and would want to ensure that sentences are meaningful enough to achieve a level of transformation in the criminal, with better options and a happier life in their reach.

Christians would be concerned about threats to the safety of offenders while incarcerated. This is because Christians believe that we are all made in God's image and have inherent dignity and worth; we are all equal in the eyes of God. Many Christians would be disturbed by the mistreatment and lack of protection for those serving a custodial sentence. An example of how Christians might take action on this is through the many churches and charities that work with those in prison, providing advocacy and support. Salvation Army prison chaplain, Carl Huggins, said, 'Whatever life throws at them; we tell them Jesus loves them and was born for them.' This suggests that protection of prisoners is paramount and that God's love for them is greater than their worst acts.

ONLINE

Go online and click the link on our Digital Zone to find out more about the Salvation Army and the work it does www.brightredbooks.nets/subjects

NON-RELIGIOUS RESPONSES TO THE MORAL ISSUES ARISING FROM PROTECTION

Utilitarian belief in the greatest happiness principle means that they would largely favour protection as a purpose of punishment as they would be more concerned with the happiness of the majority (law-abiding society) and less concerned with the unhappiness of the minority (those who do not abide by the law). However, Utilitarians would want to consider carefully the long-term consequences and would be concerned where protection was short-lived or where the offender wasn't protected.

Jeremy Bentham saw crimes as acts of mischief and punishment as itself a mischief or evil. Bentham believed it 'ought only to be admitted in as far as it promises to exclude some greater evil'. Bentham believed the primary aim of punishment should be to deter, meaning those who follow his philosophy would be concerned if the sentence did not deter, with the protection to society lasting only so long as the sentence. To this extent, Utilitarians may favour an element of the punishment to ensure a more effective deterrent. This may mean the sentence was harsher, or it could mean that the sentence incorporated rehabilitation – ensuring the offender left prison more skilled, qualified and intent on living a crime-free life. In turn, this would ensure better protection to society and would also fulfil the purpose of an effective deterrent.

Utilitarians may also be concerned about the lack of protection for incarcerated prisoners. By virtue, it is paramount that to improve one's life, you must increase the good things in the world and minimise the bad things. Utilitarians would generally concede that acceptance of the mistreatment of offenders could lead to a less caring and more brutal society that would be less happy in the long term.

THINGS TO DO AND THINK ABOUT

Working with your peers, write a first paragraph for the following essay:
Analyse non-religious responses to the moral issues arising from protection.
Some helpful hints:
- Start backwards, e.g., describe protection, then a moral issue, then a non-religious response to protection *before* analysing the response to the moral issues arising from protection.
- Structure, e.g., three knowledge and understanding points, followed by two analytical.
- Language: use language that helps develop the skill, e.g., an implication of this response is…
- Branch out: What other non-religious responses could you use? Draw on your learning in class as well as the other responses in the chapter. How might those be used in the context of protection?

MORALITY AND JUSTICE
DETERRENCE

DON'T FORGET

Earlier in this chapter, when exploring the Four Noble Truths, we learned that the Eightfold Path is central to the fourth Noble Truth and that following this path is the only way to bring an end to suffering.

WHAT IS DETERRENCE?

Deterrence is a purpose of punishment that seeks to deter would-be offenders from committing crimes in the first instance by showing them the seriousness of the consequences if they do. Deterrence can be associated with a harsh punishment in the hope that it shocks and dissuades those of a criminal mindset. For instance, those who support capital punishment believe it to be an effective deterrent because it sends a clear message that murderers will receive the very worst punishment if they choose to take the life of another.

For most people in society, punishment is a deterrent in itself. For example, the threat of a driving ban would be enough to deter individuals from drinking and driving. The majority fear the implications of a criminal record and the consequences of what a custodial or non-custodial sentence would mean for themselves and their families.

WHAT ARE THE MORAL ISSUES ARISING FROM DETERRENCE AS A PURPOSE OF PUNISHMENT?

It doesn't take an individual approach

One moral issue is that punishments intended as a deterrent take a blanket approach and do not take enough note of personal circumstances. The primary intention of this purpose of punishment is to set an example to others, with little consideration of the drivers or circumstances that caused the offender to commit the crime in the first instance. Some may say that this lacks compassion and is short-sighted in that it does not put any emphasis on tackling the root causes of crime. However, there are others who argue that if you commit a crime then you must face the consequences, even if that means an overly harsh punishment set as an example to others. Reasons like poverty or addiction are merely excuses; the majority of people affected by those factors do not live a life of crime, either because they're suitably deterred by the potential punishment or because they know it is wrong to do so.

DON'T FORGET

Should we conside that if someone was not in their right mindset, or influenced by alcohol or drugs, then there is no level of sentence that would deter them from committing the offence?

Crimes committed in the heat of the moment

Another moral issue arising from deterrence is that many crimes, particularly violent crime, are committed in the heat of moment with no thought of the consequences. This raises some questions in relation to the punishment that should follow. Should the lack of intent and irrational thought that led to the crime be taken into account when sentencing, rather than issuing a sentence with the prime purpose of deterring others along with the individual from committing the crime again?

RELIGIOUS RESPONSES TO THE MORAL ISSUES RAISED BY DETERRENCE

Source

'Criminals, people who commit crimes, usually society rejects these people. They are also part of our society. Give them some form of punishment to say they were wrong but show them they are part of society and can change. Show them compassion.'

Dalai Lama

Meaning: This source highlights the belief of many Buddhists that compassion is key in both how and why we punish. In the context of deterrence, it might suggest that the sentence must be measured; it should not ostracise the offender and it should give them an opportunity for reflection and experiences that will help them to turn their lives around.

contd

Morality and Justice: Deterrence

While Buddhists may not favour harsh or cruel punishments, they are not unaccepting of deterrence in general. The belief in Kamma is a deterrent. Buddhists understand that all actions have consequences and that unskilful Kamma will impact on future rebirths. The worst possible rebirth would be in the realm of hell and so Buddhists will work hard to act out of generosity, compassion and non-attachment to accumulate skilful Kamma. Criminal behaviour may therefore be avoided for that reason, with Buddhists committing to the five precepts to live a moral and fulfilling life.

However, many Buddhists would be concerned about deterrence as a purpose of punishment where it did not consider individual circumstances and used the offender as an example to others. In one respect, this would be harmful to those doing the sentencing: in a quest for vengeance and with a lack of compassion, the sentencer would accumulate bad karma for themselves. Additionally, it may even compromise the principle of ahimsa, doing no harm to others, as it may involve giving a severe punishment inflicting pain and suffering on the offender, where a lesser punishment may have been more appropriate.

Buddhists recognise that judgement and logical thought are impaired by anger and intoxicants, which is why they would encourage followers to observe the Five Precepts and practise meditation to develop wisdom and compassion. They would generally want individual circumstances to be considered when using sentences to serve the purpose of deterrence as this is an act of loving kindness, in keeping with their beliefs and values.

Some Buddhists may show no concern for this issue, and this may be in keeping with the politics of the country where they live, where harsh punishments like capital punishment are used and considered by society to be effective deterrents to the most serious of crimes.

NON-RELIGIOUS RESPONSES TO THE MORAL ISSUES RAISED BY DETERRENCE

Many Humanists would want to question the effectiveness of deterrence in sentencing. Prison is the most severe sentence in Scotland, and arguably the greatest deterrent, and yet recidivism rates would suggest that for many it is a revolving door and is no deterrent at all. The Scottish Prison Service puts the cost of incarceration at over £37 000 per year per prisoner. If offenders go on to reoffend, then the purpose of deterrence has not been served and prison becomes ineffective.

Humanists would be concerned where individual circumstances were not taken into account in sentencing. The British Humanist Association writes: **A more equitable life may be one of the best deterrents, and we should look at what we can do to improve the quality of life of people in those sectors of society who feel the need to turn to crime.**

This source could be interpreted to suggest that a more revolutionary approach is necessary, with less plaster sticking and more treatment of the root causes of crime to lead to a fairer and more socially just society. Where people lead happy and fulfilled lives where their needs are met and they are achieving their potential, there is little need to commit crime.

Humanists may feel that when deciding whether to use punishment as a deterrent, all evidence as to the effectiveness of that punishment should be considered. Punishment may prove an effective deterrent for some but it may not be the best response to every criminal act. A likelihood of punishment might not be the best approach for example if criminals simply do not expect to be caught or have little regard for any consequences. An example here are "crimes of passion" where criminal acts are undertaken with very little premeditation or consideration of any negative outcomes. Additionally, Humanists may feel that deterrence based on severe punishments as a means to deter criminals would mean that the punishment is then not appropriate to the crime committed.

They recognise that deterrence presents problems, including for those crimes committed in the heat of the moment. This may mean that sentences which aim to be deterrents are difficult to measure.

How do we really know how many fewer crimes would have been committed had the potential offender not been deterred by the potential consequence?

 THINGS TO DO AND THINK ABOUT

Using the information on deterrence, its moral issues, and the religious and non-religious responses, create a visual organiser like the one below:

CONNECT	EXTEND	CHALLENGE
How does this information connect to what you already know?	How does the information extend your knowledge in a different direction?	What challenge or question has come up in your mind?

65

Responses to crime

MORALITY AND JUSTICE

CUSTODIAL SENTENCES

In Higher RMPS, we explore three responses to crime:

1. Custodial Sentences
2. Non-Custodial Sentences
3. Capital Punishment

CUSTODIAL SENTENCES

A custodial sentence is usually a prison sentence, where an offender is locked up as a punishment for their crime and as a way of keeping society safe. The length of a prison sentence is dependent on the severity of the individual's crime and always involves a loss of freedom and some rights. The vision of Scotland's Prison Service is 'Helping to protect the public and reducing reoffending through safe and secure custodial services that empower offenders to take responsibility and fulfil their potential'. This indicates that the purpose is twofold: the protection of wider society as well as what is intended to be a transformative experience for the offender.

DON'T FORGET

Whilst in prison, criminals would commonly be expected to take on a job of sorts, where they would be paid a small sum of money. There may be a rehabilitation programme available to offenders, which would hopefully reduce the risk of them reoffending.

WHAT ARE THE MORAL ISSUES ARISING FROM CUSTODIAL SENTENCES?

High rates of recidivism

National statistics for Scotland highlight that reoffending rates following a prison sentence are around one in four. This increases to six in 10 for those serving sentences of less than three months. This is a moral issue because it suggests that prison isn't effective and doesn't wholly achieve its aims of reform.

Prisons are overcrowded and places of hardship

Prisons are, arguably, places of despair and human misery as offenders are kept in crowded conditions and separated from their families and the wider society. This is a moral issue as it suggests that the longer prisoners are kept in these conditions then the more likely they are to suffer from psychological harm, making them ill-equipped to deal with the pressures of society when they are released from prison. There are some people, however, who wouldn't view this as an issue. They argue that offenders deserve those poor prison conditions as a proportionate punishment for the crimes they have committed.

DON'T FORGET

Some might argue that the money spent on incarceration would be better directed towards other public services that help address the causes of crime.

RELIGIOUS RESPONSES TO THE MORAL ISSUES ARISING FROM CUSTODIAL SENTENCING

Source

'The Lord hears the needy and does not despise his captive people.'   Psalm 69:33

Meaning: God cares for those who are vulnerable or in need of salvation. This could be interpreted to suggest that His compassion extends to those in prison as we are all made in His image, capable of change and deserving of second chances.

Many Christians would favour custodial sentences where the crime was serious, and society needed to be protected from the offender. They might extend this argument to say that prison is a means of protecting serious offenders from themselves. However, Christians would likely argue that while serving a custodial sentence, prisoners should be treated with dignity and respect in a safe environment free from violence and threat.

Christians would be concerned with the **high rates of recidivism** and wouldn't typically favour custodial sentences for more minor crimes as there are fewer opportunities for rehabilitation, and they carry a higher risk of reoffending after release. Many Christians believe that while custodial sentences have their place, the primary purpose of such a sentence should be to reform the offender. The implication here is that in providing

contd

Morality and Justice: Custodial sentences

opportunities for offenders to reflect on their criminal behaviour, learn new skills and even achieve qualifications, prisoners are far less likely to reoffend on their release.

Christians would be similarly concerned where prison conditions were poor, and inmates were living in an environment that negated their basic dignity. This is because Christians believe all life is special and God-given. They believe in agape, which is unconditional love or self-giving love, and think that they should aspire to treat all people in that way.

NON-RELIGIOUS RESPONSES TO THE MORAL ISSUES ARISING FROM CUSTODIAL SENTENCING

Humanist writer Carrie Thompson speaks of Humanist views on punishment and prison. She writes that while money and poverty play a part in crime, what impacts most is the environment in which we grow up in and the love – or lack thereof – that we are exposed to. Thompson argues that where we punish people who don't know how to behave better, they can end up resenting the laws and the system that works against them. By implication, this can lead to marginalisation, stigmatisation and a cycle of reoffending. For this reason, Humanists would be concerned with the **high rates of recidivism** that are associated with prison sentences.

Most Humanists would be concerned where **prisons had poor conditions**, as they would see this as a breach of an individual's basic human rights. They might be concerned that those types of conditions would impact negatively on an inmate's mental health. Furthermore, they may be concerned that poor conditions are not conducive to rehabilitation, which they believe to the most important purpose of a custodial sentence.

THINGS TO DO AND THINK ABOUT

At Higher, you must be able to **analyse** and **evaluate** responses to the moral issues arising from sentencing. It is important that you do not simply analyse and evaluate prison or the religious/non-religious responses to prison. In the activity below, try to find and fix the mistakes.

Evaluate religious responses to the moral issues arising from custodial sentencing.

Candidate 1: Prison is a custodial sentence which involves a loss of freedom and a fixed sentence, which is dependent on the severity of the crime. An implication of prison is that is that the sentence gives the offender time to reflect on the nature of his crime and make amends for his wrongs, e.g., by apologising to the victims of his crime. I agree with prison as I think that offenders need to be taught a lesson to make them see the error of their ways and be deterred from committing any further crime, in the knowledge of the harshness of the punishment.
Mistakes: _____
A fix: _____

Candidate 2: Prison is a custodial sentence which involves a loss of freedom and a fixed sentence, which is dependent on the severity of the crime. One moral issue arising from prison is that recidivism rates are high, with 1 in 4 re-offending, suggesting that prison doesn't really deter or reform offenders. A non-religious response to this is from Humanists. They say that prison must have a strong focus on rehabilitation or it is rendered ineffective and a poor use of public money. I agree with the Humanist response as I think punishment must serve more than a punitive purpose and that offenders, often suffering from trauma and addiction, must be given opportunities to improve themselves.
Mistakes: _____
A fix: _____

DON'T FORGET

Many Christians are strongly in favour of new 'super prisons', like the proposed HMP Glasgow, which will replace Barlinnie, as those types of prison are more like a college than traditional Victorian prisons, which are no longer fit for purpose.

DON'T FORGET

A Humanist perspective is that if children haven't been taught to self-regulate their emotions, or don't have adults who lead by example, they can behave in a way that leads to offending.

MORALITY AND JUSTICE

NON-CUSTODIAL SENTENCES

DON'T FORGET

The CPO may also involve a rehabilitation programme, which helps to tackle the root cause of the crime, where it's occurred a result of alcohol or drug intoxication.

COMMUNITY PAYBACK ORDERS (CPOS)

Community Payback Orders (CPOs) give an offender a set number of hours of service to be carried out in the community. This is intended to restore and repair the damage caused by their crime and could be something like litter picking. CPOs are normally supervised. The supervision aims to change the way the person behaves by making them attend regular appointments with a criminal justice social worker. The social worker can address what makes them offend, for example, poor decision-making.

Electronic monitoring

Electronic monitoring or tagging is used in Scotland to support rehabilitation and reduce reoffending. It can be used with another community sentence as part of a considered package to support rehabilitation. Electronic monitoring enables the offender to live with their families and continue in education or employment. It usually involves a curfew, and may also include an exclusion zone. Where the offender breaks the conditions, it may result in a custodial sentence.

Fines

Fines are the most common non-custodial sentence used by Scottish courts. They are often used for lesser offences, such as driving misdemeanours, theft or a breach of the peace. Fines are dependent on the severity of the crime and judges take into consideration how much the offender is able to pay. Where fines are not paid, the offender will often be brought back to court and may be given another sentence. They may include a Victim Surcharge, which was introduced by the Scottish Government in 2019.

MORAL ISSUES ARISING FROM NON-CUSTODIAL SENTENCING

Too soft touch?

Many believe that non-custodial sentences are too soft and not nearly punitive enough. They say that this is an issue because punishment should involve an element of retribution. If no hardship is felt, then some may argue that the offender is unlikely to learn from their mistake and is more likely to reoffend. In turn, this makes society less safe, with a higher occurrence of crime. However, there are many who would take an evidence-based approach and argue that non-custodial sentences are more appropriate and proportionate to the crimes they are issued for. They may argue that alternative short-term sentences involve high recidivism rates, so we should be less concerned about the severity of the sentence and more concerned about the financial cost of a custodial sentence and the high potential for the offender to reoffend.

High rates of uncompleted sentences and unrecovered costs

Successful completion rates of CPOs are generally around 70% in Scotland, with those in employment far more likely to complete a CPO than those who are unemployed. Many people take issue with the 30% rate of incomplete CPOs and argue that justice is not being served with offenders avoiding any meaningful punishment. This may nurture in the offender a disregard for the law and result in further criminality. Electronic monitoring has a higher rate of completion at around 80%, but again, many take issue with the 20% rate of incomplete sentences. Figures from the Scottish courts in January 2022 put fine recovery at 89%. There is some concern about those fines that have not been recovered. However, because of the expense in bringing an individual to court, some cases result in no reimbursement for the taxpayer.

Morality and Justice: Non-custodial sentences

RELIGIOUS RESPONSES TO THE MORAL ISSUES ARISING FROM NON-CUSTODIAL SENTENCES

The Muslim response

Source: 'God orders justice, doing good... he forbids what is shameful, blameworthy and oppressive.'

Surah 16:90-92

Meaning: The source suggests that order and fairness are important parts of God's wishes for justice. Regarding sentencing, this source could be interpretated to understand that while criminal behaviour is shameful, harsh punishments could be considered oppressive. Other interpretations may see this source only in the context of those who chose to engage in law-breaking.

Many Muslims would be concerned if a punishment were seen as too soft touch. As God's vice-regents on the Earth, they would want to see that justice was served and that there was some restoration for the victim. Many Muslims favour sentences that are retributive in nature and serve as a deterrent to others. However, a part of this would also be ensuring that all God's creations were treated in a fair way, and they may not support excessive punishments. In this sense, if 'softer' punishments led to lower reoffending rates then they may support them.

Muslims would be concerned if sentences were incomplete and fines unrecovered, as this would be seen as justice not being served. Diyyah, in Islamic law, is the financial compensation paid to a victim of a crime, which is practised in many Muslims countries and often instead of a more serious sentence for the offender. If the fine is not paid, then Muslims may see this as a lost opportunity for forgiveness, which may lead to a desire for vengeance on behalf of the victim and their family.

NON-RELIGIOUS RESPONSES TO THE MORAL ISSUES RAISED BY NON-CUSTODIAL SENTENCING

One non-religious response to non-custodial sentences and the issues raised by them comes from the Scottish Government. In July 2021, the Auditor General reported that, prior to the COVID-19 pandemic, Scotland had one of the highest rates for incarcerations in Western Europe, with the number of prisoners exceeding the operating capacity of prisons. Since then, there was a dip in prisoner numbers in mid-2020, but they may increase again in the future.

In response to accusations that non-custodial sentences were not punitive enough, the Scottish Government might reply by looking through the lens of equity. The Vision for Justice in Scotland 2022 writes:

'We must not criminalise those who are most vulnerable in our society. We have a moral imperative to ensure that prevention and early intervention efforts enable us all to thrive in our communities...We know that to address the causes of crime Scotland's public services together must tackle societal inequalities such as child poverty, mental ill health, addiction and adverse childhood experiences.'

This source can be interpreted as the Scottish Government recognising that the causes of crime are complex and at their root lies deep inequality. This is a societal problem that must be addressed by all public services in a collaborative way. The Scottish Government may be less concerned about non-custodial responses being less punitive if they are taking a more individualistic and compassionate approach to offenders. If we address the causes of crime, we drastically reduce its occurrence.

In relation to unfulfilled sentences and unrecovered fines, the Scottish Government may wish to consider this in the context of the cost of prison compared with that of a CPO. While prison costs over £37 000 per year per prisoner, a CPO costs just £1894. Recidivism rates remain relatively high for incarcerated offenders, especially for those prisoners who serve a sentence of one year or less. Audit Scotland reports: 'Of those released from prison in 2017/2018 who had served a sentence of a year or less, 49% were reconvicted within a year, compared with 30% who completed a community service.' While the concerns about CPOs being unfulfilled may be valid, some may weigh this against the reduced reoffending rates, and see CPOs as the more effective of these two options.

 THINGS TO DO AND THINK ABOUT

Create flash cards for responses to the moral issues arising from non-custodial sentencing. Your flash cards might include:

- ✔ Pictures that will help trigger your memory
- ✔ Colour to categorise responses/issues
- ✔ Limited text: keywords with one issue/response per flash card

 ONLINE

To take a test and try another task for this topic, go to our Digital Zone at www.brightredbooks.net/subjects

MORALITY AND JUSTICE

CAPITAL PUNISHMENT

Capital punishment is the execution of a convicted offender after a legal trial, usually for a serious crime like committing a murder. Capital punishment has been abolished throughout most of the world, but there are still some countries that practise it or have it as a sentence in principle. China is believed to be the country with the highest number of executions per year, although there is no official number because China treats this information as a state secret.

TYPES OF CAPITAL PUNISHMENT

There are many different types of capital punishment; lethal injection and hanging are two of the most used methods. Lethal injection consists of an injection of three different drugs, which paralyse the heart of the offender and stop it beating. Hanging can be either long or short drop. In long drop hanging, the drop distance is determined by the weight of the offender: the less a person weighs, the longer the drop needs to be. If the drop distance is calculated correctly, the individual should die quickly, with the spinal cord being severed between the second and third vertebrae. Short drop hanging results in a slower death by strangulation and is intended to make the individual suffer. In countries like Iran, cranes are sometimes used to publicly hang offenders.

Countries with the Most Confirmed Executions in 2020 (Deathpenaltyinfo.org)

Country	Number
China	1,000s
Iran	246+
Egypt	107+
Iraq	45+
Saudi Arabia	27
United States	17
Somalia	11+

Note: Execution totals are not known for Vietnam, North Korea and Syria.

WHAT ARE THE MORAL ISSUES RAISED BY CAPITAL PUNISHMENT?

Right to life

One moral issue raised by the use of capital punishment is that it takes away a person's right to life, as outlined by Article 3 in the Universal Declaration of Human Rights. The United Nations argues that this right to life is non-negotiable and not dependent on anything else. This is a moral issue for many as they believe that the taking of life should never be used as a punishment as all life has meaning and value. However, there are others who argue that we negate our right to life when we take the life of another.

Inhumane and degrading

Another moral issue raised by capital punishment is the belief of some that it contravenes Article 5 of the Universal Declaration of Human Rights, which states: 'No one shall be subjected to torture or to cruel, inhuman or degrading treatment or punishment.' Some would argue that the death penalty constitutes a cruel and degrading punishment, with some methods being particularly torturous. They may look to examples of botched executions, often caused by poorly trained technicians and resulting in a prolonged period of pain for the offender. For some this is not an issue, because they believe that the suffering of those who commit the most heinous of crimes is not something we should be concerned about. Rather, our concern should remain with the victims and their families.

RELIGIOUS RESPONSES TO THE MORAL ISSUES ARISING FROM CAPITAL PUNISHMENT

The Christian response

Source: 'So God created man in his own image, in the image of God he created him; male and female he created them.'

Genesis 1:27

Meaning: This source could be understood as human life having something special about it, that because we are made in God's image, our lives have inherent value, meaning and purpose. As the pinnacle of God's creation, life should be treasured.

Christians may be concerned when an individual's right to life is taken, even when that person has taken the life of another. In 2008, in 'The Church and Society', The Church of Scotland wrote:

> 'We know something of the character of God and are called upon to emulate it. In particular, we know that God is compassionate. He calls us to be likewise. In this matter, our compassion must extend to victims, to offenders and to society itself. This is, at times, hard to maintain, but compassion to society will entail finding the most appropriate ways of protecting it and healing its wounds. Inflicting more violence cannot be a part of that.'

This source, and the wider report, make clear that the Church of Scotland takes a strong position against capital punishment. The source highlights that Christians are expected to act in a way that is like God Himself because they are made in His image, with compassion and without vengeance. An implication of this response is that taking away an offender's **right to life** will only create a cycle of violence that damages us as individuals and as a society. There are some Christians who may disagree with this and look to the teachings of the Old Testament to support their position.

In relation to the moral issue of capital punishment being **inhumane and degrading**, many Christians would react with concern. Sister Helen Prejean is a Catholic nun who campaigns against capital punishment in the United States of America. She writes:

> 'The secrecy surrounding executions makes it possible for executions to continue. I am convinced that if executions were made public, the torture and violence would be unmasked, and we would be shamed into abolishing executions. We would be embarrassed at the brutalization of the crowds that would gather to watch a man or woman be killed.'

This source highlights her Christian position that the death penalty is tantamount to torture. It is suggested that in killing an offender in such a violent way, we become brutalised, losing our humanity. Some argue that this is supported by the fact that those US states with the death penalty have 48% to 101% higher rates of homicide than those that do not (*The Times*); by implication, where we readily execute others, we devalue life and make it disposable.

NON-RELIGIOUS RESPONSES TO THE MORAL ISSUES RAISED BY CAPITAL PUNISHMENT

One non-religious response to the moral issues raised by the death penalty comes from Amnesty International. From their website:

> **'The death penalty is the ultimate cruel, inhuman and degrading punishment. Amnesty opposes the death penalty in all cases without exception – regardless of who is accused, the nature or circumstances of the crime, guilt or innocence or method of execution.'**

This source makes clear their position on capital punishment and how they would respond to the moral issues raised by it. Amnesty International places a significant value on basic human rights for all and campaigns tirelessly to champion those. Amnesty International believes that the **right to life** is fundamental and should never be compromised in any way. Similarly, Amnesty International takes great issue with capital punishment as a **cruel and inhumane punishment**. Amnesty International notes unfair trials in many countries along with executions for crimes, or non-crimes, such as drug offences and same-sex consensual conduct.

THINGS TO DO AND THINK ABOUT

Working in pairs or groups, conduct research to gain more in-depth knowledge of the moral issues arising from capital punishment and some religious and non-religious responses to those. You should write up your research in a presentation, which meets the following success criteria:

1. A description of the moral issues. You may wish to include a case study to exemplify your issue, e.g., a botched execution leading to suffering for the offender.
2. A description of an alternative religious/non-religious response to the ones in this chapter.
3. An analysis of the responses: What are the implications of those responses? In what ways are they similar/different to other viewpoints?
4. An evaluation: Do you agree/disagree with the responses? Give reasons to support your view.

Use of embryos

MORALITY, MEDICINE AND THE HUMAN BODY

AN OVERVIEW

To do well in this section, you need to develop a good knowledge and understanding of:

- The reproductive uses of embryos
- The therapeutic uses of embryos
- Using embryos in research

You will also need to understand the moral issues raised by each of these areas, and the religious and non-religious viewpoints on these moral issues. Before we look at each separate area, let's explore what embryos are and why the status of the embryo is important.

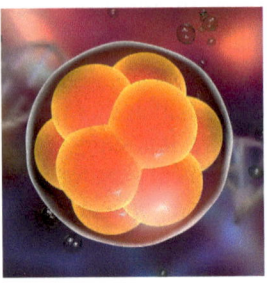

WHAT ARE HUMAN EMBRYOS?

A human embryo is a multicellular organism, which is the earliest stage of human life. The term embryo is used from conception (when sperm meets egg) until the end of the seventh week of development. From week eight the embryo is known as a foetus. In the UK, the Human Fertilisation and Embryology Authority (HFEA) regulates how embryos can be used. The Human Fertilisation and Embryology Act 1990 is the legislation that explains what can and can't be done regarding the use of embryos in the UK. It explains that human embryos must be used within 14 days of creation or until the appearance of the *primitive streak*, a groove that appears on the embryo marking the development of the inner cell mass that will form the skeleton, brain and nervous system.

The uses of human embryos raise many moral issues. Possibly the main question that causes the most moral debate is: When does human life actually begin? Depending on your answer regarding the status of the embryo, there are many different consequences for how embryos can or should be used.

ONLINE

Go to our Digital Zone at www.brightredbooks.net/subjects and click the link to find out more about the HFEA and the work that it does.

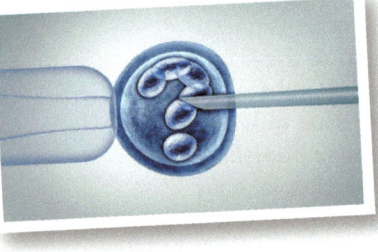

THE STATUS OF THE HUMAN EMBRYO

The 'status of the embryo' is a more sophisticated way of saying: 'What is the embryo's position regarding how much of a human being it is?' There are generally three positions to consider: *embryos are human beings*, *embryos are potential human beings* and *embryos are not human beings*, and, depending on which of these viewpoints you take, there will be implications on how you believe embryos can be used within medical ethics.

The Roman Catholic Church alongside many other (but not all) Christian churches would argue that the human life begins at conception.	Professor Michael Sandel from Harvard writes, 'one need not regard the embryo as a full human being in order to accord it a certain respect. To regard the embryo as a mere thing, open to any use we desire or devise does, it seems to me, miss its significance as potential human life.'	Peter Singer, utilitarian philosopher writes, 'If we take the fertilised egg… it is hard to get upset about its death. The fertilised egg is a single cell… with out a single anatomical feature of the being it will later become.'
Life begins at conception and an embryo is a human being. Embryos should be entitled to all rights that human being have.	Biologically the embryo has many human characteristics; it is in a process of development. It does not hold the status of being a human; however it should be respected.	The embryo is not a human being. It lacks many human characteristics, such as feeling pleasure or pain, or thinking for itself. An embryo can be treated as a means to an end without human rights.
Embryos are human beings.	**Embryos are potential human beings**	**Embryos are not human beings**

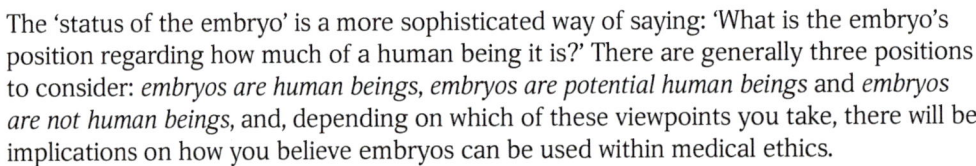

The Status of the Embryo

DON'T FORGET

For a general overview of understanding moral issues see page 50.

Morality, medicine and the human body: An overview

RELIGIOUS VIEWPOINTS ON THE STATUS OF THE EMBRYO

Religious viewpoints are extremely varied regarding the status of the embryo.

Hinduism

Most Hindus believe that an embryo should be classed as a person from conception; this is because of the Hindu belief in reincarnation and how this takes place at the moment of conception. There are certain exceptions to this. One would be saving the life of a mother at the expense of an embryo. Another could be that some Hindus believe the benefits of embryonic stem cell research can bring more benefits to humankind.

Roman Catholic Church

Like the Hindu viewpoint, but for different reasons, the Roman Catholic Church believes the embryo should be considered a person from conception, the moment that the egg becomes fertilised by the sperm.

Church of Scotland

At the General Assembly in 2006, the Church of Scotland revised their viewpoint on the status of the embryo. The Church took what they called a middle position, affirming the special status of the embryo, yet recognising the benefits of embryo research under certain circumstances.

Judaism

The majority of Jewish people would not believe that the embryo is a human at conception. Some Jews consider the embryo as a person on the 40th day of development when the soul becomes part of the embryo. Many Jews, however, believe that it is long after the embryonic stage that personhood takes place, and full personhood is not reached until the time of birth.

NON-RELIGIOUS VIEWPOINTS ON THE STATUS OF THE EMBRYO

Non-religious viewpoints usually consider the embryo to be a non-person; however, this is not always the case, with some arguing the embryo as a potential human, while others argue that the embryo is a person.

Carl Sagan

The non-religious scientist stated that 'Despite many claims to the contrary, life does not begin at conception: It is an unbroken chain that stretches back nearly to the origin of the Earth, 4.6 billion years ago.' This would be the viewpoint of the majority of secular scientists today.

Humanist Society Scotland

The Humanist Society Scotland argue that a fertilised egg has the ability to grow into a person; however, they are quite clear on their position regarding the status of the embryo, stating 'there is no brain, no self-awareness or consciousness, no way of feeling pain or emotion. An early-stage embryo is not a person and cannot suffer.'

Secular Pro-Life

Secular Pro-Life, an organisation run by three atheist women, who state that 'one of our primary goals is to hold space in the pro-life movement for atheists, agnostics, and other non-religious people who are against abortion'. They believe that the embryo is a person from the moment of conception.

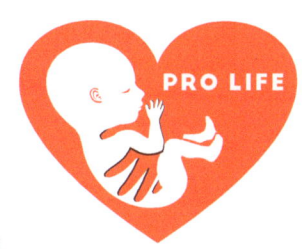

 ## THINGS TO DO AND THINK ABOUT

Exploring what you think regarding the status of the embryo, and why you think that, can set up a good foundation for exploring the rest of this unit. Have a go at answering the question below as a starting point before working through the unit.

What is a human embryo and to what extent do you believe a human embryo is a person, a potential person and not a person?

MORALITY, MEDICINE AND THE HUMAN BODY
REPRODUCTIVE 1

DON'T FORGET
Some of the guidelines propose that you must be under the age of 43 years, have been trying to get pregnant by natural means for two years, or have been receiving less invasive fertility treatment in consultation with your local GP or doctor.

ONLINE
Have a look and explore the NHS website that offers lots of information on the IVF process.

IN VITRO FERTILISATION (IVF)

In Vitro Fertilisation (IVF) is a medical process that creates an embryo outside of the body. This technique is often used by people who cannot conceive a child naturally. There are quite strict guidelines as to who can go through the IVF procedure on the National Health Service (NHS). These guidelines are regulated by an organisation known as NICE (the National Institute for Health and Care Excellence).

The NHS highlights six stages to the IVF process:

1. The natural menstrual cycle is stopped using medication.
2. Egg supply is boosted by using medication to help the ovaries produce more eggs.
3. An ultrasound scan is used to monitor the eggs and check they are maturing, with medication used to help the eggs mature.
4. The eggs are collected from the ovaries.
5. The eggs are fertilised by mixing them with sperm for a few days, this forms the embryo.
6. One or two of the embryos are placed back into the womb.

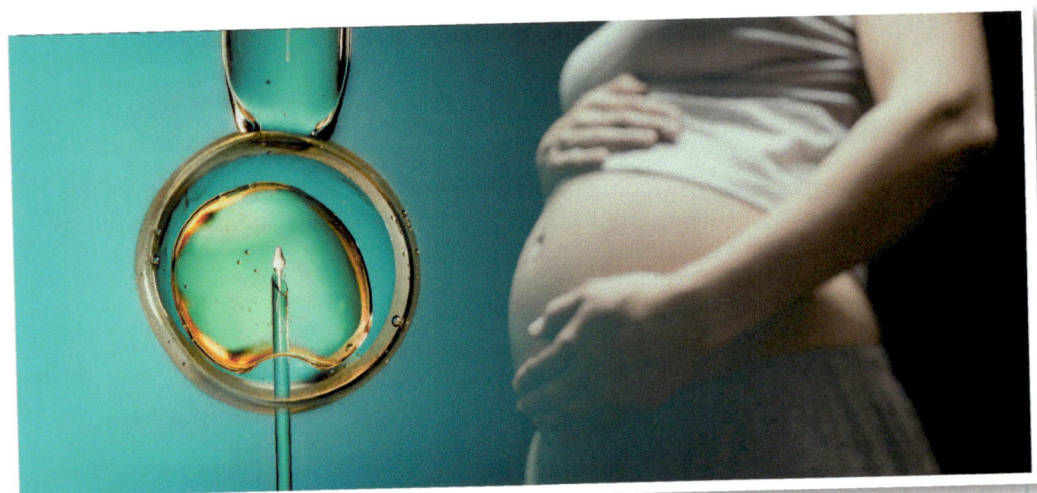

DON'T FORGET
There are no hard scientific facts concerning the point when human life has actually or will actually begin. Organisations such as the British Medical Association (BMA) view the embryo as having more rights the more they develop, highlighting that until the embryo achieves the status of a human being, it doesn't have full human rights.

WHAT ARE THE MORAL ISSUES RAISED BY IVF?

The status of the embryo

As noted in the previous topic, there are different viewpoints regarding the status of the embryo. Is the embryo a human being, a potential human being or not a human being?

If the embryo is considered a person, then the process of IVF can be called into question, as common practice means more embryos are created than are used. The treatment of those leftover embryos (explored in detail below) from the IVF process raises an ethical question if those embryos are considered to be human beings.

If the embryo is considered a potential human being it becomes harder to judge, from an ethical perspective, how the embryo might be used.

If the embryo is considered as not being a human being, then there are less ethical issues raised with how embryos are used, specifically those embryos that are additional to requirements regarding the reproductive process.

contd

Leftover embryos

As eggs are fertilised during the IVF process, there may be many embryos produced. It is common practice for one embryo to be implanted, although two embryos may be used (if the patient is slightly older or if there are questions regarding the quality of the embryo). This means that there are embryos left over and poses a question as to what should be done with the embryos that are left over. Some of the options regarding the unused embryos are:

- They may be frozen and kept for a later date.
- They may be donated to other couples unable to conceive.
- They may be donated to scientific or medical research.
- They may be destroyed.

Interfering with natural processes/playing God

There are those, usually from a religious perspective, who would argue that having children should be a natural process and if you are unable to have a family then you should just accept this. If you start to interfere with this process, then you are *playing God*. Others argue that God may have given His creation the wisdom and intellect as human beings to be able to advance the human race in this way, whilst others see God as irrelevant in the discussion as God doesn't exist and it is up to humanity to use reason and science to advance medicine in any way that will benefit us.

Eugenics/slippery slope

Eugenics is when desirable or favourable traits in offspring are selected, so that they, or indeed future races, have an improved genetic composition. Medically, on the NHS, IVF is not used to control human reproduction so that certain types of preferred people are being bred. However, there is an argument that creating embryos outside the womb could open the door to greater experimentation, which may have concerning morally questionable implications regarding what traits an individual could be born with.

Cost/equity

IVF costs can vary, but the NHS states on their website that 'one cycle of treatment may cost £5000 or more'. The NHS works on a budget, which means that money directed towards IVF treatment has an opportunity cost. The opportunity cost is that those who are waiting on other medical procedures either miss out, or that there are longer waiting lists in some areas of critical care.

Some may argue that there is more virtue and equity in putting this money into treatments that have a higher success rate or may be more beneficial for more people. Others would argue that the right to have a family overrides the cost and that if IVF was only available through private healthcare, then there are many in society who would not be able to afford the treatment.

DON'T FORGET

From 2014 to 2016, it was recorded that the success of IVF in any age range was less than 30%, gradually becoming less successful with age, with less than a 10% success rate for those older than 39 years.

 THINGS TO DO AND THINK ABOUT

Two of the other techniques that use embryos created by IVF are Pre-implantation genetic diagnosis (PGD) and Pre-implantation tissue typing (PTT), often known as saviour siblings. Have a look at the diagram below and see if you can explore these further issues for yourself. Remember, the key questions to ask are: What are they? What moral issues do they raise? And what are the religious and non-religious viewpoints towards those moral issues?

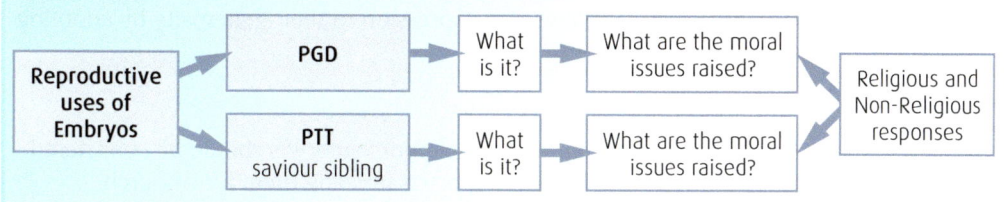

MORALITY, MEDICINE AND THE HUMAN BODY

REPRODUCTIVE 2

RELIGIOUS RESPONSES TO THE MORAL ISSUES RAISED BY IVF

Many religions believe in the sanctity of life. There will be differences, as sacred texts and beliefs differ from religion to religion. The big theme is that life is sacred as it is created by a divine or supreme being and is precious. The diagram below outlines the Christian perspective on the sanctity of life.

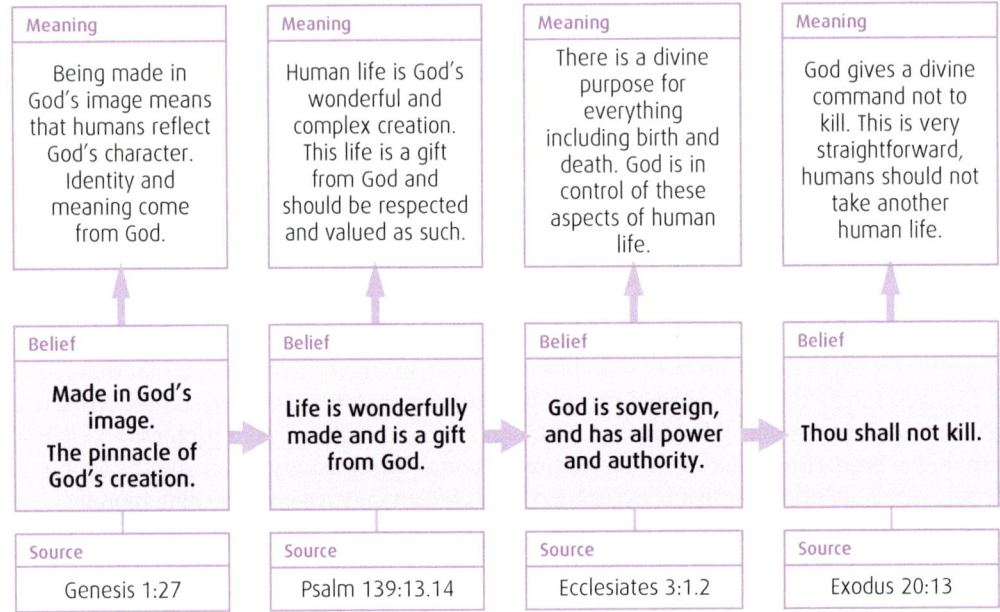

Made in God's image

Most Christians believe that God is the creator of life and has created humanity in His image, and to reflect His character. This natural and divine process could be seen to contrast with the medical process of IVF because IVF gives medical professionals the power to create life. Other Christians might respond that being made in God's image means that we have been made as thinking beings and given wisdom to be able to support and sustain life. IVF is our way of using the intellect God has given us.

Life is wonderfully made and a gift from God

A passage from the Bible explains that when an embryo is created it is wonderfully made by God in the womb. The process of IVF allows a specialist to grade the embryos and choose which ones they think are most viable and of the best quality. For some Christians, IVF turns that natural process of creation into a medical procedure, and it also seems to value some embryos more than others.

God is sovereign

Many Christians believe that God is sovereign, which means that God is in control, He has the power and authority to say what happens and when. This includes when and if you have children. The Catholic Church in its catechism suggests there are those who might not be able to have children and they 'can give expression to their generosity by adopting abandoned children'.

Thou shall not kill

As many Christians believe that life begins at conception, embryos should be considered human beings. Therefore, destroying leftover embryos or using them for research purposes would be in direct opposition to God's command not to kill.

DON'T FORGET

The Bible passage in question is from Jeremiah 1:5
Before I formed you in the womb I knew you, before you were born I set you apart; I appointed you as a prophet to the nations.

Morality, medicine and the human body: Reproductive 2

NON-RELIGIOUS RESPONSES TO THE MORAL ISSUES RAISED BY IVF

From a non-religious viewpoint, IVF is seen as a medical intervention that helps those struggling with infertility to have children. Humanists believe firmly in using reason and science to bring about benefits to humanity. Here is what the Humanists UK website says regarding IVF:

In the 20th and 21st centuries, humanity began to uncover many new medical advances with the potential to change our lives for the better – from in-vitro fertilisation treatments benefiting many kinds of couples, to the use of embryonic stem cells to cure diseases.

On these issues, scientists' efforts are often impeded by the campaigning of religious activists who have strong views about the 'sanctity' of the human body, 'playing god', or the appropriate use of human tissues.

We believe that the decision as to whether to permit any such research should be based entirely on principled ethical considerations, not religious points. We want the primary ethical consideration in scientific matters to be benefit to human beings and other living creatures.

Thinking back to the principle of utility (see p 51), **Utilitarians** may believe that, when it comes to IVF, enabling those who struggle to have children to overcome those barriers medically will bring the greatest happiness to the greatest number of people.

Many would argue that allowing IVF protects human rights (such as the right to have a family) and allows greater autonomy, which ultimately promotes happiness across most of society. Like many secular scientists, Eugenie Smith is of the opinion that embryos cannot be considered persons.

Smith writes 'If a zygote (the earliest stages of the embryo just after conception) is just a cell, and cells die regularly, then the answer to whether it is ethically permissible to destroy it is yes.'

Brave new bioethics - Eugenie Scott

If we consider this viewpoint against many of the moral issues that are raised by IVF, then it would appear that most secular scientists should have no problem with IVF because of their response on the status of the embryo and leftover embryos.

ONLINE

Go to our Digital Zone at www.brightredbooks.net/subjects and click the link to explore this issue further.

DON'T FORGET

Remember, Utilitarians believe that actions are considered right if they promote happiness or pleasure and they are wrong if they produce unhappiness or pain.

THINGS TO DO AND THINK ABOUT

1 Have a look at this example to see how beliefs lead to viewpoints and then how those viewpoints interact with the moral issues:

It says in the Bible in Exodus 20, 'you shall not murder' (belief), therefore **most Christians believe that it is to wrong take the life of another human being** *(viewpoint). This means when it comes to* **the moral issue of the status of the embryo** *(moral issue), if you believe that life begins at conception, using an embryo in any other way than creating a human being would be considered wrong or could not be morally justified. This viewpoint would also mean that many Christians would disagree with IVF as one of the moral issues raised is* **the leftover embryos** *(moral issue), if those leftover embryos are used for research or discarded as many are, then Christians would be against the process as this would be viewed as destroying life.*

We can see here that the Christian viewpoint – 'It is wrong to take the life of another human being' – has something to say about the status of the embryo and leftover embryos.

Have a look at some of the religious and non-religious viewpoints highlighted above and see if you can match them up as responses to some of the identified moral issues with IVF.

77

MORALITY, MEDICINE AND THE HUMAN BODY
THERAPEUTIC USES OF EMBRYOS

DON'T FORGET

Currently, there is a high expectation for the use of hESCs in medical treatment with an enormous amount of research taking place, but there are presently very few clinical uses for treating humans with embryonic stem cells.

DON'T FORGET

Whilst it is believed that these human stem cells have great potential, to date they have only been used for research purposes, with no evidence of them being used as part of therapeutic treatment for humans.

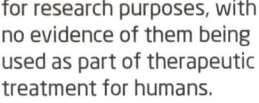

DON'T FORGET

In 1997, Dolly the sheep was the first known cloned mammal, as part of research undertaken at the Roslin Institute in Scotland. Since then, there have been many advancements in reproductive cloning, with scientists cloning animals such as cats, dogs, horses, rabbits and rats.

ONLINE

Go online to out Digital Zone at www.brightredbooks.net/subjects to find out more about another breakthrough in reproductive cloning which took place in Shanghai in 2018.

HUMAN EMBRYONIC STEM CELLS

The word therapeutic means *medicine or medical treatments used for healing disorders or diseases*. Embryos can play an important role as they are the source of human embryonic stem cells (hESCs), which can be used to treat certain disorders or diseases. Small numbers of hESCs can be taken from the human embryo and cultured in a laboratory, where they are divided to make copies of themselves for a long period of time. hESCs are very valuable in medicine because of their unique properties: not only can they continue to divide and renew themselves for long periods of time, they are also undifferentiated or unspecialised cells. This means that they have the ability to differentiate into many different specialised cell types such as brain, bone marrow or heart cells, which could then be used to treat diseases such as heart disease, Parkinson's disease and leukaemia.

THERAPEUTIC CLONING

Another way that embryos can be created, in order to generate hESCs, is through therapeutic cloning. The process involves an egg cell being given by a donor. This egg cell has its nucleus removed and it is replaced with a nucleus from the patient's cell. The cell is then stimulated to divide and develops into an embryo. After four or five days, stem cells are removed and cultured for therapeutic use.

While there are moral issues raised by the practice of therapeutic cloning, many argue that research involving therapeutic cloning will lead the way to human reproductive cloning, which for some creates a greater moral issue to navigate. Therapeutic cloning and reproductive cloning share many of the same techniques and processes, the main difference is that they are used to bring about different purposes. Therapeutic cloning aims to create embryonic stem cells for therapeutic treatments, while reproductive cloning aims to develop that embryo to create a complete copy of the mammal.

WHAT ARE THE MORAL ISSUES RAISED BY THE THERAPEUTIC USES OF EMBRYOS?

As the therapeutic uses of embryos still rely on the use and ultimate destruction of human embryos, the **status of the embryo** remains a central moral issue, as does the moral issue of **interfering with natural processes and playing God**. Embryonic stem cells can also be created as a hybrid human and animal cell which for many has ethical concerns.

The supply of human eggs

If the embryos are not left over from IVF, then human egg cells need to be donated as part of the process. As part of the natural monthly cycle, a woman will usually only produce one or two eggs; to increase the number of eggs produced then stimulatory medicines are taken, which can cause harm. The surgery itself to retrieve the eggs isn't considered complex, but like any surgery it can be dangerous. There are moral concerns about putting a person's health at risk to create embryos that will be used for research.

The embryo as a commodity

The HFEA stipulates that it is illegal to pay for egg donation in the UK, with donors able to receive compensation of up to £750. There are, however, other countries that will pay much more in the line of compensation, with a quick internet search finding some private companies in the USA offering to pay $10 000 plus expenses per cycle. There are also press releases highlighting the black-market trade in human egg cells, in which women are recruited and paid to produce eggs that are harvested then sold to illegal fertility agencies.

contd

Morality, medicine and the human body: Therapeutic uses of embryos

Means to an end
There is a moral argument that creating human embryos for research purposes and to harvest embryonic stem cells is simply a means to an end. The embryo is not in any way important; it is the result of the embryonic stem cells for therapy that matters. Many consider this to be morally wrong.

Human cloning
The thinking that research involving therapeutic cloning may lead to human reproductive cloning brings with it several ethical concerns. Issues such as the loss of life, identity and eugenics mean that many believe human cloning is morally unjustified.

DON'T FORGET

Have a look at the previous section on the reproductive uses of embryos to remind yourself of these two moral issues, which will be at the centre of any debate regarding the treatment of embryos.

RELIGIOUS RESPONSES TO THE MORAL ISSUES RAISED BY THE THERAPEUTIC USES OF EMBRYOS

The sanctity of life
Have a look at the sanctity of life in the religious responses to the moral issues raised by IVF. What responses would those four beliefs generate with the moral issues raised by the therapeutic uses of embryos?

The Church of Scotland
As we discovered earlier by looking at the religious responses regarding the status of the embryo, the Church of Scotland have taken up a middle position, stating that the embryo should have a special status, although there are 'recognised potential benefits of embryo research under limited circumstances'. They also urged the government to encourage research into other sources of stem cells so that the use of embryos could be avoided.

The Church of England
The Church of England holds a similar view that research using embryonic stem cells should not be ruled out, however, it would be better to find an alternative source for stem cells that avoided the destruction of embryos.

The Roman Catholic Church
In a piece of writing known as *Dignitas Personae*, the Roman Catholic Church outlined that the use of embryonic stem cells presented serious problems. The Church also condemned therapeutic cloning, stating that 'It is gravely immoral to sacrifice a human life for therapeutic ends'. Creating embryos with the intention of destroying them is 'incompatible with human dignity'. This is a direct response to the moral issue of using embryos as a means to an end.

NON-RELIGIOUS RESPONSES TO THE MORAL ISSUES RAISED BY THE THERAPEUTIC USES OF EMBRYOS

As leftover embryos from IVF are a source of embryonic stem cells, some of the responses to the moral issues raised by the reproductive uses of embryos will also apply to the therapeutic uses of embryos.

Utilitarianism
Thinking back to the Utilitarian position on page 51, consider the consequences of the moral issues raised by the therapeutic uses of embryos. If the consequences of an action bring more pleasure or happiness – than pain – then a Utilitarian is likely to be in favour of taking that action. As the embryonic stem cells are to be used to treat illness and disease, thereby reducing human suffering and pain, then the Utilitarian viewpoint would approve of the therapeutic uses of embryos.

The British Medical Association (BMA)
The BMA is an independent trade union that represents doctors throughout the UK. The BMA is very strongly in favour of the therapeutic uses of embryos and embryonic stem cells. Furthermore, the BMA also approves of therapeutic cloning and using hybrid human and animal cells to develop human embryonic stem cells.

DON'T FORGET

Utilitarian philosopher **Peter Singer** explains '[I]f embryos are to be used to remove stem cells and the stem cells are then going to be used for research and then destroyed, not allowed to develop...into a child, I really don't see much need to regulate that.'

DON'T FORGET

The BMA states: 'This research, carried out under the control of the Human Fertilisation and Embryology Authority (HFEA), has the potential to improve our understanding of and treatment for many very serious medical conditions.'

THINGS TO DO AND THINK ABOUT

Evaluation is one of the key skills needed in the Higher RMPS course. Remember that evaluation is your reasoned opinion. When giving a reasoned opinion, it is useful to think of it as have I 'SAID' enough to get my point across. Remember that 'SAID' stands for: Strengths and Weaknesses; Agree or Disagree; Impact; Drawbacks or Benefits. **Evaluate** the religious and non-religious responses to the moral issues raised by the therapeutic uses of embryos.

MORALITY, MEDICINE AND THE HUMAN BODY
RESEARCH

ONLINE

Go online to our Digital Zone and click the link to see the HFEA's project summaries.

THE USE OF EMBRYOS IN RESEARCH

As we have seen, in the UK, it is the HFEA that regulates how embryos can be used. This is for reproductive and therapeutic purposes, as well as any research projects that use embryos. The HFEA website lists all the embryo research projects currently taking place in the UK. It is worthwhile keeping an eye on the HFEA website as this type of research is always progressing and developing. We are going to look at the summaries of two current research projects taking place in the UK regarding embryos.

Genetic profiling in embryos (University College London)

Early human development is very complex and often there are genetic abnormalities that arise in the early human embryo. The work being carried out at the University College London has shown that many embryos created in the laboratory using the IVF process will have at least some cells with chromosomal abnormalities. The consequences of these abnormalities are thought to be why so many IVF embryos die. This project looks at comparing the genetic profiles of the embryos to try and understand why some embryos develop well and why some embryos do not progress beyond a few cells.

Embryo growth (Imperial College London)

When embryos are being selected to be used as part of the reproductive process it is the 'best' embryo that is chosen for implantation. Currently, embryos are selected on their structure and shape. This project is investigating and analysing those other factors that would provide the most viable embryos and improve the methods of embryo selection.

WHAT ARE THE MORAL ISSUES RAISED BY THE USE OF EMBRYOS IN RESEARCH?

It is important to remember that, with any topics surrounding the use and treatment of embryos, the **status of the embryo** will always be raised as a moral issue. Research into embryos will include the destruction of embryos, so whether you believe the embryo to be a person or not will have important consequences. Have a look back through the other sections and make sure you can explain the different viewpoints on the status of the embryo and what this would mean regarding using embryos in any scientific research.

Means to an end

Much of this research is exploratory. It helps scientists and the medical profession to find out more about embryos. The result for each embryo being used is not going to directly lead to the birth of a human or to help someone who is suffering, so the embryo is only being used as a means to an end. In other words, the embryo itself is not valued as an embryo, it is only important because it is useful in achieving an aim.

Slippery slope

In issues of ethics or morality, the **slippery slope argument** is one that is concerned with the future consequences, or things that might happen later because of what is permitted just now. Some people question whether some of the research into embryos represents a slippery slope concerning what could happen in the future. Have a think about issues such as **eugenics** and **animal/human hybrid embryos** and why some people might think this is acceptable, whilst for others it could cause problems moving forward.

Morality, medicine and the human body: Research

WHAT ARE THE RELIGIOUS RESPONSES TO THE MORAL ISSUES RAISED BY THE USE OF EMBRYOS IN RESEARCH?

The sanctity of life

The sanctity of life is a religious argument that runs through this topic. Remember the four key beliefs: that humans are **Made in God's image**, that **Life is wonderfully made and a gift from God**, that **God is sovereign** and the command that **thou shall not kill**. Have a look back at the **Sanctity of life** section in Reproductive uses of embryos (see pages 76-77).

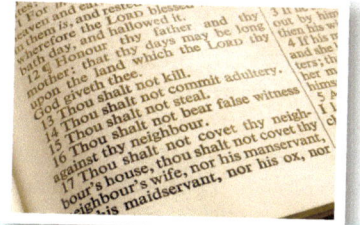

The Church of Scotland

The Church of Scotland believes that the embryo should have special status, although there are also 'recognised potential benefits of embryo research under limited circumstances'. So, it very much depends on the circumstances of the research, and the fact that the Church of Scotland uses the phrase 'limited circumstances' suggests that many of its members do not agree with destroying embryos from many of the research projects that are taking place.

Sikhism

Sikhism has contrasting views when it comes to embryo research. Some Sikhs believe that because research into embryos means that those suffering from illness or experiencing pain could be helped by the therapeutic uses of stem cells, then it should be allowed. The research could be considered as **Sewa**, which is acting selflessly to help others. However, other Sikhs disagree with using embryos for research because of their views on the status of the embryo. Many Sikhs believe that from conception humans have what is known as an **atma**, or a soul, so embryo research, as it would destroy an embryo, is against their beliefs.

WHAT ARE THE NON-RELIGIOUS RESPONSES TO THE MORAL ISSUES RAISED USING EMBRYOS IN RESEARCH?

Utilitarians

The Utilitarian philosopher Peter Singer views the embryo as having no special status, and wrote 'If we take the fertilised egg... it is hard to get upset about its death. The fertilised egg is a single cell... without a single anatomical feature of the being it will later become'. Therefore, he sees no problem in using embryos for the purposes of research. Remember, **Utilitarians** make moral decisions by thinking through the possible consequences of actions, wanting to bring about as much happiness or pleasure as is possible and to minimise pain, so therefore would hope that the consequences of the research into embryos would bring about more happiness as we develop our understanding of how embryos can be used.

The **BMA** is very much in favour of using embryos for research. The quote given earlier is very relevant here: the BMA said '[Embryo] research, carried out under the control of the Human Fertilisation and Embryology Authority (HFEA), has the potential to improve our understanding of and treatment for many very serious medical conditions'.

Secular Pro-Life is a non-religious pro-life group. In a piece of writing entitled *A secular case against abortion*, they write 'Life begins at fertilization...This is not a religious premise; it is a biological fact, attested to in countless biology and embryology texts and affirmed by the majority of biologists worldwide'. The view that they hold on the status of the embryo would mean that many within the organisation would be against destroying embryos for research.

 ### THINGS TO DO AND THINK ABOUT

1. The four key beliefs of the sanctity of life are that humans are **Made in God's image**, that **Life is wonderfully made and a gift from God**, that **God is sovereign** and the command that **Thou shall not kill**. If someone believed these statements and took them as the basis for their beliefs then how would they respond to how embryos should be treated for research?

2. Having gone through each section concerning the uses of embryos, have a go at these two 20-mark questions; remember that the breakdown for the 20-mark question is 10 marks for knowledge and understanding, 5 marks for analysis and 5 marks for evaluation.

   A) *'The use of embryos can never be justified.'* To what extent do you agree with religious responses to this statement? (20 marks)

   B) *'The use of embryos can always be morally justified.'* To what extent do you agree with non-religious responses to this statement? (20 marks)

Organ donation

MORALITY, MEDICINE AND THE HUMAN BODY

CONSENT

DON'T FORGET

The word 'consent' can be thought of like the word permission; therefore, to consent is to give permission.

DON'T FORGET

The NHS encourages people to sign up to the organ donation register so that their decision is recorded. They are also advised to have conversations with their families so that they are aware of their decision and can therefore ensure that their wishes are respected when they die.

DON'T FORGET

In 1979, Spain implemented a presumed consent system that is recognised as having the highest rate of donation in the world. Austria, which legalised presumed consent in 1982, saw its organ donation rate quadruple by 1990.

ONLINE

Click the link on our Digital Zone at www.brightredbooks.net/subjects and have a look at the Organ Donation Scotland website for some more information on the current system in Scotland and some of the real-life stories associated with the issue of organ donation.

INFORMED OR PRESUMED

Whenever someone dies, their organs and tissue can be passed on to save, or improve, the lives of others. Globally, there are different systems regarding how organ transplantation works and even within the UK there is different legislation regarding organ donation, specifically regarding the issue of consent. With regards to organ donation there are two main systems or types of consent, these are known as informed consent (opt in) and presumed consent (opt out).

Informed consent

If the system is one of informed consent, then to become an organ donor when you die, you must at some point have informed the government/NHS of your decision to be an organ donor by asking to be added to the organ donation register. This is sometimes known as an opt-in system. If you do not sign up to the register and **'inform'** the government/NHS of your decision then the NHS cannot use your organs or tissue. In the UK, under informed consent, if you have not made a decision regarding organ donation, a specialist nurse will work with your family so that they have the opportunity to provide the most up-to-date information regarding your views on being a donor, which will be respected.

Presumed consent

If the system is a presumed consent system, then it is **'presumed'** that you are an organ donor, unless you have expressed to the government/NHS that you do not want to donate your organs when you die. This is sometimes known as an opt-out system. In the UK, the main system of consent is a **'soft presumed'** system, where it is presumed you are an organ donor; however, a specialist nurse will still talk to close family members about your views on donation. If family members are not aware that you wished to be a donor, then they can override the system of presumed consent and stop the donation from taking place.

One of the main challenges facing organ donation is that there is always a waiting list: globally the demand for organs is always much greater than the supply. The issue of consent has a big impact on the supply of organs, with the belief that presumed consent systems increase the numbers of organ donors. The *Journal of Ethics* published by the American Medical Association states that 'the [informed consent] model has not been shown to be effective in increasing the supply of organs to a level anywhere near that of the demand'. However, the presumed consent system often tells a very different story: for instance, see the examples of Spain and Austria in the *Don't Forget* feature to the left.

CONSENT IN SCOTLAND

The system of consent changed in Scotland in March 2021, moving from a system of informed consent to a system of soft presumed consent. The Scottish Government highlighted that the reason for the change was 'to save and improve lives'. With only around 1% of people dying in a way that makes organ donation possible, the Scottish Government wants to maximise the opportunity of using those organs and tissue to help others in need.

WHAT ARE THE MORAL ISSUES RAISED BY INFORMED AND PRESUMED CONSENT?

Vulnerable in society

There are those in society who are considered vulnerable and might not understand the changes in legislation or the need to act if they do not wish their consent to be presumed with regards to organ donation. Is it morally correct to change the system of consent if these vulnerable people are at a disadvantage and do not know their options within the system? The soft opt-out system in Scotland seems to accommodate for this by excluding those **under the age of 16**, adults who **lack the capacity to understand the new law** and adults who have **lived in Scotland for less than 12 months** before they die. Some might question if these measures are sufficient to ensure that all those who are vulnerable are protected.

Autonomy

Autonomy means being able to make decisions about donation for yourself when and if you want. For some, changing from an informed system to a presumed system means that autonomy is more limited, because now they have to act and inform the NHS and make them aware of their decision not to be a donor; it is a choice they didn't have to make before but now may be forced to make. For others, patient autonomy is being increased by the change to presumed consent. Most of the religious and non-religious viewpoints we explore, and society at large, are in favour of organ donation and of helping those in need; therefore, a change to presumed consent aligns with the majority point of view and reflects their personal decision in the law.

Rights

The system of consent has a huge impact on human rights. One right that everyone has is the **right to privacy**, and opting in or opting out means that you have to declare your position on organ donation to others. In an informed system, if you didn't want to be an organ donor you could keep your views or beliefs private; however, if you don't want to be an organ donor and the system moves to one of presumed consent then you must give up your right to privacy by making the NHS aware of your decision. Another way in which consent can impact rights is that not consenting to be an organ donor, or asking to opt out from a presumed system, may be seen as selfish in that it denies those who need a transplant the **right to life** or **the right to social service** (medical care).

Medical integrity

Medical integrity concerns the relationship between the patient and the doctor. Doctors take an oath called the Hippocratic oath and promise to uphold certain moral standards and to do no harm to patients. If every patient was to become a donor, then is there a risk that doctors would begin to see dying patients as a collection of spare parts that can be used to help many other patients? Would this compromise the relationship between the patient and their doctor and the care that they give? Doctors in the past have expressed a wish to gain the consent of the family even if the patient hasn't opted out of being a donor, to maintain integrity in the donation process.

Giving

An informed consent system means that those who opt in have an opportunity to give (donate) something to someone as an act of generosity. In a presumed system that option is taken away, as rather than donating your organ, you are simply not objecting that it is being taken from you. This removes an opportunity for kindness and compassion towards others.

Does it increase the supply of organs?

One of the main reasons that governments want to move from an informed to a presumed system of organ donation is to increase the supply of organs. We have seen that in countries like Spain and Austria the presumed consent system does just that; however, in other countries this hasn't always been the case. In 1997, Brazil moved to a system of presumed consent, but later had to return to a system of informed consent. Donations did not increase because the country didn't have the infrastructure to keep a record of recipients and inform them when a donor became available. So sometimes simply changing the system isn't always the answer.

 THINGS TO DO AND THINK ABOUT

Make a set of flashcards and test yourself on the different types of consent as well as the moral issues that are raised by consent and organ donation.

MORALITY, MEDICINE AND THE HUMAN BODY
RESPONSES TO THE MORAL ISSUES

RELIGIOUS RESPONSES TO THE MORAL ISSUES RAISED BY INFORMED AND PRESUMED CONSENT

Sanctity of life

Sanctity of life is always central to the **Christian** response in medical ethics. Think about the four main beliefs regarding the sanctity of life: that humans are **Made in God's image**, that **Life is wonderfully made and a gift from God**, that **God is sovereign** and the command that **Thou shall not kill.** How would someone who held these beliefs respond to organ donation and the issues raised regarding consent? Most Christians overwhelmingly support organ donation, as Dr Barry Morgan, Archbishop of Wales, explains: 'Giving organs is the most generous act of self-giving imaginable'. Think about how these beliefs might interact with some of the moral issues we have explored.

Church of Scotland

The Church of Scotland released a leaflet entitled *Transplantation: Opting-in or opting-out for organ and tissue donation?* In the leaflet they state that 'It would be immoral not to do everything ethical to prolong and improve the quality of lives of those in need of transplant'; however, the leaflet also states that it is important to consider that 'such a change could discriminate against groups who might not be aware of any change, through lack of knowledge or understanding'. The Church of Scotland also said that there would need to be clear evidence that changing the system would provide more organs for transplantation.

Hinduism

The Hindu faith views organ donation as a very positive thing. Hasmukh Velji Shah, who is an International Trustee for the World Council of Hindus, explains 'that which sustains life should be accepted and promoted as Dharma (righteous living). Organ donation is an integral part of our living'. It is worthwhile to note that many Hindus view organ donation as *Daan*, which means 'selfless giving', and selfless giving/*Daan* is one of the 10 Niyamas (virtuous acts) important to Hindu practice. A question that might be raised is whether moving to a system of presumed consent takes away that ability to 'selflessly give'?

NON-RELIGIOUS RESPONSES TO THE MORAL ISSUES RAISED BY INFORMED AND PRESUMED CONSENT?

The British Medical Association (BMA) has been a supporter of the law changing to a soft opt-out (presumed consent) system for organ donation. They state 'we believe this is the best option for the UK to reduce the shortage of organs and save lives'.

Remember that **Humanists** make moral decisions based on reason, empathy and a concern for other human beings. The **Humanist** response is very much in favour of a system of presumed consent and Humanists have campaigned for a change to the legislation in the UK. On the Humanist website it states that:

'(Humanists UK) campaign for a move away from an "opt-in" system of consent to donating organs in favour of a "soft opt-out" system where a deceased person over the age of 16 is presumed to have consented to their organs being donated, unless they had specifically stated otherwise and their family members know of no prior objection.'

This is because Humanists believe that '[a]n opt-out system increases the number of organs available for transplant, saving lives'.

Classical **Utilitarianism** would state that moral decisions should be made in a way that takes into account the consequences of our actions, whilst doing the greatest good for the majority of society. It would make sense then for Utilitarians to be in favour of a system of presumed consent. As the Utilitarian philosopher and bioethicist Jacob M. Appel states, 'Presumed consent generates many more available organs'. The consequences of many more available organs would be a society where there is a greater opportunity for life-saving transplant surgery.

An **Egoist** is someone who will perform a moral action only if it maximises their own self-interest. As a moral theory, egoism is very different from Utilitarianism, as the egoist only considers themselves: they are not interested in the welfare of others. You could find that an egoist would be in favour of informed consent because it would mean that if they ever needed an organ then there would be a greater supply available; however, when it comes to actually giving up their own organs and becoming a donor, an egoist might not have a preference as they have nothing to gain regarding their own welfare.

THINGS TO DO AND THINK ABOUT

Analysis is a key skill in RMPS. One way that we can analyse is to compare things and draw out similarities and differences. Compare some of the religious and non-religious responses from this section, making sure to refer to the **similarities** or **differences** between the responses.

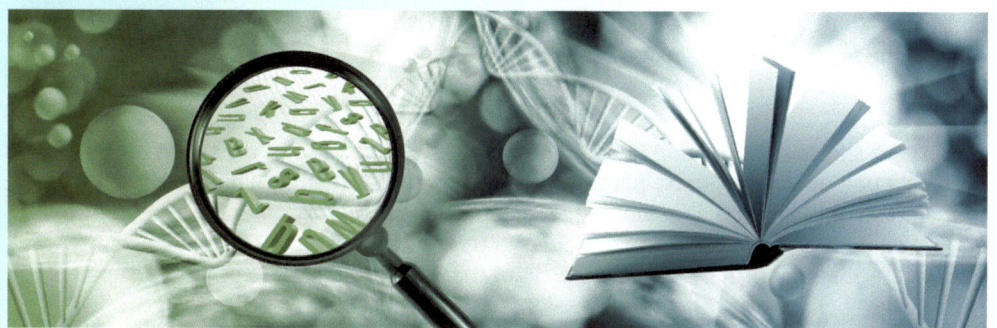

MORALITY, MEDICINE AND THE HUMAN BODY

BEATING AND NON-BEATING HEART DONATION

BEATING HEART DONATION

Organ donation that takes place after **brainstem death** (when the brain stops functioning) is known as **beating heart donation.** A ventilator takes over the breathing process, pumping oxygen into the lungs, keeping the circulatory system functioning until the transplant team can remove the organs, extending the viability of these organs and lengthening the time for transplantation to another patient.

Non-heart beating donation

Organ donation that takes place after **circulatory death** (when the heart stops working) is known as **non-heart beating donation**. This type of donation is categorised as either controlled or uncontrolled retrieval. Controlled retrieval happens after the withdrawal of life-sustaining treatments to someone who is critically ill in hospital. Uncontrolled retrieval happens after an unexpected cardiac arrest; patients are often dead upon arrival at the hospital. Advancements in medical science means that **non-heart beating donation** has increased significantly in the last 10 years, and currently the NHS have found that hearts donated after circulatory death prove to be successful.

DON'T FORGET

When organs are donated after brainstem death this is known as **beating heart donation.** When organs are donated after circulatory death it is known as **non-heart beating donation**.

DON'T FORGET

Organs such as the liver and pancreas are very vulnerable to interrupted blood supply, but it is now believed that lungs donated from non-heart beating donors have a greater chance of success.

WHAT ARE THE MORAL ISSUES RAISED BY BEATING HEART DONORS?

Dead donor rule

The dead donor rule means that organs cannot be taken until the patient has been declared dead. There is still controversy around confirming how we establish that someone has actually died. For some this is when the brain stops working or the heart stops beating, although not everyone is in agreement. Another important issue to consider is whether the cause of death is actually the removal of the organs. The brainstem is the control centre for how the body functions. After it stops working then it is only a matter of time before all the body's functions stop working, including the heart. Removing the organs has to happen whilst the heart is still beating; however removing the organs will inevitably cause death, so is removing the organs killing the patient or simply quickening an inevitable process?

Personhood

There is some controversy regarding beating heart donors and whether they are actually dead when their organs are removed. A person may be past the point of no return when brainstem death has been established, but the argument remains that they can be considered to be a dying person rather than a dead person. If the organs retrieval team remove the organs at this point, is that dehumanising the donor?

Respect

Due to the shortage of beating heart donors, there is concern that the dying patient is seen as a potential set of spare parts to help others rather than as a person. Being treated in this way could be seen as removing an element of the dignity and respect patients should be entitled to. Is the dying patient still treated with care, the same care as those who will receive the organs? Some may claim that this could lead to compromising the relationship between healthcare professionals and patients.

DON'T FORGET

The lack of success is mainly due to the interrupted blood supply between the time of death or end of treatment and the removal of the organs.

DON'T FORGET

Beating heart donors often simply look like they are sleeping as the ventilator is keeping them breathing, so saying goodbye can be traumatic for family and friends.

DON'T FORGET

There is also the issue of respect for the dying patient's family, which must also be taken into consideration.

WHAT ARE THE RELIGIOUS RESPONSES TO THE MORAL ISSUES RAISED BY BEATING HEART DONORS?

As we have explored earlier, most religions are in favour of organ donation as it is a compassionate act and is seen as a virtuous (morally excellent) thing to do. As Dr Desmond Biddulph, the chairman of The Buddhist Society UK, explains:

'Giving is the greatest of Buddhist virtues…What loss do I suffer to give an unwanted organ after my death to give another person life?'

The Jewish response

David Katz, Board of Deputies of British Jews, states: 'The issue of brainstem death is still highly controversial amongst those who interpret Jewish law'.

Some orthodox Jews would be of the opinion that beating heart donation should not be allowed, as to remove organs at this point would be to end that person's life. Rabbi Elyashiv, known as one of the most important Rabbis in Israel until his death in 2012, wrote this regarding a beating heart donor who was classed as brain dead: 'It is our view that it is absolutely not permissible to remove any of his organs; and to do so would involve the taking of a life'. **Other Jewish leaders would respond differently**. Rabbi Jerome Davidson, past president of the Synagogue Council of America, has acknowledged that there can be 'grey areas'; however, for him **compassion** is very important, and there is no need to keep someone alive if they are suffering and there is no hope of renewal, so brainstem death becomes an acceptable definition of death. The Rabbi states: 'It becomes clear that when there is no hope, it is permissible to cease artificial ventilation, tube feeding, and water feeding if the person is just being kept alive in a state that is not really living at all'.

The Islamic response

Islam is not unlike the Jewish response with regards to beating heart donors. **Some Muslims view brain death as an in-between state between life and death** and believe that life support needs to continue, so would disagree with beating heart donation. Others, however, such as the International Islamic Fiqh Academy (an international Islamic organisation dealing with Islamic law), came to the conclusion that, in a time when there was a great need for organ donors, a person can be pronounced legally dead when either the heart stops, or when the brain completely stops all vital functions.

WHAT ARE THE NON-RELIGIOUS RESPONSES TO THE MORAL ISSUES RAISED BY BEATING HEART DONORS?

Think back to Utililitarianism on page 51. As organs from **beating heart donors** are thought to be in better condition and more transplantable than those that come from **non-heart beating donors,** many Utilitarians would be in favour of using organs from beating heart donors as the consequences would maximise happiness for those in need of an organ transplant.

Humanism

The Humanist response to beating heart donors is complex. A famous case regarding brainstem death was that of Jahi McMath, a 13-year-old who was pronounced brain dead in hospital. The medical professionals wanted to remove her from the ventilator not long after the diagnosis of death was made by both doctors and a judge. Medical professionals had also attempted to speak to the family about organ donation as a next step. Her family, however, refused to accept the diagnosis of death and fought to keep her on life support. In an article on Jahi McMath, the American Humanist Association concluded that 'Leaving the decision up to the family is the most practical, especially because there is no consensus among scientists, philosophers, and bioethicists on the definition of death'. When it comes to brainstem death, specifically in this situation, respecting the views of family and next of kin would allow Humanists to make a moral decision based on empathy and concern for other human beings.

THINGS TO DO AND THINK ABOUT

Analyse [religious responses to] the moral issues raised by beating heart donors.

You can remove the bit in brackets and replace it with [non-religious responses to] or [moral issues raised by]. You can also swap out the beating heart donors with other issues such as living donors, assisted dying and reproductive uses of embryos, etc.

> **DON'T FORGET**
> The main religious concern with beating heart donors is not the donation of organs, but whether the donor is actually dead.

> **DON'T FORGET**
> If the person is considered dead from brainstem death, many Jews would view it as compassionate to allow their organs to help save the life of another.

> **DON'T FORGET**
> Muslims who follow this line of thought would have no issue with beating heart donors and would see it as supporting the Qur'anic teaching on the importance of saving a life.

> **DON'T FORGET**
> The main thinking behind **Utilitarianism** is what we call *the principle of utility*, which states that actions are right if they promote happiness or pleasure and wrong if they produce unhappiness or pain.

> **DON'T FORGET**
> Withdrawing life-sustaining treatment in this instance might not bring the greatest happiness to the greatest number of people. This shows how complex the **Utilitarian** response can be.

> **DON'T FORGET**
> Humanists don't believe in faith, nor do they follow the teachings of a higher supreme being when considering their moral actions. Humanists make moral decisions based on reason, empathy and a concern for other human beings.

MORALITY, MEDICINE AND THE HUMAN BODY

LIVING DONORS

Living donors are people who have decided to donate organs while they are still alive. The most common organ donated by living donors is the kidney; a healthy person can live a pretty normal life with only one kidney. About one-third of all kidney transplants in the UK are from living donors. Living donors can also donate a part of their liver, as well as tissue and bone. More than 1000 people across the UK donate a kidney or part of a liver each year.

LIVING DONATION

Living donation has a few key terms that, when understood, bring a bit of clarity to the living donation process. **Directed donation** is when a person makes a donation to someone they know; this could be a family member or friend. One issue with directed donation is that the donor is not always a suitable match for the patient they wish to help; in these circumstances the donor and patient take part in what is known as **paired or pooled donation**. This is a sharing scheme that enables kidneys to be 'exchanged' with other pairs in a similar situation.

There is also what is known as **altruistic donation**; the term altruism is whenever someone shows selfless concern for the wellbeing of others. Altruistic donation could take one of two forms. It could be **directed altruistic donation**, when a donor offers their donation to a specific person they don't know but may have read about in the news or heard about on social media, or it could be **non-directed altruistic donation**, when a donation is made to a stranger.

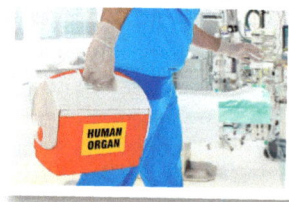

ONLINE

Organ Donation Scotland has a great website with excellent Scottish-specific information on what it means to be a living donor as well as further information on organ donation in general. Click the link on our Digital Zone at www.brightredbooks.net/subjects

WHAT ARE THE MORAL ISSUES RAISED BY LIVING DONORS?

Coercion

Is the living donor giving altruistically (selfless concern for the wellbeing of others), or do they feel coerced (forced into it) by outside pressures, such as emotional pressure, threats or illegal payments, etc.?

Organs as a commodity

Organ transplant commercialism and the black market for organ donation create the issue of organs becoming a commodity in great demand. Does living donation open up the opportunity for the buying and selling of organs? Is organ commercialism morally justified or morally wrong? The illegal black-market trade in organs is an area of great concern. Pope John Paul II said 'Accordingly, any procedure which tends to commercialize human organs or to consider them as items of exchange or trade must be considered morally unacceptable, because to use the body as an object is to violate the dignity of the human person'.

Risk

It is clear that a living donor is putting themselves forward for a medical procedure that involves a risk to their own health and wellbeing. Is it morally justified to put yourself in harm's way for the good of someone else?

Principle of non-harm

Doctors take the Hippocratic oath, which has as a principle to 'first do no harm'; is operating or performing surgery doing harm and putting the donor at risk? If so, is it ever morally justifiable for a doctor to put a donor at that risk?

Morality, medicine and the human body: Living donors

WHAT ARE THE RELIGIOUS RESPONSES TO THE MORAL ISSUES RAISED BY LIVING DONORS?

The Roman Catholic Church encourages organ donation and their response to living donors would be similar. A recent article indicated that the Catholic Church had consistently encouraged its followers to consider organ donation as it considers the act of donating organs (before or after death) as both a gift and an intrinsic good. The **Canadian Catholic Bioethics Institute**, however, does offer some considerations, stating that 'the recipient's need must be serious with no other treatment options, the benefit to the donor must be proportionate to the risk taken by the donor and there must be free and informed consent from the donor without coercion'.

Many **Muslims** would have a similar response to the **Roman Catholic view** on living donation. The **Institute of Islamic Jurisprudence** states that 'living/altruistic organ donation is permissible provided harm to the donor is negligible or relatively minor that it does not disrupt the life of the donor'. This illustrates that the issues concerning risk and harm are key to the morality of the decision.

ONLINE

The NHS has a great video playlist on YouTube exploring all issues of organ donation and the Islamic faith. You can view it by clicking the link on our Digital Zone www.brightredbooks.net/subjects

WHAT ARE THE NON-RELIGIOUS RESPONSES TO THE MORAL ISSUES RAISED BY LIVING DONORS?

Humanism is in favour of organ donation and Humanists would have no problem with people becoming living donors. Living donation would allow Humanists to show empathy and concern for other human beings, values that are central to a Humanist. **Coercion** and **risk** are two moral issues that must, however, be considered alongside the Humanist response. In a written memorandum to Parliament a few years ago, the **British Humanist Association (BHA)** said that individual choice was central to living donation. If someone wants to be a living donor, they must 'have enough information to make a rational choice for herself about the risks of such a procedure to her wellbeing and life compared with the benefits to the wellbeing and health of the person needing that organ'. This means that Humanists would support living donation provided it is the donor's personal choice (i.e., they are not being coerced) and the donor understands the risks that are involved. The same memorandum also endorsed the 'ban on sale of organs', highlighting that the **BHA** objects to organs being a commodity that can be bought and sold.

DON'T FORGET

Think about how a **Utilitarian** and an **Egoist** make moral decisions. What would these philosophical responses look like with regards to living donation?

 ## THINGS TO DO AND THINK ABOUT

Similar to the 10-mark analysis question in the last section, you can also create some evaluation questions using a similar structure. These questions allow you to evaluate either the responses or moral issues raised by a topic. Again, it's quite straightforward to write these questions yourself to practise your **evaluation** skills. Use the same template as before, swapping analyse for evaluate;

Evaluate [religious responses to] beating heart donors.

You can simply take out the bit in brackets and replace it with [non-religious responses to] or [moral issues raised by]. You can also swap out the beating heart donors with other issues in the medical ethics section, such as living donors, assisted dying and reproductive uses of embryos, etc.

End of life

MORALITY, MEDICINE AND THE HUMAN BODY
ASSISTED DYING 1

EUTHANASIA AND ASSISTED DYING

Euthanasia comes from two Greek words 'eu' meaning good or well, and 'thanatos' meaning death. So, euthanasia can roughly be translated as 'good death'. It is the act or practice of allowing an individual to die, sometimes at their own request and other times because of the decision of medical professionals, close family or next of kin, when the individual is unable to make a decision for themselves. The intention is to give the patient as painless a death as possible when they are suffering unbearably from an incurable disease or illness. Another term that you may see used is the term mercy killing.

Assisted dying is a form of euthanasia and refers to cases where the person who is going to die needs help to die and asks for someone to help them. An example of this may be getting drugs for that person and putting those drugs within their reach so they can administer them. Helping someone to end their life in this way is illegal in England and Wales under the Suicide Act 1961. In Scotland there is no specific crime of assisted dying; however, helping someone to die could lead to you being prosecuted for culpable homicide or even murder. **Physician-assisted dying** is assisted dying that involves a physician (medical doctor); the physician assists the patient by providing a means to die such as providing medication for the patient, who will then use this to end their own life.

You may see the terms assisted dying and assisted suicide used interchangeably. The UK and Scottish Government don't make any distinction between the terms; however, many groups that support assisted dying state the terms are different, arguing that the term assisted dying refers only to those who are terminally ill, whilst assisted suicide would include those who are not terminally ill as well.

ONLINE

Go online to our Digital Zone and click the link to find out more about the work of Dignity in Dying www.brightredbooks.net/subjects

WHAT ARE THE MORAL ISSUES RAISED BY ASSISTED DYING?

Look back to the CRAVE framework on pages 50 and 51 and attempt to think through what moral issues might arise with the topic of assisted dying. Try this out for all the issues raised in the 'End of Life' section of the course. There are very important issues, which are listed below. If you look closely, you will see that the first letter of each issue gives you the acronym ACDC, which might make it easier to remember.

Autonomy

The word **autonomy** comes from the Greek auto-nomos, which translates as self-rule and means being able to make decisions for yourself. If human beings can control every aspect of their lives, such as how we live, spend our money or what job we do, then the question remains, does it make sense that we should have the right to decide when and how our lives end?

Dignity in Dying patron, Sir Patrick Stewart, has argued 'We have no control over how we arrive in the world but at the end of life we should have control over how we leave it'. Sir Patrick Stewart is highlighting the importance of autonomy when it comes to the end of life. In his view humans should have control over those difficult decisions about how and when their life should end. Others may believe that when it comes to matters of life and death, we shouldn't have the autonomy to interfere with natural processes; many religious followers would take this further and believe that everyone has a divine plan and that only God or a divine power has the authority to give and take away life, those decisions are out of people's control.

contd

Morality, medicine and the human body: Assisted dying 1

Compassion

Compassion means showing sympathy and concern for the sufferings of others. This is one of the oldest and most debated moral issues regarding euthanasia and assisted dying. For many it seems very simple that as human beings we should try to reduce the suffering of others. As a humane society, therefore, we should show compassion and provide ways for individuals to end their pain and suffering through ending their lives in ways and means that are appropriate. Others however would argue that more compassion is shown through caring for people as they journey through the final stages of life. Providing good **palliative care** and improving this provision to control pain for the patient is seen by some as more compassionate than assisting someone to end their life.

Dignity

The term **dignity** means the right that a person has to be valued and respected and this is a very complex moral issue with regards to assisted dying. Having to rely on the help of other people to do what many consider straightforward everyday tasks such as eating, washing and using the toilet might be unimaginable, but for many this loss of dignity is a key factor in wanting to legalise assisted dying. Many would argue that not having assisted dying as an option whenever someone comes to the end of their life means that people may go through pain, suffering and a loss of dignity that they would rather avoid. If someone is terminally ill, allowing that person to control how and when they die means they are treated with greater dignity.

Others, however, such as those who believe in the sanctity of life, argue that allowing assisted dying and letting someone choose to end their life is undignified and actually devalues and disrespects life. As before, those who oppose assisted dying would argue that **palliative care,** which doesn't just treat pain at the end of life, but also offers spiritual, social and psychological support until death happens naturally, values and respects the person in a holistic way and is more dignified than assisted dying.

Control

Another moral issue in the assisted dying debate is that of **control**. Many argue that there are already countries where assisted dying has been legalised, and legislation exists which allows assisted dying to take place in an appropriate and just way. There are, however, those who question whether legislation and laws can control an issue that often isn't black and white and has many shades of grey.

In 2015, MSPs in Scotland rejected the Assisted Suicide (Scotland) Bill: 82 MSPs voted against and 36 voted for. There was significant support to see the law changed, although a Holyrood committee had concluded that the proposed legislation had several flaws and the **Law Society of Scotland** raised a concern that the proposed changes to the law lacked clarity, stating 'Lack of such clarity leads to ambiguity and leaves the legislation open to interpretation'.

THINGS TO DO AND THINK ABOUT

Assisted dying, like many of the issues we explore in medical ethics, is a serious issue and a real issue. It is something that impacts many people daily, and so we have to approach it with thoughtful understanding. There are deliberately no studies in this section, but there are many examples that can be explored to understand the personal importance of this issue, to patients, but also for their families and the medical professionals involved. One way to do this is to first read the story and then use CRAVE to analyse or break the case study down (have a look back to the 'Using the CRAVE framework to explore moral issues' section).

You can, of course, use the internet to do your own search for cases, but two to consider to begin with are:

- Noel Conway – Dignity in Dying
- Alison Davis – Care Not Killing

MORALITY, MEDICINE AND THE HUMAN BODY
ASSISTED DYING 2

WHAT ARE THE RELIGIOUS RESPONSES TO THE MORAL ISSUES RAISED BY ASSISTED DYING?

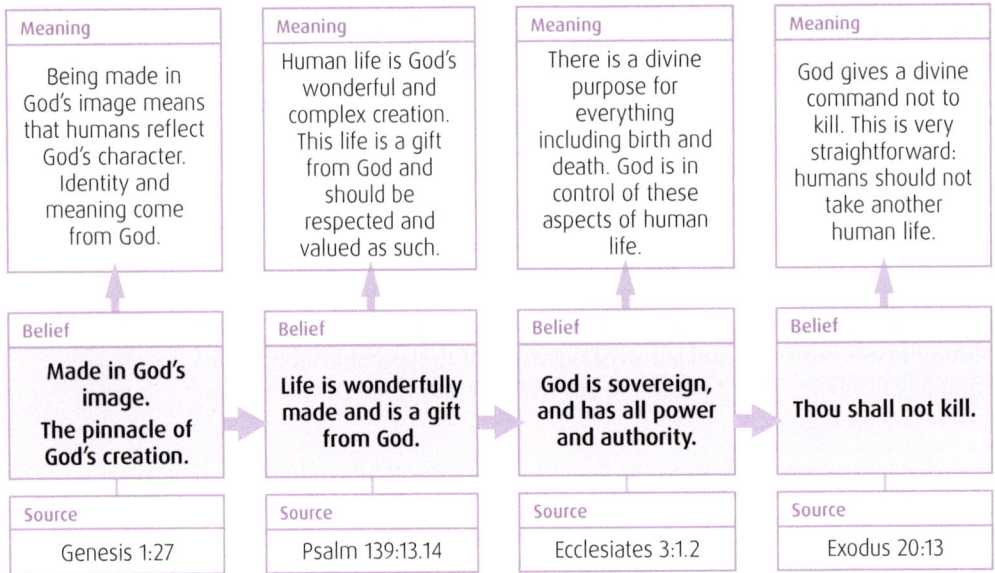

Just as we have seen in the other sections of Morality, medicine and the human body, understanding the sanctity of life is key to understanding the religious responses to assisted dying. As we explored earlier in the section, and as is outlined in the table, what is important is the religious belief (the coloured boxes), where it comes from (the source) and what this means with regards to the issue (in this case assisted dying and the moral issues it raises).

Christianity

As we understand more about the concept of the sanctity of life, we can conclude that the **general Christian** response is that assisted dying is wrong. The **Catechism of the Catholic Church** is quite clear on its teaching regarding euthanasia and suicide. It highlights that humans are stewards of a life which God has given; it is not theirs to dispose of. It also states that if suicide is carried out to set an example it can be considered a scandal and any voluntary co-operation (or assisting) in suicide is contrary to the moral law.

The **Church of Scotland** argued against the Assisted Suicide (Scotland) Bill in 2015. Of great concern was the impact that legalising assisted dying would have on the way society views its weakest and most vulnerable citizens. With regards to the moral issue of autonomy, the **Church of Scotland** is of the opinion that community is more important, they state 'instead of an individualistic approach to personal autonomy ("It's my life and I can choose how and when to end it") the interdependence of community life is more important'. This highlights the views of the church that decisions regarding the end of life do not just affect the terminally ill person, but also the family, medical professionals and the understanding of all of society.

Not all Christian viewpoints however oppose assisted dying. **Desmond Tutu, the Archbishop emeritus of Cape Town** in South Africa has made it clear in several media publications that terminally ill people 'should have the right to choose a dignified assisted death'. Tutu stated 'I have been fortunate to spend my life working for dignity for the living. Now I wish to apply my mind to the issue of dignity for the dying.'

Other church leaders have also reviewed their position on assisted dying. **Lord Carey, former Archbishop of the Church of England**, stated 'In strictly observing the sanctity of life, the Church could now actually be promoting anguish and pain, the very opposite of a Christian message of hope'.

Islam

Many Muslims are also opposed to assisted dying. The **Muslim Council of Britain** have said that '[legalising assisted dying would] in our collective view, fundamentally shift the emphasis away from the preservation of life, which should be cherished and protected, to viewing life as a commodity, to be dispensed with when deemed of little value'. Similar to the views held by the Church of Scotland, the Muslim Council of Britain explained that those approaching the end of their life are among the most vulnerable members of society and legalising assisted dying removes safeguards and puts their fundamental rights at risk.

WHAT ARE THE NON-RELIGIOUS RESPONSES TO THE MORAL ISSUES RAISED BY ASSISTED DYING?

Non-religious responses to assisted dying are quite mixed. There are many similarities with religious responses, as most (if not all) non-religious organisations and groups hold the belief that life is valuable, that people should have the right to life (not to be killed) and that society should protect the most vulnerable. However, many believe that patient autonomy is important, with some believing it is more important than anything else, and that each individual should be in control of their death.

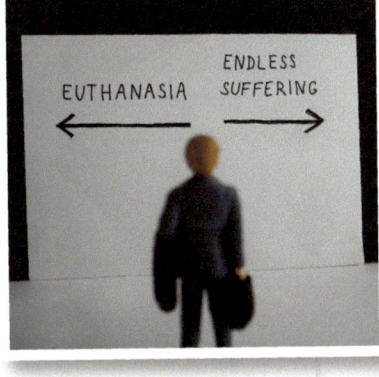

The Humanist Society Scotland believes that personal autonomy is key in end-of-life decisions, stating 'we are in favour of the right to choose to end one's own life, subject to appropriate qualifications and safeguards'. Speaking to the Scottish Parliament during the proposal of the Assisted Dying Bill in 2015, Dr Bob Scott highlighted the reasons why the Humanist Society Scotland supported assisted dying. Dr Scott explained that when suicide comes as a consequence of mental illness or emotional turmoil it is a tragedy; assisted dying, however, is different, as this is when decisions are made by sane individuals who have calmly decided to end their lives because of **incurable illness and unbearable suffering**, and that can be appropriate. He went on to explain that **tolerance** should lie at the heart of legalising assisted dying, we should be tolerant of the measured conduct of others, even although their decisions might go against our personal values.

Dignity in Dying is a national organisation campaigning to legalise assisted dying in the UK. Similar to the Humanist view, **they believe in the importance of autonomy** and that dying people should be in control of how and when they die. The organisation is quite clear that assisted dying should only be an option for those who are terminally ill (diagnosed as having six months or less to live) and mentally competent, so therefore not as wide reaching as other organisations who believe it should include those with incurable illnesses. **Dignity in Dying** believes that allowing dying people to control their death safely in the comfort of their own home would guarantee the patient a safe and peaceful death. They believe this would **bring greater dignity than the alternatives**, which include paying thousands of pounds to travel abroad or risking a painful death by ending their lives themselves.

 ONLINE

The Not Dead Yet website has some content that is worth reading to appreciate why it opposes assisted dying. The website can be accessed by clicking the link on the Digital Zone www.brightredbooks.net/subjects

The British Medical Association (BMA), the independent trade union that represents doctors from across the UK, has a policy position of **neutraliity**. The BMA reached the conclusion that the continuing improvement in palliative care allows patients to die with **dignity**. The organisation also has an important role in listening to and protecting doctors and has stated that if any type of euthanasia was legalised there should be a clear distinction between the doctors who would and would not be involved in the practice.

Not Dead Yet is a disability rights group with members in the USA and UK. It opposes making assisted dying legal and believes it is a deadly form of discrimination.

Some of the reasons Not Dead Yet is in opposition to assisted dying include:

- The implications for disabled people if assisted dying is added to the list of medical treatment options.
- The unreliability of a doctor's prognosis that patients are terminally ill (i.e., will die inside six months).
- The expansion of the law to include those with an incurable illness, not just those who are believed to be terminal.
- The main reasons why many physicians issue lethal prescriptions in specific places in the USA concern disability issues, for example a loss of autonomy, being less able to engage in activities, the loss of bodily functions, loss of dignity and the feeling of being a burden. These are issues that many people with disabilities face in their lives, and the stigma associated with them is one of the primary reasons for enacting assisted dying laws.

 THINGS TO DO AND THINK ABOUT

Create your flashcards (and then use them properly). Go through the content and pick out the key information about the topic, the moral issues, the religious and non-religious responses and then test yourself or your classmates on what you understand.

MORALITY, MEDICINE AND THE HUMAN BODY

VOLUNTARY AND NON-VOLUNTARY EUTHANASIA 1

Before we begin to explore the different types of euthanasia it is important to remember a few key things. Euthanasia is

- Intentionally ending a person's life to stop pain and suffering
- Illegal in all forms in the UK, although it is legal in other countries
- Very complex with different approaches, methods and medical terminology
- Met with very different responses because of the many moral issues it raises.

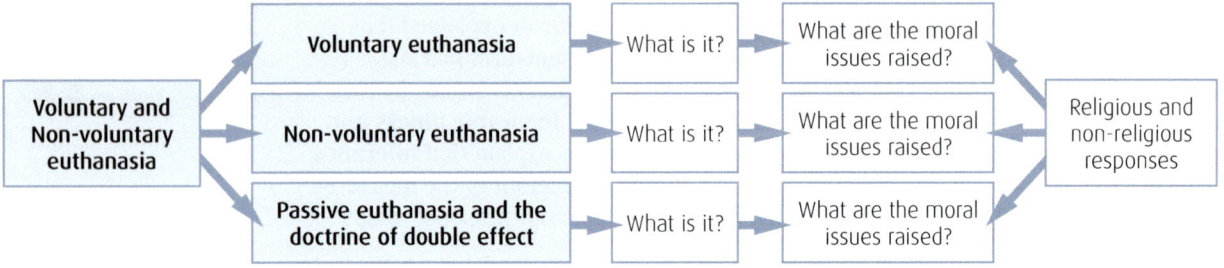

DON'T FORGET

The Groningen Protocol is an extremely controversial piece of legislation. Those who oppose it regard it as an attempt to legalise the intentional killing of infants, whilst others believe that the Protocol is a success in ending the unbearable and constant pain that some infants experience and don't have a voice to end.

VOLUNTARY AND NON-VOLUNTARY EUTHANASIA

Voluntary euthanasia is when someone wants to end their life and asks for this to happen. An example of this is when a dying patient refuses medical treatment, asks for life-sustaining treatment to be withheld or withdrawn, makes a choice to die by some specific means (refusing to eat) or asks for help to end their life (assisted dying – which we have already explored in depth).

Non-voluntary euthanasia is when someone is unable to make a decision about their condition and someone else makes that decision for them. A distinction must be made between **active and passive** non-voluntary euthanasia. **Active non-voluntary euthanasia** is when someone has either acted towards or deliberately done something to end a patient's life, such as administering a lethal substance to a patient; this type of euthanasia is generally seen as illegal throughout the world, with the exception of the Groningen Protocol.

In the Netherlands, voluntary euthanasia has been common practice for the last 30 years. However, more recently, in 2004, **the Groningen Protocol** was established to allow **active non-voluntary euthanasia to take place**. The Protocol provides guidelines on ending the life of infants under the age of 1. This example of active non-voluntary euthanasia is acceptable under Dutch law if certain criteria are met: the infant must be going through hopeless and unbearable suffering; there is consent from the infant's parents; consultation has taken place with medical professionals; and there is careful execution of the termination of life. The Protocol raises many moral issues, many of which you will be able to come up with yourself using the CRAVE framework and some of which we will explore as we move on.

PASSIVE NON-VOLUNTARY EUTHANASIA

Passive non-voluntary euthanasia is whenever a doctor or other medical professionals either choose not to do something that would keep the patient alive or withdraw treatment that is keeping the patient alive. The cases when passive non-voluntary euthanasia could take place include

- if the person is in a coma with no chance of recovery
- if the person is in a permanent vegetative state (PVS)
- if the person is terminally ill, in unbearable pain and suffering and cannot communicate with others.

contd

This passive approach to euthanasia, where treatment is not given to the patient or is withdrawn, is known as a **Non-Treatment Decision (NTD)**. Medical professionals will consult with the patient's family before agreeing on an NTD.

The doctrine of double effect

The doctrine of double effect is an ethical principle that states when doing something good, there might be a morally bad side effect. However, provided the bad side effect wasn't intended, the initial good act can still be seen as morally good. The **doctrine of double effect** is used at times with regard to the topic of euthanasia to justify a patient's death. It may be that a doctor has to administer a lethal dose of pain relief to relieve a patient's pain and suffering; however, the side effect could be that the patient's life is shortened or ended.

WHAT ARE THE MORAL ISSUES RAISED BY VOLUNTARY AND NON-VOLUNTARY EUTHANASIA?

In the earlier section we looked at some of the moral issues raised by, and the responses to, assisted dying, which gives us an understanding of voluntary euthanasia. So, let's now turn our attention to the moral issues raised by non-voluntary euthanasia.

Autonomy

For many the key point about the right to die is that it is a personal choice. The patient has the **autonomy to ensure that any decision is voluntary**. However, when it comes to **non-voluntary euthanasia all autonomy is removed** as the patient is unable to give consent. Therefore, it might very well be the case that choices that are made by family members or medical professionals on behalf of the patient are different from the choices that the patient would make themselves.

Virtue

If something is of virtue it shows high moral standards. Some would argue that to choose to take the life of another person is not a morally good choice. Ending someone's life does not exemplify high moral standards and is made even worse when it is something that they have not consented to. Others, however, believe that putting an end to a situation where someone is in unbearable pain and suffering and can't make a decision for themselves is, morally, a good thing to do. The patient may well want to end their own life, they just can't communicate that, so others have a duty to act on their behalf. The fact remains that, because the patient can't voice their own decision on the matter, there will always be a debate with regards to what is right and wrong in any particular situation. If a patient makes an **advance decision to remove treatment (ADRT)** then there is a little more clarity regarding their wishes if there comes a point when they can't communicate these themselves; we will explore ADRT further in another section.

Duty to care

In the UK, doctors have a duty to care for their patients and are also, as the General Medical Council states, 'personally accountable for your professional practice and must always be prepared to justify your decisions and actions'. Some doctors may feel that their duty to care means that they should do whatever is within their power to end any intolerable pain or suffering a patient is going through; in this scenario non-voluntary euthanasia could be seen as an act of compassion. If non-voluntary euthanasia was made legal then it would protect doctors, with the result that carrying out such an act of compassion would not see a doctor being prosecuted.

Other doctors may believe that it is their responsibility to attempt to sustain life at all costs and any type of euthanasia should never be an option. The BMA surveyed thousands of medical professionals and the overwhelming response was that doctors would not be willing to administer drugs with the intention of ending a patient's life, even if the law changed to make it legal. Would legalising non-voluntary euthanasia change a 'duty to care' to a 'duty to kill'?

 ## THINGS TO DO AND THINK ABOUT

This chapter has been full of important terminology that is key to your understanding of euthanasia. Take some time to create a glossary of the key terms, write down these keywords or terms and then add the definition or explanation.

Euthanasia	Non-voluntary	NTD
Assisted dying	Passive	Doctrine of double effect
Voluntary	Active	ADRT

MORALITY, MEDICINE AND THE HUMAN BODY

VOLUNTARY AND NON-VOLUNTARY EUTHANASIA 2

WHAT ARE THE RELIGIOUS RESPONSES TO THE MORAL ISSUES RAISED BY NON-VOLUNTARY EUTHANASIA?

Christianity

The Catholic Church's response to voluntary and non-voluntary euthanasia is that it is wrong. The **Congregation for the Doctrine of the Faith**, the body responsible for protecting Catholic doctrine based at the Vatican in Rome, recently released a letter stating that 'euthanasia is a *crime against human life* because, in this act, one chooses directly to cause the death of another innocent human being'. The letter goes on to declare that 'Euthanasia, therefore, is an intrinsically evil act, in every situation or circumstance'. The Catholic Church does, however, believe that rejecting aggressive or disproportionate medical treatments that have little hope of positive results is allowed. They believe that this is not the same as euthanasia, it is simply the acceptance of the human condition as it faces death. Others, however, might claim that this withdrawal or denial of treatment could be defined as passive non-voluntary euthanasia.

The **Church of Scotland** oppose euthanasia, arguing that dying is a natural process and those who become vulnerable through illness or disability deserve special care and protection and proper end-of-life care does this much better than euthanasia. These views come from the beliefs that the church has in the sanctity of life (which we have explored).

Sikhism

Sikh teaching also shares some similarities with Christianity with regards to **opposing euthanasia** as Sikhism teaches that all life is sacred and is given by God. The Guru Granth Sahib states that 'Everyone comes here at the Lord's command, leaves in his will and remains merged, too, in the Lord's will'. This means that humans cannot choose the time when life ends; it is decided by God. Interestingly, some Sikhs will also use this passage from the Guru Granth Sahib as an argument **in favour of passive non-voluntary euthanasia**, as keeping someone alive who has no chance of recovery is prolonging life for longer than God intended.

Buddhists

Buddhists are generally against all forms of euthanasia due to the teachings of the five precepts; this Buddhist guide to ethical issues states as its first precept that 'I undertake to abstain from taking life'. Some Buddhists argue that voluntary euthanasia could be seen as a compassionate act and is in line with the teachings of the Noble Eightfold Path; however, others believe that any type of active or non-voluntary euthanasia might bring about negative Kamma for the patient and for anyone assisting their death. Suffering at the end of life could be seen as the consequence of previous negative Kamma and any attempt to remove this suffering will simply delay it until a future life: the suffering is simply something that the person must work through.

WHAT ARE THE NON-RELIGIOUS RESPONSES TO THE MORAL ISSUES RAISED BY NON-VOLUNTARY EUTHANASIA?

The BMA's stance is that voluntary and non-voluntary euthanasia, as well as physician-assisted suicide, should not be legalised in the UK. The BMA's policy is debated and voted on nationally by elected members from the medical profession across the UK. They believe the further development of high-quality palliative care is what allows patients at the end of their lives to die with dignity, not any form of euthanasia. They believe that doctors have a **duty to care** for patients, and want to protect doctors, and have stated that if any type of euthanasia was legalised there should be a clear distinction between those doctors who would and those who would not be involved in the practice.

Humanists are in support of legalising assisted dying and voluntary euthanasia across the UK; however, the organisation does not offer much of a response towards non-voluntary euthanasia. **The Humanist Society Scotland**, however, is very clear in its views that personal choice is central to any issue at the end of life, and personal choice is something that is not offered under non-voluntary euthanasia. One organisation that the Humanist Society Scotland advocates on its website is the charity **Friends at the End**. This non-religious organisation is very clear in its terminology, explaining the differences between assisted dying and euthanasia, and in response to non-voluntary euthanasia, explains 'We do not advocate for euthanasia, where someone else, usually a doctor, administers the life-ending medication'.

Dignity in Dying is very clear as to what it is campaigning for and what laws it wants to see changed: assisted dying legalised for terminally ill, mentally competent adults. Dignity in Dying is also very clear with its response to euthanasia, explaining 'We do not campaign to change the law to allow doctors to end the lives of their patients, known as euthanasia, or to legalise assisted dying for people who do not have capacity to make the decision for themselves'. So, Dignity in Dying does not support non-voluntary euthanasia.

Utilitarian views on voluntary and non-voluntary euthanasia are varied: some believe that legalising both would bring the greatest good to the greatest number of people, whilst others oppose this. The well-known Utilitarian philosopher **Peter Singer** argues in favour of voluntary euthanasia and in some cases non-voluntary euthanasia. Singer argues his point based on the quality of life of the patient and whether those at the end of their lives can still be considered persons due to a lack of self-awareness and not being capable of reasoning. If the patient can no longer be considered a person, then Singer believes that they aren't entitled to the same rights as others. This debate surrounding personhood has important consequences when it comes to the moral issues of autonomy and virtue; take some time to explore what these might be for you.

THINGS TO DO AND THINK ABOUT

Read through the content on the moral issues, religious responses and non-religious responses and do a brain dump for each of these key bits of content.

MORALITY, MEDICINE AND THE HUMAN BODY

END-OF-LIFE CARE 1

ONLINE

To explore this in more detail, click the link on our Digital Zone and have a look at the Scottish Government's anticipatory care planning toolkit online www.brightredbooks.net/subjects

END-OF-LIFE CARE

End-of-life care is the care that you receive when you are nearing the end of your life. For some, end-of-life care will begin days before the end of their life, while for others it may begin months, or possibly years, before their life ends. The NHS considers patients to be approaching the end of life when they are 'likely to die within the next twelve months, although this is not always possible to predict'.

Planning for the end of life

Thinking about and planning the care you would like at the end of life is something that can happen long before death. It is something that is often avoided as it can involve difficult decisions, as well as imagining yourself in a scenario or situation that is uncomfortable, and you would rather not. However, with regards to the issue of **autonomy**, having things in place can ensure that your wishes are respected as well as possibly making things easier for family members and medical professionals as they don't have to speculate what it is you would have wanted to happen if, for whatever reason, you can't communicate this to them. This is important in the euthanasia debate, specifically the debate around passive non-voluntary euthanasia and the withdrawal of treatment. Some of the things that can support planning for the end of life include:

- Advance Care Planning (ACP): advance or anticipatory care planning is a record of the decisions you have made about the care you wish to receive at the end of your life. It is made in partnership with family and healthcare professionals. The Scottish Government explains that advance care planning is important as it gives 'person centred care, dignity, choice and control'.
- Advance Decision to Refuse Treatment (ADRT): this is a decision that you can make in writing to refuse a specific type of treatment in the future. This includes life-sustaining treatments such as ventilation and infection-fighting antibiotics. ADRTs must be written, signed by you and signed by a witness; they are legally binding provided they comply with the Mental Capacity Act (you have the mental capacity to make these decisions), are valid and apply to the specific medical condition.
- Do Not Attempt Cardiopulmonary Resuscitation (DNACPR) order: this is a legal document that informs any medical team not to attempt CPR if you have a heart attack or cardiac arrest. Most patients never regain the physical or mental health they had before resuscitation, with some having brain damage or going into a coma.
- Power of attorney: this is a legal document that allows you to appoint one or more people (as attorneys) to make decisions on your behalf when you can't. If you do not have a power of attorney in place then, when it comes to healthcare, doctors ultimately make decisions for you in line with what they think are your best interests.

Palliative care

Palliative care is included within end-of-life care and exists to improve the quality of life of terminally ill patients. It is often seen as holistic care as it doesn't just manage the pain and physical suffering that is faced by the patient but also offers psychological, social and spiritual care.

Palliative care is available in a number of different environments that are significantly different. The four main environments are:

- Palliative care in hospitals: hospital palliative care is delivered over a short period of time by a specialist palliative care team. They will work alongside the patient and devise a plan for the patient to receive further care at a care home, a hospice or in their own home. This care is provided by the NHS in the UK.
- Palliative care in care homes: care homes with specially trained staff can offer palliative care. Many believe it is a calmer environment than a hospital in which to receive care, and not having to move makes things more comfortable for the patient. Most care homes are privately run and can be expensive.

contd

Morality, medicine and the human body: End-of-life care 1

- Palliative care in hospices: these are designed to be pleasant places where terminally ill patients can receive care and spend time with their friends or family. Some will spend many weeks at a hospice, while others might attend for the day (often to give respite to family members) and then return home. Many hospices also have facilities for families to stay with patients overnight. Hospices in Scotland are funded by charities.
- Palliative care at home: this allows patients to stay at home and receive palliative care. Depending on the situation, palliative care nurses may make arranged visits during the day, stay overnight or move into the home on a full-time basis.

Palliative care is also seen as care that goes beyond the individual patient, benefiting the family of the patient as well. The World Health Organisation (WHO) explains that 'addressing suffering involves taking care of issues beyond physical symptoms. Palliative care uses a team approach to support patients and their caregivers. This includes addressing practical needs and providing bereavement counselling.'

WHAT ARE THE MORAL ISSUES RAISED BY END-OF-LIFE CARE?

Cost

One of the big moral issues raised with end-of-life care, specifically palliative care, is the cost. All types of palliative care are expensive, but as we have seen, palliative care happens in many different environments with different providers, so the burden of that cost lands on different people. Some have asked **'should all palliative care be free?'** When patients are admitted to a private care home there is a cost that the patient must pay; if they can't afford this then choices for care can be limited. However, others could argue that we live in a consumer society that is filled with financial choices every day: those who have the money to pay for things can and those who can't do without.

There is also the **opportunity cost** when palliative care is funded by the NHS. The NHS doesn't have an endless supply of money, so when money is spent on palliative care other alternatives don't receive that funding. Many believe that we have a duty to care for those at the end of their lives and to make that time as comfortable as possible. Others are of the opinion that this money should be spent on things such as research or medical interventions for those at the beginning of their lives rather than those at the end of theirs. Cost also has a part to play in **the legal debate with assisted dying**.

Virtue

You would have to go a long way to find someone who suggested caring for someone at the end of their life wasn't a virtuous act. There are, however, other things to consider. Some would argue that **forcing palliative care on people when they don't want it** shows a lack of compassion, and that care becomes even less compassionate when people would rather stop that care for the alternative of assisted dying, but are legally denied that choice – some non-religious organisations view this as a removal of their personal autonomy. Others, however, argue that palliative care brings **a greater moral good** than the alternative of assisted dying **as it is more holistic** (psychological, social and spiritual care) and also supports the family or caregivers with things such as bereavement counselling, whereas assisted dying simply deals with the patient's pain.

Mental health and wellbeing

There is a big difference of opinion here. Advocates of palliative care believe that it provides the best care for patients at the end of their life, including psychological care for the patient. However, those who want assisted dying legalised believe that palliative care without the option of assisted dying is simply drawing out an inevitable death, which is detrimental to a patient's mental health and wellbeing.

THINGS TO DO AND THINK ABOUT

Go online to our Digital Zone for this topic to see our essay writing diagram and use it to turn the quotes online into a paragraph that you could use in an exam-style essay.

DON'T FORGET

Palliative care is often seen and referred to as an alternative to euthanasia and assisted dying. Some would agree that this is the case, whilst others, specifically advocates of assisted dying, would argue that it should be a 'both and' situation rather than an 'either or', with the terminally ill being allowed to access good quality palliative care until the time of their choosing to die.

DON'T FORGET

An opportunity cost is the alternatives that are missed out on when one thing is chosen.

DON'T FORGET

Some would argue that if people had their choice respected to end their lives rather than continue with what could end up being a long period of palliative care then money could be saved and spent elsewhere.

MORALITY, MEDICINE AND THE HUMAN BODY

END-OF-LIFE CARE 2

WHAT ARE THE RELIGIOUS RESPONSES TO THE MORAL ISSUES RAISED BY PALLIATIVE CARE?

Buddhism

Central to Buddhist belief and practice is the understanding that suffering is a part of human existence and that **true liberation only comes from ending that suffering**. This fits in with the principles and practices of good palliative care and its holistic approach at supporting people to navigate suffering. Therefore, it is not surprising that **most Buddhists are in favour of palliative care**. As part of that care, a Buddhist would encourage the practice of meditation to support mental health and wellbeing and the recognition that human existence is painful and filled with unsatisfactoriness.

Christianity

The **Church of Scotland** is very much in favour of palliative care as the only option at the end of life. They state that 'the Christian tradition provides us with structures of hope, meaning and new possibilities even in the midst of pain and suffering'. This shows the importance of living life even as death approaches. The Church explains that end-of-life care should not focus on the actual moment of death but rather that end-of-life period and if this period is to be the focus, rather than a moment, then 'it is best realised through the palliative care model of holistic care – physical, psychological, spiritual, social – with positive objectives which will enhance the remaining days of the patient, and of relatives and carers'.

Many other Christian traditions mirror this thinking as it upholds the sanctity of life. **The Catechism of the Catholic Church** indicates that palliative care is a special form of disinterested charity and, as such, should be encouraged. Care and preservation are the number one priority for the Catholic Church, as the catechism goes on to explain that 'we are obliged to accept life gratefully and preserve it for his honour and the salvation of our souls. We are stewards, not owners, of the life God has entrusted to us. It is not ours to dispose of.'

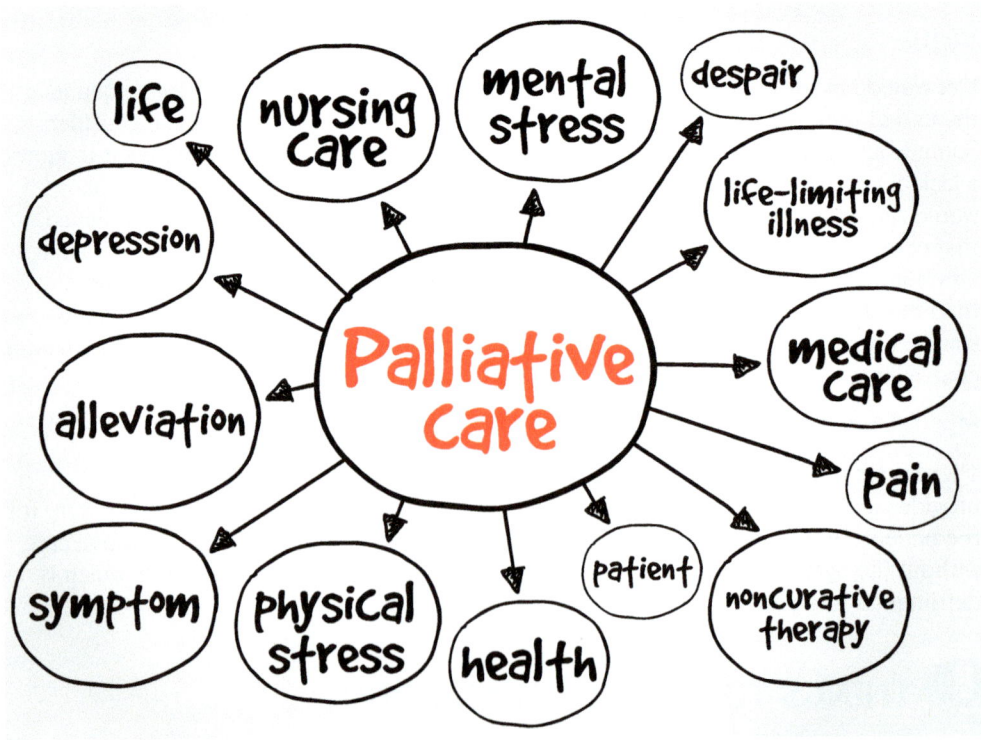

Morality, medicine and the human body: End-of-life care 2

WHAT ARE THE NON-RELIGIOUS RESPONSES TO THE MORAL ISSUES RAISED BY PALLIATIVE CARE?

As we have seen in previous topics, **the BMA** is against legalising any form of assisted dying or euthanasia and is very much in favour of palliative care. Its policy states that the BMA 'believe that the ongoing improvement in palliative care allows patients to die with dignity'. The BMA does not, however, believe that the system of end-of-life care is perfect in the UK, and a few years back undertook a significant project to explore the provision of care in the UK. Some of the key points put forward were:

- Although there are examples of excellent end-of-life care throughout the UK, there is considerable variation depending on where you live and what your illness is.
- To address the inconsistencies across the UK in end-of-life care there would need to be significant changes and investment.
- For the provision of services to be fairer the government needs to make end-of-life care a priority.

These findings suggest that, currently, for palliative care to be fairer and more consistent across the UK, a considerable amount of further resources and money are needed, impacting the issue of cost explored earlier.

The **Humanist Society Scotland** believes that assisted dying should be legalised, but not that it should exist as an alternative to palliative care. Quite the contrary, in fact, the Humanist Society Scotland has called for investment in palliative care and wishes to raise awareness through its 'end-of-life charter' so that everyone who wishes to access high-quality palliative care in Scotland has a right to do so. **Dignity in Dying** also believes that assisted dying should be legalised, but similarly to the Humanist response, it should not be at the expense of palliative care. Rather palliative care should be available as support for the dying patient until the point when the dying patient chooses to end their life. This gives the dying patient **full autonomy** to decide when care begins and when care ends

THINGS TO DO AND THINK ABOUT

Having now worked your way through each of the issues in the end-of-life sections, have a go at this **20-mark** question. Remember the split is 10 marks for knowledge and understanding, 5 marks for analysis and 5 marks for evaluation – knowledge and understanding is important but what you do with that knowledge is equally important.

'Palliative care should be the only option available at the end of life.'

To what extent do you agree?

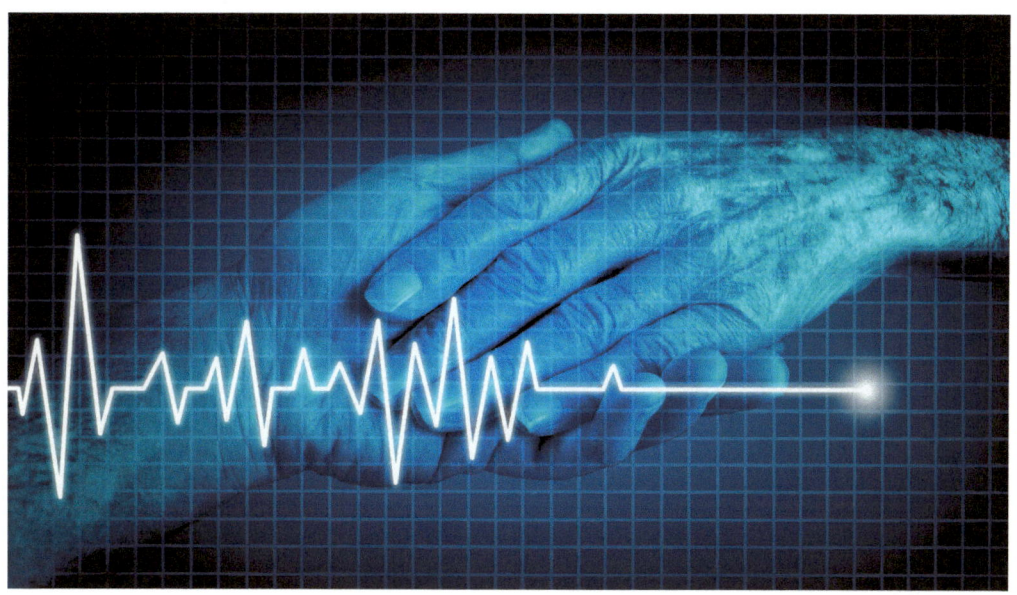

ORIGINS. WAS THE UNIVERSE AND LIFE CREATED?

RELIGIOUS AND SCIENTIFIC APPROACHES

This unit explores the religious and philosophical question 'Was the Universe and life created'? When answering this question in an exam there are usually three scenarios:
- A question with a focus specifically on the origins of the Universe.
- A question with a focus specifically on the origins of life.
- A question on 'Origins' that requires you to focus on both.

DIFFERENT APPROACHES

When it comes to the question of origins, there are two main responses to explore: the scientific response and the religious response. It is completely acceptable to explore other religious creation stories and compare them with scientific explanations. One useful way of approaching these responses is to think about them on a spectrum rather than in two distinct camps.

At the opposite ends of the spectrum there are two very different views. At one end are the viewpoints of Literalist Christians, such as Young Earth Creationists, while at the other end there are the viewpoints of the Scientific Materialists (that are often synonymous with the New Atheism movement). However, across the spectrum there is a range of viewpoints, some of which are difficult to categorise as specifically scientific or specifically religious. For example, many religious followers don't discard science, some scientists are very religious or others have no issues with religion. However, there are specific ways that knowledge is acquired that are unique to both and we understand these as scientific reasoning and religious reasoning.

DON'T FORGET

We will mostly focus on religious responses from Christianity because extensive coverage of all religious responses would make for a huge book!

DON'T FORGET

Understanding scientific and religious reasoning gives us a valuable insight into how both sides **gather and interpret their evidence**.

DON'T FORGET

Religious reasoning would suggest that, through the process of revelation, God has revealed key information that allows a Christian an insight into the origins of our Universe.

RELIGIOUS REASONING

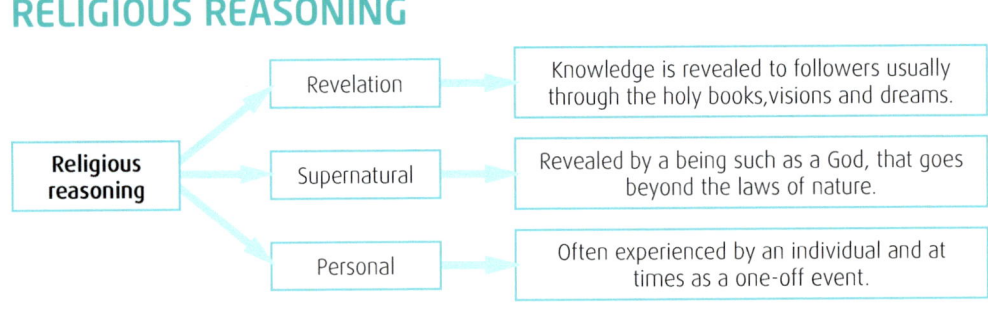

Religious reasoning or belief is gathered through experience and divine revelation. Divine revelation is knowledge that is revealed to humans by God. To an extent, it is supernatural, as the God who reveals the knowledge is a divine being who is beyond the laws of nature. This type of reasoning can also often be a very personal thing, experienced by individuals as a one-off event; therefore, believing in its validity requires an element of faith.

LIBERAL AND LITERALIST CHRISTIANS

Almost all Christians have one thing in common **regarding their beliefs on the origins of the Universe and life: they believe that God was ultimately responsible for the creation of the Universe.** However, that's not to say that all Christians believe the same thing, because their beliefs on this issue can be dramatically different. The differences in belief depend to how they interpret the Bible, specifically what has been revealed in Genesis. The question isn't 'if' God did it, but 'how' God did it.

contd

Origins. Was the Universe and life created: Religious and scientific approaches

Christian Literalists

Christian Literalists – also called Literal Creationists or Fundamentalists – interpret the account of creation in Genesis literally. This means they believe that scripture is 'God breathed' and cannot be added to or taken away from. The creation narrative in Genesis simply reads that God created the Universe and all that it contains in six 24-hour days, before resting on the seventh day. A fundamentalist approach would maintain that no interpretation is needed. They often reject scientific theories because they do not appear in the Bible. Many argue that scientific theories have been wrong before, and consequently, the Big Bang theory and the theory of evolution are no different. They argue that the evidence may well have been misinterpreted or that scientists are stuck in their ways, have their own agenda, or are completely blind to any other possibilities.

Liberal Christians

Liberal Christians adopt a symbolic or metaphorical interpretation of the Genesis account. To a Liberal Christian, these scriptural accounts are myths or stories that have been handed down from generation to generation. The accounts show that God is ultimately responsible for the creation of the Universe; however, when taken in context, they are interpreted with the understanding that the writers of these accounts were recalling these stories long before the emergence of modern science. Many Liberal Christians would argue that these accounts are rich in meaning but not in scientific fact. They would also hold that God has given his followers an intellect that allows for knowledge and understanding of the world around them to develop as time goes on.

Pope Francis adopts a liberal standpoint; 'When we read about Creation in Genesis, we run the risk of imagining God was a magician, with a magic wand able to do everything. But that is not so. The Big Bang, which today we hold to be the origin of the world, does not contradict the intervention of the divine creator but, rather, requires it. Evolution in nature is not inconsistent with the notion of creation, because evolution requires the creation of beings that evolve.'

SCIENTIFIC REASONING

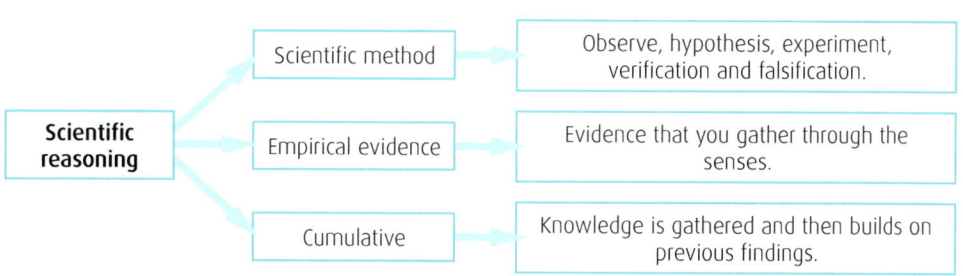

Scientific reasoning relies on what is understood as the scientific method which has five key stages:

- Observe - You observe what is happening in the world around you.
- Hypothesis - You construct a hypothesis as an idea or proposition.
- Experiment - You test your hypothesis to see if it is true.
- Verification - An analysis of the results of the experiment and retesting.
- Falsification - The understanding that new findings might bring future explanations that could disprove your initial hypothesis.

This method relies on empirical evidence, that is, evidence acquired by the senses or by observation. This type of evidence is testable, and this is one of the major differences when compared with the faith or belief required for revelation, which is understood to be untestable in this way. Scientific reasoning is also cumulative as there is an understanding that successive additions will probably come along as new empirical evidence comes to light.

THINGS TO DO AND THINK ABOUT

1. 'Religious reasoning is more convincing than scientific reasoning in the origins debate.' To what extent do you agree? Remember you need a mix of knowledge and understanding (KU), analysis (A) and evaluation (E).

DON'T FORGET

A good grasp of how Literalist and Liberal Christians interpret scripture is important because we will examine their interpretations of Genesis 1 and 2 when we explore the philosophical question: **Was the Universe and life created?**

DON'T FORGET

Ken Ham, founder of Answers in Genesis, states that 'There is a book that tells us where everything—including atoms and consciousness—came from. It is no mystery to Christians who accept the clear teaching of Scripture; everything was created by God in six, literal, 24-hour days about 6000 years ago.'

DON'T FORGET

Many Christian Literalists believe that modern scientific theories like evolution and the Big Bang theory exist to test their faith in God, or that these theories are being used by Satan to diminish or destroy their Christian beliefs.

DON'T FORGET

Most Liberal Christians will accept scientific theories such as the Big Bang theory and evolution, believing that our Universe is, as modern science would suggest, billions of years old and the Earth we find ourselves on is an 'old Earth'.

DON'T FORGET

As Stephen Hawking explained: 'Before we understand science, it is natural to believe that God created the Universe. But now science offers a more convincing explanation.'

ORIGINS. WAS THE UNIVERSE AND LIFE CREATED?

ORIGINS OF THE UNIVERSE – THE RELIGIOUS APPROACH

The religious explanation for the origins of the Universe is quite simply that **the Universe was created**. How the Universe was created varies dramatically from religion to religion and, as we will see from the liberal and literalist views within the Christian perspective, can also be interpreted differently within a religion as well. Christians are united in the belief that God created the Universe; the difference arises from how God did it, which depends on how the creation story in the Bible is interpreted.

THE BIBLE: GENESIS, CHAPTER 1

Genesis, Chapter 1, is the most significant biblical passage when it comes to the origins of the Universe. The chapter gives a blow-by-blow account of the six days of creation. It is useful to learn the story from Genesis 1 in its entirety as all six days of creation are useful to learn. Remember, though, that the first four of these days are specifically about the creation of the Universe, with days five and six being about the creation of life.

The six days of creation – Genesis Chapter 1, verses 1 to 27

1 In the beginning God created the heavens and the earth. 2 Now the earth was formless and empty, darkness was over the surface of the deep, and the Spirit of God was hovering over the waters. 3 And God said, "Let there be light," and there was light. 4 God saw that the light was good, and he separated the light from the darkness. 5 God called the light "day," and the darkness he called "night." And there was evening, and there was morning—the first day. 6 And God said, "Let there be a vault between the waters to separate water from water." 7 So God made the vault and separated the water under the vault from the water above it. And it was so. 8 God called the vault "sky." And there was evening, and there was morning—the second day. 9 And God said, "Let the water under the sky be gathered to one place, and let dry ground appear." And it was so. 10 God called the dry ground "land," and the gathered waters he called "seas." And God saw that it was good. 11 Then God said, "Let the land produce vegetation: seed-bearing plants and trees on the land that bear fruit with seed in it, according to their various kinds." And it was so. 12 The land produced vegetation: plants bearing seed according to their kinds and trees bearing fruit with seed in it according to their kinds. And God saw that it was good. 13 And there was evening, and there was morning—the third day. 14 And God said, "Let there be lights in the vault of the sky to separate the day from the night, and let them serve as signs to mark sacred times, and days and years, 15 and let them be lights in the vault of the sky to give light on the earth." And it was so. 16 God made two great lights—the greater light to govern the day and the lesser light to govern the night. He also made the stars. 17 God set them in the vault of the sky to give light on the earth, 18 to govern the day and the night, and to separate light from darkness. And God saw that it was good. 19 And there was evening, and there was morning—the fourth day.

20 And God said, "Let the water teem with living creatures, and let birds fly above the earth across the vault of the sky." 21 So God created the great creatures of the sea and every living thing with which the water teems and that moves about in it, according to their kinds, and every winged bird according to its kind. And God saw that it was good. 22 God blessed them and said, "Be fruitful and increase in number and fill the water in the seas, and let the birds increase on the earth." 23 And there was evening, and there was morning—the fifth day. 24 And God said, "Let the land produce living creatures according to their kinds: the livestock, the creatures that move along the ground, and the wild animals, each according to its kind." And it was so. 25 God made the wild animals according to their kinds, the livestock according to their kinds, and all the creatures that move along the ground according to their kinds. And God saw that it was good. 26 Then God said, "Let us make mankind in our image, in our likeness, so that they may rule over the fish in the sea and the birds in the sky, over the livestock and all the wild animals,[a] and over all the creatures that move along the ground." 27 So God created mankind in his own image, in the image of God he created them; male and female he created them.

Genesis 1:1-27, NIV Bible

DON'T FORGET

There are many translations of the Bible available today. The NIV (New International Version) or NRSV (New Revised Standard Version) are good places to start when looking at the scriptural accounts in Genesis in English.

ONLINE

Go online to our Digital Zone at www.brightredbooks.net/subjects and click the link to watch a video about creation.

contd

Origins. Was the Universe and life created: Origins of the Universe — the religious approach

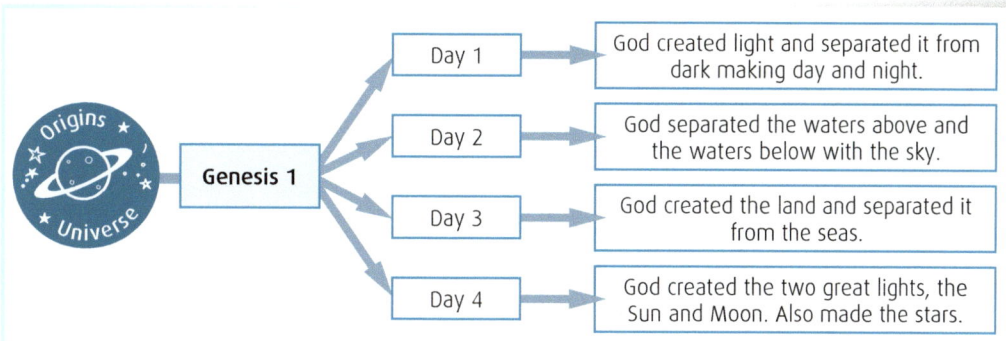

LITERALIST INTERPRETATIONS OF GENESIS 1

Literalist Christians believe that Genesis, Chapter 1, is literally true. The Universe and the Earth were created by God exactly as written in Chapter 1 of Genesis. Each day begins with morning and ends with evening and spans a period of 24 hours. Interpreting Genesis in this way means that most Literalist Christians believe that the Earth is relatively young in age. This viewpoint is often known as **'Young Earth Creationism'** and the general belief is that the Earth is about 6000 years old. The date upon which Young Earth Creationists believe the Earth began is often credited to an Irish archbishop called James Ussher. Ussher used a literal understanding of the Bible to work backwards through the Old Testament and he reached the conclusion that God's creative work began on 23 October 4004 BC. Whilst not all Literalist Christians agree entirely with Archbishop Ussher, most of them believe that the Earth is less than 10 000 years old.

LIBERAL INTERPRETATIONS OF GENESIS 1

Liberal Christians approach Genesis 1 in a more symbolic or metaphorical way. Liberal Christians believe Genesis 1 tells them that God was responsible for creating the Universe and the Earth, but most of them believe that Genesis 1 isn't conclusive as regards 'how' God did it. Liberal Christians do not agree with the literal understanding that each day in Genesis 1 is an actual 24-hour day, but rather that one day is more likely to represent a period of time, perhaps spanning thousands or millions of years: this is a specific liberal viewpoint that is known as **'Day Age Creationism'**. Day Age Creationists point to other biblical passages that hint at God's days not being an exact 24 hours in length; for example, as written in 2 Peter 3:8, 'With the Lord a day is like a thousand years, and a thousand years are like a day'.

THINGS TO DO AND THINK ABOUT

1. Within these liberal and literalist viewpoints, which one does the best job at convincing you that God could have been involved in the origins of the Universe? In your answer include:
   - The strengths within that viewpoint that makes it so convincing
   - The drawbacks that make it less convincing.

2. Alongside 'Young Earth' and 'Day Age' Creationism sit 'Old Earth' and 'Gap' Creationism. Use a search engine to find out about these viewpoints and see how they align with the Literalist and Liberal Christian responses.

ORIGINS. WAS THE UNIVERSE AND LIFE CREATED?

ORIGINS OF THE UNIVERSE – THE SCIENTIFIC APPROACH

THE BIG BANG

If you ask a scientist where our Universe came from then the most common answer will of course be that it wasn't created and began with the Big Bang. Almost 100 years ago an astronomer called Georges Lemaître theorised that our Universe began from a single point and expanded to what we observe as our Universe today. Some call this starting point the singularity. Other scientists are of the opinion that this exact starting point is unknown and possibly unknowable with the evidence we have. What scientists do know however is that from this point 13.8 billion years ago the Universe would expand in every direction to where it is today. All space, all time, all matter and all energy were born with the Big Bang.

The expansion grew from something smaller than the size of an electron to a universe a little smaller than we have today in a fraction of a second. The initial energy from the expansion formed the primordial elements hydrogen and helium, and the gases cooled to form galaxies, stars and planets.

EVIDENCE FOR THE BIG BANG

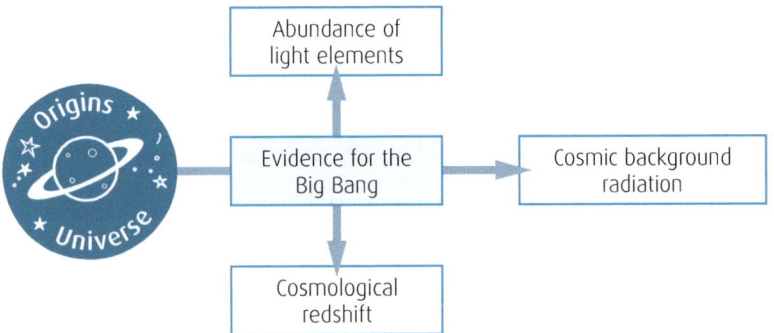

An abundance of light elements

If there was a massive expansion 13.8 billion years ago, scientists believe that we would have found evidence of lots of the lighter elements in our periodic table in our Universe. Scientists believe there would be an abundance of hydrogen and helium (those lighter elements) found in our Universe. You'll never guess what: there is an abundance of light elements such as hydrogen and helium in our known Universe!

Cosmic background radiation

This was first detected as excess noise when two telecommunications workers, Penzias and Wilson, were building a radio receiver. Most scientists believe this excess noise, which is actually radiation, is the remaining or leftover heat from the expansion/explosion that was the Big Bang 13.8 billion years ago.

contd

Cosmological redshift

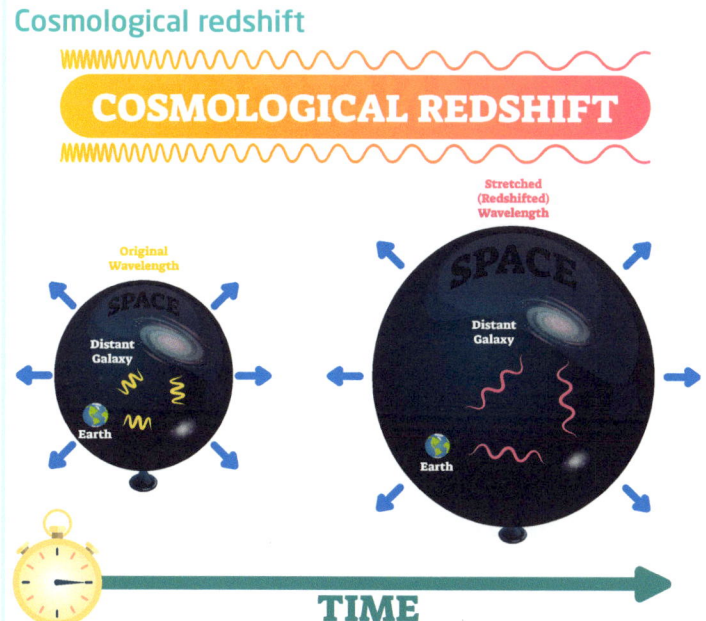

Redshift tells us that not only is our Universe expanding but that it is expanding from a central point. It works because as light or radiation is given off from a light source the wavelength will increase and show up on the red end of the spectrum. So, in simple terms, red lights in the Universe show that those light sources are moving away from us.

DID THE UNIVERSE HAVE A BEGINNING? AND OTHER THEORIES...

Whilst the Big Bang remains the most widely accepted scientific theory regarding the origins of the Universe, it is not the only scientific theory on the table. One issue that cosmologists (a fancy word for people who study the Universe) face with the Big Bang theory is how our Universe expanded so uniformly. The Universe's curvature is incredibly flat, to almost perfection, when it really shouldn't be, as there should be areas that are much denser than others. Some scientists have put forward theories of a cyclic universe (sometimes known as oscillating universe theories), which means that our Universe is part of an infinite and eternal series of expansions and contractions. These scientists believe that the expansions and contractions of each universe is what accounts for the uniformity in our present Universe. The significance of an eternal cyclic universe would be that our Universe wouldn't need to have a beginning, it would simply have always existed.

Another scientific alternative suggests that the Universe may have its origins in a series of mini-bangs rather than one big bang. This is the theory that nucleosynthesis created a series of mini-bangs, linked to quasar injections and 'white holes'. These white holes are capable of creating matter in clusters and superclusters and creating the Universe over a period of time.

 ## THINGS TO DO AND THINK ABOUT

1. Create an acronym to help you explain the Big Bang theory. Try and pick out at least four key points of knowledge.

2. How convincing is the Big Bang theory as an explanation for the origins of the Universe?

   Write as many developed points as you can for this question and try to include at least one point of knowledge, analysis and evaluation in your developed point.

3. Create a flashcard for each piece of evidence associated with the Big Bang.

ORIGINS. WAS THE UNIVERSE AND LIFE CREATED?

WHAT ARE THE STRENGTHS AND WEAKNESSES OF THE EXPLANATIONS?

THE STRENGTHS AND WEAKNESSES OF THE LITERALIST CHRISTIAN VIEW

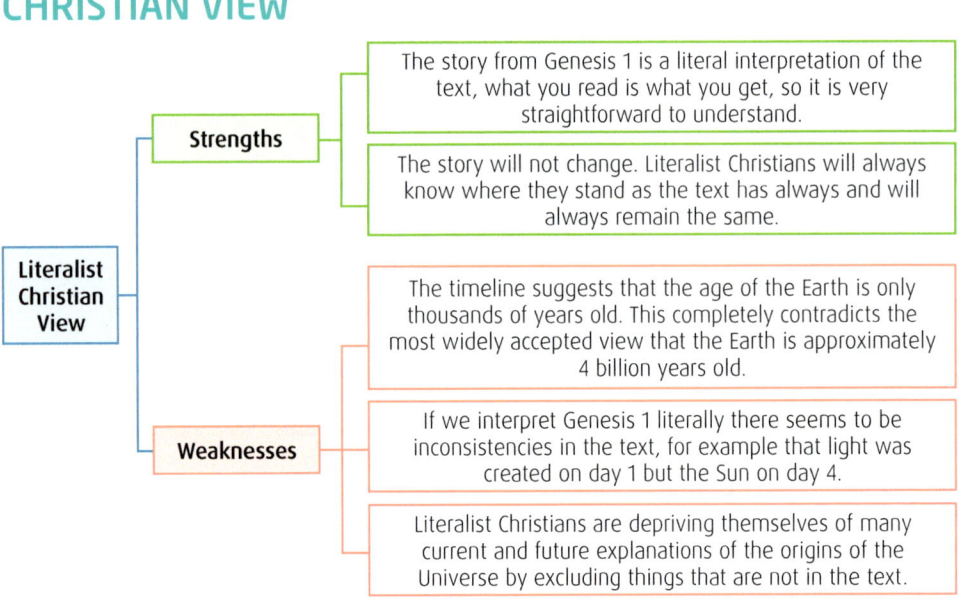

THE STRENGTHS AND WEAKNESSES OF THE LIBERAL CHRISTIAN VIEW

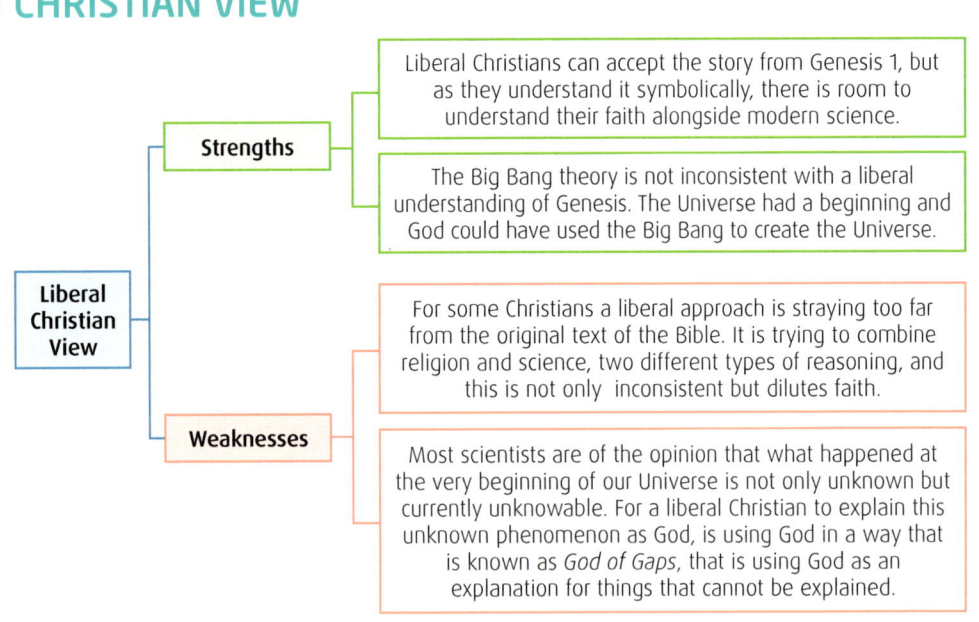

Origins. Was the Universe and life created: What are the strengths and weaknesses of the explanations?

THE STRENGTHS AND WEAKNESSES OF THE SCIENTIFIC VIEW

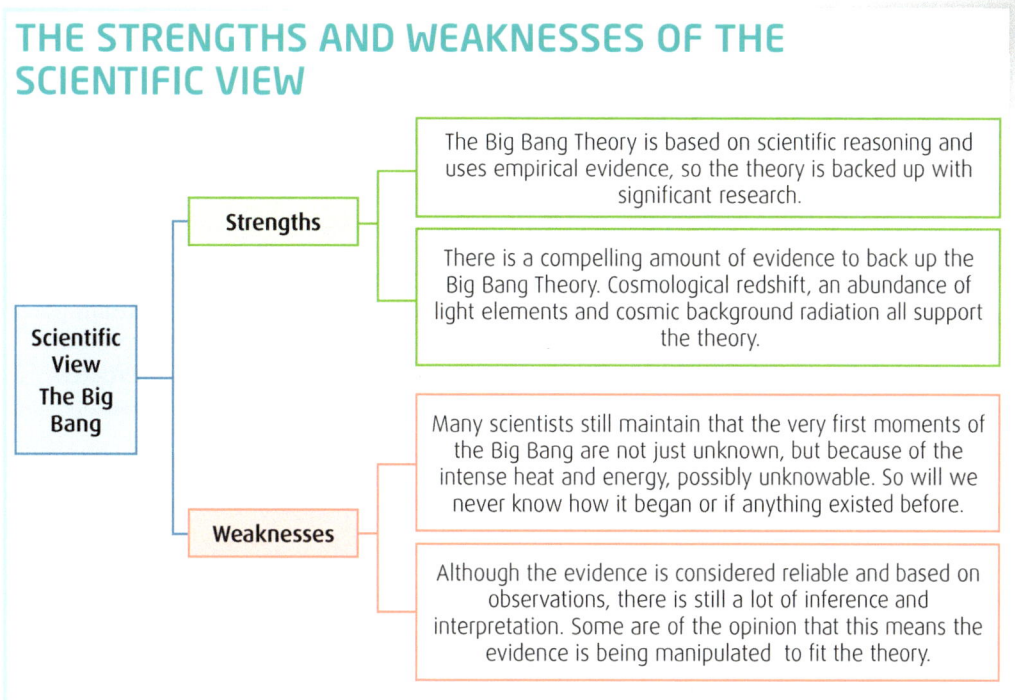

- **Scientific View – The Big Bang**
  - **Strengths**
    - The Big Bang Theory is based on scientific reasoning and uses empirical evidence, so the theory is backed up with significant research.
    - There is a compelling amount of evidence to back up the Big Bang Theory. Cosmological redshift, an abundance of light elements and cosmic background radiation all support the theory.
  - **Weaknesses**
    - Many scientists still maintain that the very first moments of the Big Bang are not just unknown, but because of the intense heat and energy, possibly unknowable. So will we never know how it began or if anything existed before.
    - Although the evidence is considered reliable and based on observations, there is still a lot of inference and interpretation. Some are of the opinion that this means the evidence is being manipulated to fit the theory.

 THINGS TO DO AND THINK ABOUT

1. Create a set of flashcards for all three viewpoints, highlighting the strengths and weaknesses.

2. Using the strengths and weaknesses for all three, play devil's advocate and write three developed points that explain why:
   - Literalist Christian viewpoints are the best explanation for the origins of the Universe as opposed to Liberal viewpoints and the Big Bang theory.
   - Liberal Christian viewpoints are the best explanation for the origins of the Universe as opposed to Literalist viewpoints and the Big Bang theory.
   - Scientific viewpoints of the Big Bang are the best explanation for the origins of the Universe as opposed to Liberal viewpoints and Literalist viewpoints.

ORIGINS. WAS THE UNIVERSE AND LIFE CREATED?

ORIGINS OF LIFE – RELIGIOUS AND SCIENTIFIC APPROACHES

THE RELIGIOUS APPROACH

The religious explanation for the origins of life is that life was created by God. How life was created varies dramatically from religion to religion and, as we will see from the liberal and literalist views within the Christian perspective, can also be interpreted differently within a religion as well. Christians are united in the belief that God created life; their differences concern how God did it, which comes down to how the creation story in the Bible is interpreted.

The Bible - Genesis, Chapter 2

Genesis, Chapter 2 is the most significant biblical passage when it comes to the origins of life. The chapter gives an in-depth account of how God created life.

> *The creation of life – Genesis, Chapter 2: A summary from the NIV*
>
> *5 Now no shrub had yet appeared on the earth and no plant had yet sprung up, for the Lord God had not sent rain on the earth and there was no one to work the ground, 6 but streams came up from the earth and watered the whole surface of the ground. 7 Then the Lord God formed a man from the dust of the ground and breathed into his nostrils the breath of life, and the man became a living being.*
>
> *8 Now the Lord God had planted a garden in the east, in Eden; and there he put the man he had formed. 15 The Lord God took the man and put him in the Garden of Eden to work it and take care of it. 18 The Lord God said, "It is not good for the man to be alone. I will make a helper suitable for him." 19 Now the Lord God had formed out of the ground all the wild animals and all the birds in the sky. He brought them to the man to see what he would name them; and whatever the man called each living creature, that was its name. 20 So the man gave names to all the livestock, the birds in the sky and all the wild animals. But for Adam no suitable helper was found.*
>
> *21 So the Lord God caused the man to fall into a deep sleep; and while he was sleeping, he took one of the man's ribs and then closed up the place with flesh. 22 Then the Lord God made a woman from the rib he had taken out of the man, and he brought her to the man. 23 The man said, "This is now bone of my bones and flesh of my flesh; she shall be called 'woman,' for she was taken out of man. 24 That is why a man leaves his father and mother and is united to his wife, and they become one flesh. 25 Adam and his wife were both naked, and they felt no shame.*
>
> *Summary of Genesis 2: 5–25 - a Summary*

Literalist interpretations of Genesis 2

Literalist Christians believe that Genesis, Chapter 2, is literally true. Life was created by God exactly as it says in Genesis, Chapter 2 (and a little bit from Chapter 1 as well). God lifted the dust of the ground and formed Adam in His image, breathing the breath of life into his nostrils. When it came to Eve, God put Adam to sleep and removed one of his ribs and with this rib God created Eve. Adam and Eve as the first humans are where all humans have come from. Literalist Christians believe that God created life according to its kind, the wild animals, livestock, birds, sea creatures and human beings are all specific 'kinds' of life created by God. It is because of this that there is no room for evolutionary theory. Any genetic change only happens within certain boundaries; for example, a dog can breed with another type of dog, but the offspring is still considered a dog – a kind of animal that God created.

contd

DON'T FORGET

Remember that we also looked at the creation story from Genesis 1 when exploring the origins of the Universe. This passage is also useful for the origins of life, although remember it's only days five and six that are relevant to life.

ONLINE

Go online to our Digital Zone at www.brightredbooks.net/subjects and watch the first two minutes of the video link there.

DON'T FORGET

Evolutionary theory is not mentioned in the biblical text and thus Literalist Christians consider it to be a test of faith or regarded as the current accepted theory from scientists (although incorrect). They believe that scientists have been wrong in the past and the proposal of evolutionary theory is a misreading of the evidence.

Origins. Was the Universe and life created: Origins of life — religious and scientific approaches

Liberal Interpretations of Genesis 2

Liberal Christians will interpret Genesis 2 in a more symbolic or metaphorical way. They believe that Genesis 2 tells them that God was responsible for creating life, but most believe Genesis 2 isn't conclusive regarding 'how' God did it. This allows many Liberal Christians to accept the theory of evolution alongside scripture. There are different ways that Liberal Christians will approach the theory. Many '**Old Earth Creationists**' believe that God created life and He also guides the process of evolution as it develops. Other Liberal Christians adopt a stance called '**Theistic Evolution**', which states that God started the process of evolution but plays a passive role as it progresses from the original creation event.

> **DON'T FORGET**
>
> The main thing to remember is that this symbolic understanding of the Bible allows for the scientific theory to be accepted alongside it.

THE SCIENTIFIC APPROACH

The scientific explanation for the origins of life comes from the theory of evolution. The theory explains that **gradually** over a long period of time an organism **adapts** or changes into a different and often more complex form. **Variations** or differences are present among species and some of these variations mean certain individuals have traits that are better suited to their environment; these advantageous traits allow some members of a species to survive better than others: this is known as **survival of the fittest**.

These advantages are said to occur naturally; hence this process is understood as **natural selection**. Charles Darwin is said to have used the term 'natural selection' in contrast to 'artificial selection'. Darwin used the example of pigeon breeding, which was a common hobby when he was alive. He explained that a pigeon breeder would choose different pigeons to mate to produce offspring with different traits. He suggested evolution was different because it happened by natural selection; it was an unaided natural process.

Evidence for Evolution

Fossils
Fossils are organisms that used to be alive and that have been turned into rock. Fossils form in layers in sedimentary rocks, with the oldest in the bottom layers and the youngest on top. Fossils become more complex, in the upper layers.

Embryonic similarities
It is often difficult to tell species of animals apart at the embryonic stage. The embryos of mammals, fish and birds are often very similar. An example are the embryos of a fish and of a human. Both embryos have gill slits; in humans they disappear before birth, whereas in fish they develop into gills.

Common features across species
Horses, donkeys and zebras have similar bodies that are structured in similar ways. This shows that all three came from a common ancestor. When animals share physical features because of a common ancestor they are said to be homologous. Another example are the forelimbs present in birds, humans and whales, where the organisation of the bone structure is very similar, once again indicating a common ancestor.

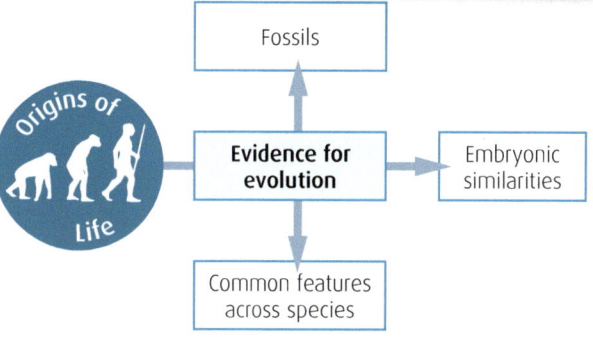

THINGS TO DO AND THINK ABOUT

1. Within the liberal and literalist viewpoints above, which one does the best job at convincing you that God could have been involved in the origins of life? In your answer, include the strengths within that viewpoint that makes it so convincing and the drawbacks that make it less convincing.
2. Create an acronym to help you explain the theory of evolution. Try and pick out at least four key points of knowledge (the text in **bold** should help you).
3. How convincing is the theory of evolution as an explanation for the origins of life?

   Write as many developed points as you can for this question and try to include at least one point of knowledge, analysis and evaluation in your developed point.

> **ONLINE**
>
> Go to our Digital Zone at www.brightredbooks.net/subjects to explore how Charles Darwin came up with the theory of Evolution by natural selection.

ORIGINS. WAS THE UNIVERSE AND LIFE CREATED?

STRENGTHS AND WEAKNESSES OF RELIGIOUS AND SCIENTIFIC APPROACHES

WHAT ARE THE STRENGTHS AND WEAKNESSES OF THE LITERALIST CHRISTIAN VIEW?

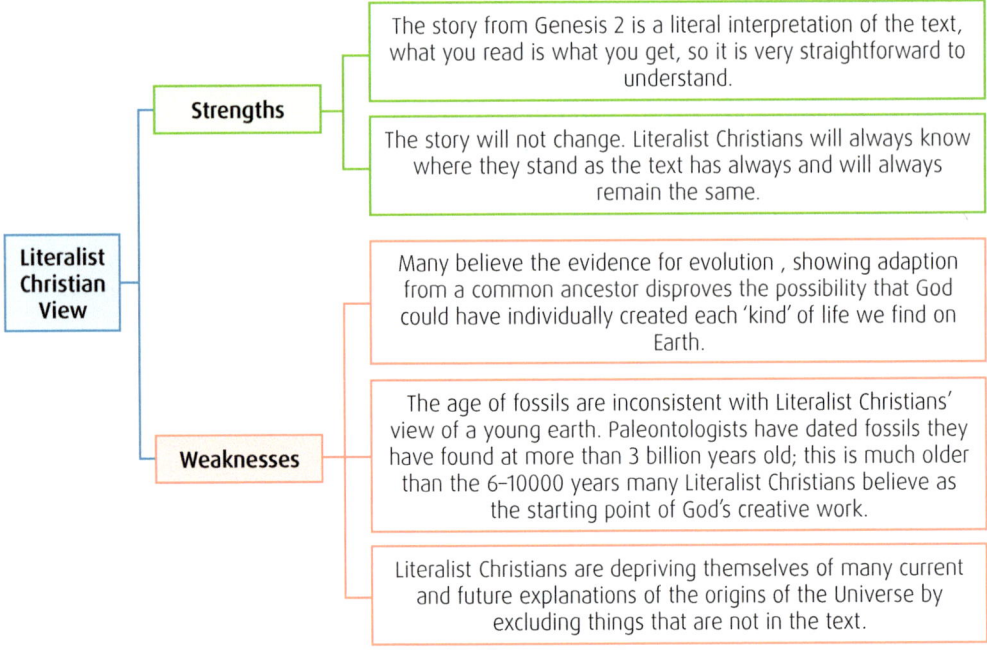

Literalist Christian View

Strengths
- The story from Genesis 2 is a literal interpretation of the text, what you read is what you get, so it is very straightforward to understand.
- The story will not change. Literalist Christians will always know where they stand as the text has always and will always remain the same.

Weaknesses
- Many believe the evidence for evolution, showing adaption from a common ancestor disproves the possibility that God could have individually created each 'kind' of life we find on Earth.
- The age of fossils are inconsistent with Literalist Christians' view of a young earth. Paleontologists have dated fossils they have found at more than 3 billion years old; this is much older than the 6–10000 years many Literalist Christians believe as the starting point of God's creative work.
- Literalist Christians are depriving themselves of many current and future explanations of the origins of the Universe by excluding things that are not in the text.

WHAT ARE THE STRENGTHS AND WEAKNESSES OF THE LIBERAL CHRISTIAN VIEW?

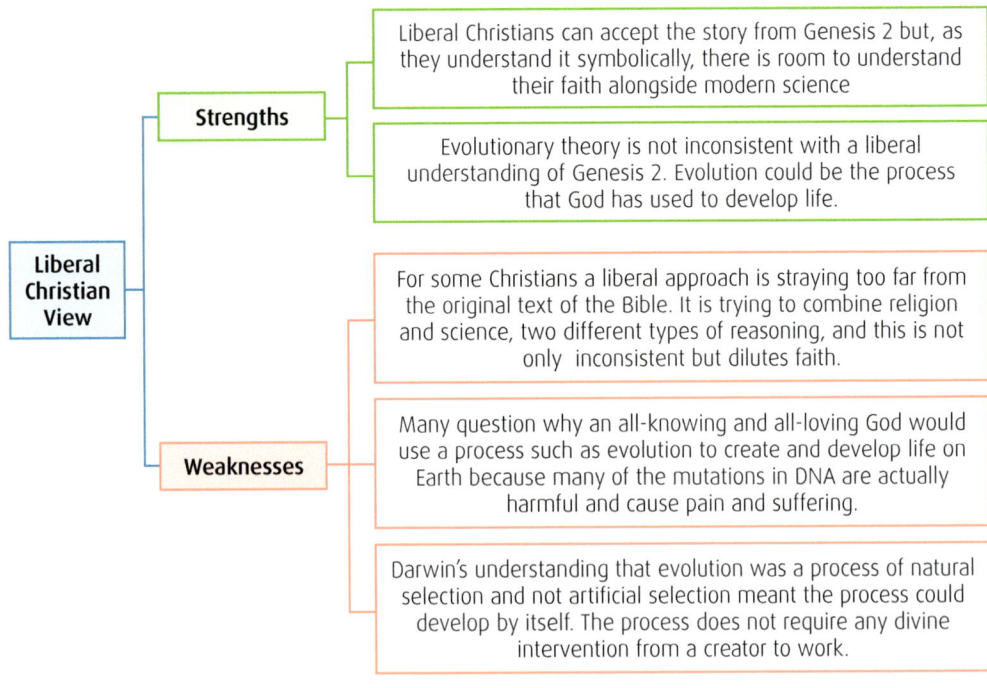

Liberal Christian View

Strengths
- Liberal Christians can accept the story from Genesis 2 but, as they understand it symbolically, there is room to understand their faith alongside modern science
- Evolutionary theory is not inconsistent with a liberal understanding of Genesis 2. Evolution could be the process that God has used to develop life.

Weaknesses
- For some Christians a liberal approach is straying too far from the original text of the Bible. It is trying to combine religion and science, two different types of reasoning, and this is not only inconsistent but dilutes faith.
- Many question why an all-knowing and all-loving God would use a process such as evolution to create and develop life on Earth because many of the mutations in DNA are actually harmful and cause pain and suffering.
- Darwin's understanding that evolution was a process of natural selection and not artificial selection meant the process could develop by itself. The process does not require any divine intervention from a creator to work.

Origins: Was the Universe and life created: Strengths and weaknesses of religious and scientific approaches

WHAT ARE THE STRENGTHS AND WEAKNESSES OF THE SCIENTIFIC VIEW?

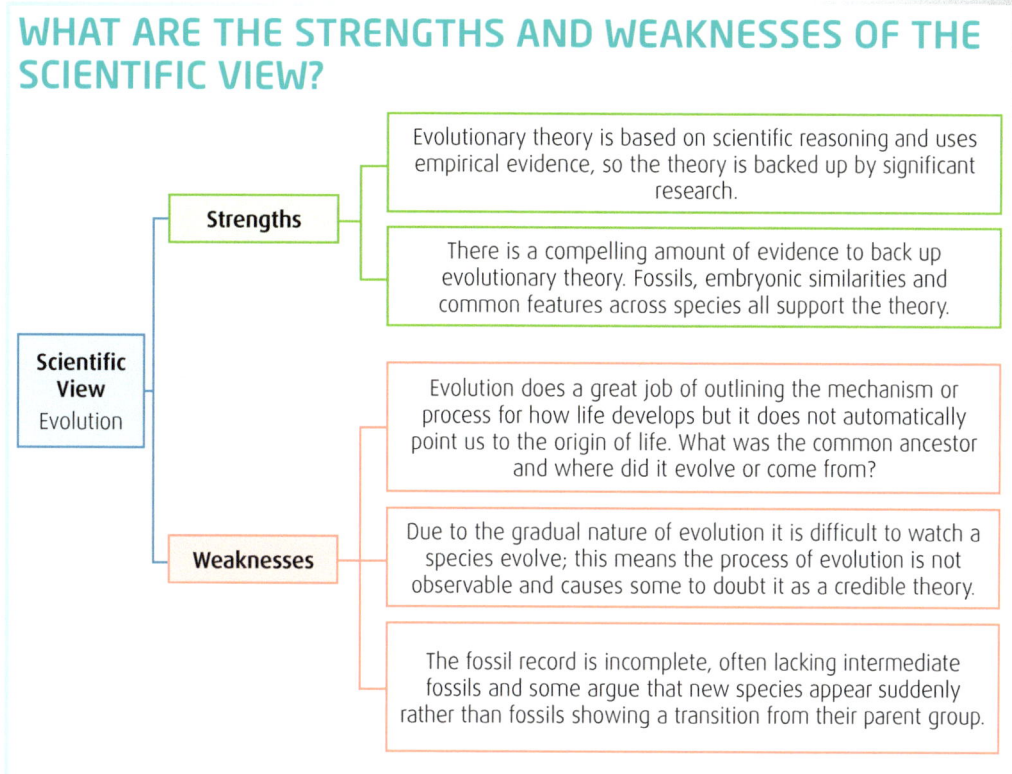

Scientific View — Evolution

Strengths
- Evolutionary theory is based on scientific reasoning and uses empirical evidence, so the theory is backed up by significant research.
- There is a compelling amount of evidence to back up evolutionary theory. Fossils, embryonic similarities and common features across species all support the theory.

Weaknesses
- Evolution does a great job of outlining the mechanism or process for how life develops but it does not automatically point us to the origin of life. What was the common ancestor and where did it evolve or come from?
- Due to the gradual nature of evolution it is difficult to watch a species evolve; this means the process of evolution is not observable and causes some to doubt it as a credible theory.
- The fossil record is incomplete, often lacking intermediate fossils and some argue that new species appear suddenly rather than fossils showing a transition from their parent group.

THINGS TO DO AND THINK ABOUT

1. Create a set of flashcards for all three viewpoints, highlighting their strengths and weaknesses.

2. Using the strengths and weaknesses for all three viewpoints, play devil's advocate and write three developed points that explain why:
   - Literalist Christian viewpoints are the best explanation for the origins of life as opposed to Liberal viewpoints and the scientific viewpoint of evolution.
   - Liberal Christian viewpoints are the best explanation for the origins of life as opposed to Literalist viewpoints and the scientific viewpoint of evolution.
   - The scientific viewpoint of evolution is the best explanation for the origins of life as opposed to Liberal viewpoints and Literalist viewpoints.

THE EXISTENCE OF GOD

DOES GOD EXIST?

The Existence of God unit explores the religious and philosophical question 'Does God exist?' In this unit we will look at the religious arguments that try to prove the existence of God, mainly the cosmological and teleological arguments (however, you may wish to explore others) and the non-religious challenges to these arguments.

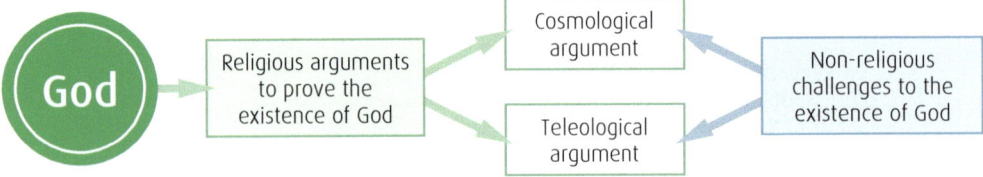

AN OVERVIEW

The main topics that you will encounter in this unit are:

- What arguments/theories do religious people use to prove the existence of God?
- What evidence do religious people use to support these arguments/theories?
- What are the strengths and weaknesses of evidence/arguments/theories?
- What arguments/theories do non-religious people use to challenge the existence of God?
- What evidence do non-religious people use to support these arguments/theories?
- What are the strengths and weaknesses of evidence/arguments/theories?
- Can either religious or non-religious arguments/theories provide conclusive proof about the existence of God?

Past questions in this section have had a focus on:

- Religious arguments that try to prove God exists and their strengths and weaknesses; these religious arguments are often in the form of:
  - Cosmological arguments
  - Teleological arguments
- Criticisms or challenges of the religious arguments used to prove God exists and their strengths and weaknesses.
- Non-religious arguments that challenge the existence of God and their strengths and weaknesses.

UNDERSTANDING WHAT WE ARE LOOKING FOR…

What do we mean by God? Have a think about this. Many people over the last 1500 years (if St Columba's story is to be believed) have spent time in search of the Loch Ness Monster. Now, if the rumours are true, then Nessie is **identified** as a large being with a long neck and at least one hump on its back. If someone was to go in search of the Loch Ness Monster to prove that Nessie exists, this information is important. It's important because it would give them guidance as to what they are searching for. If they were successful in their search to find a monster in Loch Ness, they could compare the monster they have found with their understanding of Nessie. Who knows, in this quest they might have found Tessa, who isn't Nessie at all but a very different monster than the one being sought in the first place! **Defining** the being we are trying to prove exists is very important.

contd

The existence of God: Does God exist?

Which brings us to our topic, the existence of God and our important question: Does God exist? Before we make a start in our search for a divine being called God, we must **define** what that God is like, or, as we would say in RMPS, **identify** the characteristics or attributes of God. Just like our example with Nessie above, we want to make sure we have a clear idea of what we are looking for and be confident that if we find it, we have found that being, and not something else.

The idea of God has a rich history. Many claim Hinduism as the world's oldest religion. Hinduism celebrates the idea of many gods; however, these gods are considered to be the many different forms of the same divine being. The ancient Greek and Norse religions were known as polytheistic, meaning they worshipped many different gods, each of whom had different attributes. Now, the God we are looking for is known as the God of classical theism. This is the God most commonly associated with the Abrahamic religions of Judaism, Christianity and Islam. The attributes of the God of classical theism follow below.

Omniscient

The English word omniscient comes from the Latin words 'omni' meaning all and 'sciens' meaning knowledge. Therefore, **omniscient means that God is all-knowing** and has unlimited knowledge about everything.

Omnipresent

The English word omnipresent comes from the Latin words 'omni' meaning all and 'praesent' meaning present. Therefore, **omnipresent means that God can be anywhere and everywhere at the same time.**

Omnipotent

The English word omnipotent comes from the Latin words 'omni' meaning all and 'potens' meaning powerful. Therefore, **omnipotent means that God is all-powerful.**

Omnibenevolent

The English word omnibenevolent comes from three Latin words, 'omni' meaning all, 'bene' meaning good and 'volens' meaning willing. Therefore, omnibenevolence means God is all-good or all-loving.

Necessarily existent

A being that is **necessarily existent** is often thought of as the opposite of a being that is **contingent**. If a being is contingent that means that it is able to not exist. The God of classical theism is not contingent but necessary, which means that this being cannot not exist. We will look at this again later in some of our arguments.

Eternal

God has and **will always exist**. This means that God is timeless and existed before time began.

A simple acronym to remember these attributes is **ONE**. **O** – Omnis, **N** – Necessary, **E** – Eternal.

So now we know what it is we are looking for when we refer to the term God, let's have a look at our question. Does God exist?

THINGS TO DO AND THINK ABOUT

1. Why is it important at the outset to **identify** what the God of classical theism is like?
2. Create your own acronym that helps you to explain the attributes of the God of classical theism.
3. Using your acronym that explains the God of classical theism, create a flashcard for each attribute (letter of your acronym) and use them to help you learn the attributes.

THE EXISTENCE OF GOD

THE COSMOLOGICAL ARGUMENT 1

RELIGIOUS ARGUMENTS AND EVIDENCE

The cosmological argument is one of the most well-known arguments that religious people use in an attempt to prove that God exists. The word *cosmos* is a Greek word meaning **universe or world**, and the argument uses human experiences of our **Universe or world** to make the case that God exists. Arguments like this, which are based on using our experiences of the world around us, are known as **'a posteriori'** arguments.

As well as being an a posteriori argument, the cosmological argument is also an **inductive** argument. An inductive argument tries to build a case that will lead us to a conclusion. It is important to note that an inductive argument can't **prove** its conclusion, it can only **persuade** us that its conclusion is **reasonable**.

THE CLASSICAL COSMOLOGICAL OR FIRST CAUSE ARGUMENT

Over the years the cosmological argument has been presented in many different forms and promoted by many different people. Before the birth of Jesus, the ancient philosopher Plato and his student Aristotle defended the idea of a first cause (the cosmological argument is also known as the **first cause argument**). Famously, the thirteenth-century Catholic priest Thomas Aquinas wrote about it as part of his **'five ways'** to prove God exists and it is still used through to the present day with theologians such as William Lane Craig defending their versions of the argument.

As you study the cosmological argument you may notice slight variations of it; however, very simply, it states:

1. Everything that exists has a cause of its existence.
2. The Universe exists.
3. Therefore, the Universe has a cause.
4. That first cause is God.

We are going to explore the cosmological argument through three different lenses, St Thomas Aquinas' Three Ways, Leibniz and the principle of sufficient reason, and the Kalam cosmological argument.

ST THOMAS AQUINAS' COSMOLOGICAL ARGUMENT

Arguably the most famous version of the cosmological argument was put forward by the Italian philosopher and Catholic priest **St Thomas Aquinas**. Aquinas wrote a book called *Summa Theologiae* that contains his 'five ways', which are five arguments that try to prove the existence of God. The first three of his five ways are what we know as Aquinas' cosmological argument. These are **the arguments from motion, from causation and from contingency**.

The argument from motion - Aquinas' first way

To really grasp Aquinas' first argument from motion it helps if we think of motion as you would in physics, that is, motion is the idea that an object changes its position over time. Before an object changes position, that object is not in motion, it is at rest. It has the potential to move, however, and we call this a state of potentiality. When that object actually moves it is changing position and changes to a state of actuality. Aquinas argued that whenever something is in motion (changed from potentiality to actuality) it has to have been put into motion by another. This chain of motion or change cannot go back forever: you eventually arrive at the first mover, who is God. Keeping it simple like this gives a good understanding of the argument. Other books and articles argue Aquinas' view of motion is a much broader one. As well as motion meaning a change in position, over time, it could also be considered as a change of any kind. Ultimately, when thinking of motion, the move from potentiality to actuality is the really important thing to remember.

Aquinas uses two examples in *Summa Theologiae* to help explain his argument: the change fire brings to wood and the motion the hand brings to a staff. Aquinas outlined **the impact that fire has on wood** to explain what he means when something is changed or **moved from potentiality to actuality** and how that change can only be brought about by something external to itself. Generally speaking, a piece of wood is not hot; however it has the potential to be hot, but it only actually becomes hot when it is changed by the fire. With regard to the staff and the hand, Aquinas' point is that this long wooden object sits at rest and is only moved when the hand, **something external to itself, moves it.**

The argument from causation - Aquinas' second way

Aquinas argued that in our world there is an order of efficient causes. Things can't cause themselves. They are caused by something else. This chain of causes cannot go backwards infinitely so there must have been a first cause and Aquinas said this was God.

contd

The existence of God: The cosmological argument 1

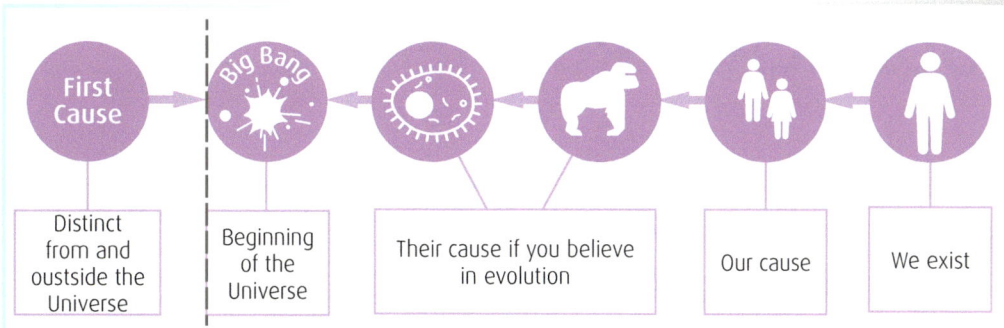

The argument from contingency – Aquinas' third way

At the beginning of this chapter when exploring the attributes of God, we highlighted that the God of Classical theism is understood as a **necessary being – a being that cannot not exist** and does not depend on another being to bring it into existence. This is the opposite of a **contingent being** – a being that is able to not exist, or in simple terms, something that comes into existence and also goes out of existence.

In his third way Aquinas argued that our world is made up of contingent things (things that at some points don't have to exist and are dependent on some other being bringing them into existence). Aquinas believed that all beings could not be contingent, because if this was the case nothing would exist. Aquinas writes, 'if everything is possible not to be, then at one time there could have been nothing in existence. Now if this were true, even now there would be nothing in existence, because that which does not exist only begins to exist by something already existing.' **Therefore, there had to be a being that was not contingent** but was necessary and **for Aquinas this necessary being was God**.

KALAM COSMOLOGICAL ARGUMENT

According to William Lane Craig, one of the most recent theologians to develop the Kalam cosmological argument, 'taken literally, Kalam is simply the Arabic word for speech and was used to mean the statement of an intellectual position or the argument upholding such a statement'. Theologian William Lane Craig outlines the value of **Saadia ben Joseph's** thinking on the Kalam argument. Saadia, an important Jewish philosopher who lived in between Al Kindi and Al Ghazali, explained **that time must be finite and cannot be infinite**. Saadia argued that the present moment has obviously arrived and therefore existence has traversed the time series: however, if time was infinite moving backwards then existence could never reach the present moment. Therefore, **Saadia concluded that the world and time must have had a beginning**.

This thinking allowed Craig to make a subtle change to previous cosmological arguments, which for many makes the argument easier to defend. Previous cosmological arguments state that 'everything that exists has a cause', but the subtle change introduced with the Kalam cosmological argument was 'everything that **begins to exist** has a cause'. As God never began to exist, then he doesn't need a cause. Simply stated

- Everything **that begins to** exist has a cause.
- The Universe began to exist; therefore, the Universe has a cause.
- This chain of causes can't go infinitely backwards.
- Therefore, there must be a first uncaused cause.
- This first uncaused cause is God.

DON'T FORGET

Fire and wood
'But nothing can be reduced from potentiality to actuality, except by something in a state of actuality. Thus that which is actually hot, as fire, makes wood, which is potentially hot, to be actually hot, and thereby moves and changes it.'
St Thomas Aquinas – Summa Theologiae

DON'T FORGET

The staff and the hand
'As the staff moves only because it is put in motion by the hand.'
St Thomas Aquinas – Summa Theologiae

DON'T FORGET

The argument has an Arabic name because the Kalam cosmological argument most likely began with the thinking of two Muslim scholars, **Al Kindi (AD 801-873) and Al Ghazali (AD 1056-1111)**.

ONLINE

Go online to our Digital Zone to read about Gottfried William Leibniz, a German philosopher famed for his principle of sufficient reason www.brightredbooks.net/subjects

THINGS TO DO AND THINK ABOUT

1. There are several terms within this unit that need to be defined. Being able to explain some of these key terms will help you to really grasp the topic and understand it. A good way to do this is to create a glossary (almost like a brief dictionary). Using some of the words that are in bold, create your own glossary for the key vocabulary within the cosmological argument. (You can add to your cosmological argument glossary with the next section on challenges to the cosmological argument.)

THE EXISTENCE OF GOD
THE COSMOLOGICAL ARGUMENT 2

CHALLENGES TO THE COSMOLOGICAL ARGUMENT

Circular logic

One major challenge that is given in opposition to the classical cosmological argument is that it contains what philosophers call circular logic. Looking at the argument below, if we are to argue that the first cause is God (the 4th bullet point), but then put God back into the start of the argument as something that exists (the 1st bullet point), then **we have to ask the question: What caused God?** The best that could possibly be argued here is that God caused God, which doesn't sound very reasonable and as mentioned above is just going round in circles.

1. Everything that exists has a cause of its existence.
2. The Universe exists.
3. Therefore, the Universe has a cause.
4. That first cause is God.
5. Therefore, God exists, but according to premise 1, God now needs a cause.

It is at this point that religious people would state that the Kalam cosmological argument gives a simple solution to this challenge by arguing that the argument should start with the premise – Everything that begins to exist. This means that as God is eternal, God has no beginning and therefore the first premise does not apply. Many religious thinkers will use this to challenge the criticism brought about by circular logic.

BERTRAND RUSSELL VERSUS FREDERICK COPLESTON: THE FALLACY OF COMPOSITION

In 1948, the BBC hosted a radio debate between Frederick Copleston (a Jesuit priest) and Bertrand Russell (philosopher and atheist). **Copleston** used a version of Aquinas' argument from contingency to justify that God could be the only explanation for the existence of our Universe. In his argument he explained that **as the world was made up of the totality of all contingent things, it would therefore itself be contingent** and consequently the reason for its existence had to exist external to it, and that reason was the necessary being, God.

Russell disagreed with Copleston and argued that to say this was just like saying because every human being has a mother then the human race must have a mother, which is clearly absurd. **This is known as a fallacy of composition, inferring that something is true of the whole, because it is true of the parts of the whole** (an idea that also appears in Hume's *Dialogues Concerning Natural Religion*, which we will look at in more detail in criticism of the Teleological Argument). Russell argued that the Universe itself was self-coherent and did not need an external explanation, the Universe was simply a brute fact; his famous words are **'the universe is just there and that is all'**.

DAVID HUME'S OBJECTIONS

David Hume was a Scottish philosopher born in 1711 who had many objections against the cosmological argument. First, **Hume challenged the very idea of causes and effects**. Hume concluded that just because cause and effect happen a specific way now or in the past, it doesn't mean that this will always be the case. If we were to assume that this will be the case, we would have to also assume that nature is uniform, but this is not the case. As Michael Palmer explains, 'The repetition of instances which leads us to the belief that A causes B, in turn reinforces our expectation – or what Hume calls a habit or custom –

> **ONLINE**
>
> Go to our Digital Zone at www.brightredbooks.net/subjects and click the link to listen to part of the Russell/Copleston debate

contd

The existence of God: The cosmological argument 2

that the same will occur in the future. But **the expectation that the relation between A and B will persist does not establish that it will.**' Aquinas expected causes and effects to happen in a specific way, assuming that the world was rational, but he only assumes it is rational and provides no evidence for it.

Second, Hume also **challenges Aquinas' idea of God being the necessary first cause** and argues why the Universe cannot be self-caused. As Hume writes in *Dialogues Concerning Natural Religion*, 'But further, **why may not the material universe be the necessarily existent Being**, according to this pretended explication of necessity?'

IMMANUEL KANT

Immanuel Kant was a German philosopher who lived at the same time as David Hume. One of his most influential pieces of writing was the *Critique of Pure Reason*. In this book he explains why arguments from cause and effect do not support the existence of God as a first cause. Kant concluded that because God as the first cause exists outside our Universe, this transcends any experience that we may have, and therefore we can have no knowledge of who God is, or what He has done. According to Kant, **the cosmological argument fails because it tries to reason a first cause that is beyond the world of sense-experience;** us mere mortals cannot come to any conclusions about things that go beyond the world of sense experience.

THE BIG BANG THEORY

The Big Bang theory is explored in detail on pages 106-107, but it explains that before our Universe came into existence there was nothing, no time, matter, space or energy. Nothing. From this nothingness, approximately 13.8 billion years ago a singularity expanded to give us everything we currently have in our Universe today. The Big Bang theory gives a scientific explanation for the existence of our Universe, and since the theory was established, it has been used to both support and refute the argument that God exists. One modern scientist who uses the Big Bang to argue against the existence of God is Stephen Hawking; he asks the question: 'Did God create the quantum laws that allowed the Big Bang to occur? I have no desire to offend anyone of faith, but I think science has a more compelling explanation than a divine creator.' Hawking is of the opinion that the Universe could simply have popped into existence without any need for an external necessary first cause such as God.

Another scientific theory that undermines the cosmological argument is the oscillating universe theory, which explains that our current Universe may be one of an infinite series of expanding and contracting universes. If this is the case then there is no beginning to the Universe and therefore no first cause.

THINGS TO DO AND THINK ABOUT

1. Using the Cornell note taking technique, create a note for each of the following criticisms of the cosmological argument, making sure to explain the criticism and any key thinkers involved:
   - Circular logic
   - The fallacy of composition
   - David Hume's challenges:
     - Working backwards from causes and effects
     - God as the necessary existent being.
   - Immanuel Kant
   - The Big Bang theory.

2. Have a go at this exam-style question, which builds on your developed points from the last section.

   'The cosmological argument is enough to prove that God exists.'
   To what extent do you agree? (20 marks)

THE EXISTENCE OF GOD
THE TELEOLOGICAL ARGUMENT 1

RELIGIOUS ARGUMENTS AND EVIDENCE

The word teleological comes from the Greek word **teleos**, which means purpose or end. The Teleological Argument therefore asserts that the natural world is directed towards a purpose or end by God. It is often simply referred to as the design argument and argues that **the Universe exhibits evidence of design, which implies that there is a designer, and that this designer is God.**

Many influential thinkers throughout history have explained that our Universe displays some sort of order, complexity or design. King David (1010 BC), quoted in the Christian Bible and the Jewish Tanakh, says 'The heavens declare the glory of God; the skies proclaim the work of his hands'. The Greek philosopher, Socrates (470 BC), was quoted as saying 'With such signs of forethought in these arrangements, can you doubt whether they are the works of chance or design?'

Like the cosmological argument in the previous section, **teleological arguments are a posteriori**, meaning that they are based on observations on the world around us, and they are also **inductive**, meaning they try to build a case that will lead us to a conclusion; remember that they can't **prove** their conclusion, but can only **persuade** us that any conclusion is **reasonable**.

Also, like the cosmological argument earlier, you may notice slight variations of the design argument; however, stated very simply, it is pretty much as follows:

- The Universe displays purpose, regularity and complexity.
- This purpose, regularity and complexity suggests the appearance of design.
- The appearance of design implies there was a designer.
- This designer of the Universe is God.

We are going to explore four different variations of the design argument, namely, William Paley's design argument, St Thomas Aquinas' fifth way, the anthropic principle and the argument from Intelligent Design.

WILLIAM PALEY

One of the most popular forms of the design argument comes from William Paley (1743–1805). Paley was an English theologian and philosopher, and in his book *Natural Theology* he puts forward **an argument based on a simple analogy** to argue for a designer God. In his book he writes:

'In crossing a heath, suppose I pitched my foot against a stone, and were asked how the stone came to be there; I might possibly answer, that, for any thing I knew to the contrary, it had lain there for ever: nor would it perhaps be very easy to show the absurdity of this answer. But suppose I had found a watch upon the ground, and it should be inquired how the watch happened to be in that place; I should hardly think of the answer which I had before given, that, for any thing I knew, the watch might have always been there. Yet why should not this answer serve for the watch as well as for the stone? why is it not as admissible in the second case, as in the first? For this reason, and for no other, viz. that, when we come to inspect the watch, we perceive (what we could not discover in the stone) that its several parts are framed and put together for a purpose... the inference, we think, is inevitable, that the watch must have had a maker: that there must have existed, at some time, and at some place or other, an artificer or artificers who formed it for the purpose which we find it actually to answer; who comprehended its construction, and designed its use.'

And then, in Paley's application of the argument, comes his analogy, *'for every indication of contrivance, every manifestation of design, which existed in the watch, exists in the works of nature; with the difference, on the side of nature, of being greater and more, and that in a degree which exceeds all computation'.*

The existence of God: The teleological argument 1

So, Paley's analogy was simple: if you were to walk across a field and stumble upon a watch you would come to the conclusion that **this complex object hadn't simply appeared like a stone, but rather had been created for a purpose by a designer.** Paley then explained that **when we observe the natural world** around us, just like the designed watch, **we also see design and purpose but to an even greater extent,** which implies that it too was created for a purpose by a designer.

A summary of Paley's argument would be:

- A watch is complex and is put together for a particular purpose.
- We can compare this to the natural world, which is even more complex.
- We know that a watch is the product of a designer.
- Like effects have like causes.
- Therefore, the natural world must be the product of a designer.
- That designer is God.

Paley then uses **the example of the human eye** as further evidence of a complex object, found in the natural world, that has been designed for a particular purpose. In **comparing it to a telescope**, Paley suggests that both the eye and the telescope have been designed with the specific purpose of seeing, and these complex arrangements, in the natural world, lead us to the conclusion of an intelligent designer.

Using the evidence of design to suggest that parts of the natural world have been put together for a particular purpose, just as William Paley does here, is known as arguing from **design qua purpose,** with the word qua being Latin for 'as relating to'.

Paley also argued from **design qua regularity**, or 'design as relating to regularity', which means to argue that **the regularity and order found in our Universe suggests that the Universe has a designer.** Paley believed that the planets within our solar system obeyed certain universal laws; in line with Newton's understanding of science and astronomy, they behaved in this way because they were designed to do so – for Paley this type of order and regularity could not have happened by chance, it must have been designed and this designer was God.

AQUINAS' FIFTH WAY

Aquinas also argues from **design qua regularity** with his version of the design argument, which comes from his book *Summa Theologiae*. When we explored Aquinas' cosmological argument, we looked at ways one, two and three – now we are looking at his **fifth way to prove that God exists**. Aquinas writes:

'The fifth way is taken from the governance of the world. We see that things which lack intelligence, such as natural bodies, act for an end, and this is evident from their acting always, or nearly always, in the same way, so as to obtain the best result. Hence it is plain that not fortuitously, but designedly, do they achieve their end. Now whatever lacks intelligence cannot move towards an end, unless it be directed by some being endowed with knowledge and intelligence; as the arrow is shot to its mark by the archer. Therefore some intelligent being exists by whom all natural things are directed to their end; and this being we call God.'

St Thomas Aquinas – *Summa Theologiae*

Aquinas is arguing that natural bodies in our Universe, which lack intelligence, act towards a purpose or end. Aquinas believed that these **natural bodies would not be able to act towards their end unless they were directed by an intelligent being**. The example Aquinas gives is that of an archer shooting an arrow. The arrow needs to be directed by the archer to reach its target in the same way that unintelligent natural bodies need directed towards their end by an intelligent being, and Aquinas believed that intelligent being was God.

 ## THINGS TO DO AND THINK ABOUT

The initial task when exploring the cosmological argument is to create a glossary (almost like a brief dictionary). Start a new section in your glossary using some of the keywords or terms that are in bold in this section; this will enable you to keep a record of the key vocabulary within the Teleological Argument. (You can add to your Teleological Argument glossary with the next spread on challenges to the argument.)

121

THE EXISTENCE OF GOD
THE TELEOLOGICAL ARGUMENT 2

THE ANTHROPIC PRINCIPLE

The word anthropic means involving humankind or human existence, and **the anthropic principle** is a design argument that suggests that **the Universe is so finely tuned for human existence that it is as if the Universe has been designed so that it could sustain human life.** Any small changes in the natural constants around us, such as the force of gravity or the mass of a proton or an electron, and it would be very unlikely for any life to have developed on the Earth. In 1971, the theoretical physicist and mathematician (and Christian) Freeman Dyson, writing in *Scientific American*, explained 'As we look out into the universe and identify the many accidents of physics and astronomy that have worked together to our benefit, it almost seems as if the universe must in some sense have known we were coming'.

The British theologian, F. R. Tennant (1866–1957), has been credited for his work on developing the anthropic principle. His influential book *Philosophical Theology* outlines three types of natural evidence in favour of the world being designed:

- First, the world can be analysed in a rational manner or rationally understood.
- Second, the fitness (or ability) of our inorganic (not consisting of living matter) world to minister to (be able to sustain) life.
- Third, '*progressiveness in the evolutionary process culminating in the emergence of man, with his rational and moral status*', which, simplified, means the way in which evolution has progressed to bring about intelligent human life.

Therefore, Tennant's argument can be summarised like this: it is possible for us to imagine a world full of chaos, but that is not what we have, we have a world that we can understand rationally, and that world appears designed in such a way that intelligent life can exist – so therefore a designer God must exist.

More modern developments of the anthropic principle have seen it grouped into two categories, **the weak anthropic principle** and **the strong anthropic principle.**

- **Weak anthropic principle:** The Universe must possess the properties that allow for the existence of observers. In other words, the circumstances in our Universe are such that it is highly possible that life would emerge. This suggests our Universe has an appearance of design but may simply be natural laws working over a very long time.
- **Strong anthropic principle:** The Universe has been fine-tuned or designed to bring about human life. So, the circumstances in our Universe are such that it is inevitable that life would emerge. This suggests that a designer is at work and has designed a universe with the ultimate purpose of sustaining human life.

This brings us back to the issue we explored at the very beginning, which is whether the appearance of design is different from actual design. Many scientists and philosophers will agree that our Universe has an appearance of design; however, an *appearance of design* does not confirm *actual design* or indeed the religious idea of a designer.

The existence of God: The teleological argument 2

INTELLIGENT DESIGN

The Intelligent Design movement emerged towards the end of the twentieth century in direct opposition to Darwinism and it proposes that an intelligent cause is responsible for the diversity and complexity of life, rather than unguided natural selection, as suggested by the theory of evolution. Its supporters claim that **intelligent design** is a scientific theory; it does not simply use the Bible as a scientific text. The movement believes that Darwinism is an inadequate framework for biology and they oppose it on scientific and philosophical grounds.

The Discovery Institute, one of the leading intelligent design organisations, defines intelligent design as *'a theory of biological origins and development. Its fundamental claim is that intelligent causes are necessary to explain the complex, information-rich structures of biology, and that these causes are empirically detectable. To say intelligent causes are empirically detectable is to say there exist well-defined methods that, on the basis of observational features of the world, are capable of reliably distinguishing intelligent causes from undirected natural causes.'*

The movement is quite clear that it uses science to discover or identify 'intelligence' without speculating about the nature of that intelligence; however, many who oppose the movement believe it to be a pseudo-scientific version of creationism, and that it is really trying to prove that God is that 'intelligence'.

One of the scientific ways in which the movement explains that it detects intelligent causes is through Michael Behe's (Professor of Biochemistry) Irreducible Complexity. Behe concluded that it is impossible to remove any of the component parts of an irreducibly complex system and for it to still maintain its functionality. This is important as it challenges the theory of evolution. Darwin stated in *On the Origin of Species* that, 'If it could be demonstrated that any complex organ existed, which could not possibly have been formed by numerous, successive, slight modifications, my theory would absolutely break down'. Behe argues that irreducibly complex systems, such as his example of the bacterial flagellum, could not come from slight successive modifications of an earlier system because if it was missing any of its parts it wouldn't function, and this therefore disproves the theory of evolution as a blind natural process.

 ## THINGS TO DO AND THINK ABOUT

Make some developed points on this 'exam-style' question:

In what ways does the Teleological Argument attempt to prove that God exists?

Remember we haven't looked at the criticisms of the Teleological Argument so the full 20-mark essay will come at the end of the next section. See how many developed points you can create.

Outline all the versions of the Teleological Argument listed and add them to your selection of flashcards for revision.

THE EXISTENCE OF GOD

THE TELEOLOGICAL ARGUMENT 3

NON-RELIGIOUS ARGUMENTS AND EVIDENCE

David Hume – *Dialogues Concerning Natural Religion*

David Hume (1711–1776) was a Scottish philosopher who, in his book *Dialogues Concerning Natural Religion*, argues against the idea that our Universe was designed by the God of classical theism. The book is written as a dialogue between different characters, so it reads as a conversation.

Disanalogy

A disanalogy is whenever differences are pointed out between two things that are being compared in an analogical argument. If there are several relevant differences between the two things being compared then the argument can become severely weakened. Hume argues that the difference between human-made things and things that occur naturally is too great and that this type of analogy does not work or is unsound. Therefore, if we have a look at Thomas Aquinas' fifth way and the example he gives of the archer and the arrow as an analogy for a purpose-giver and natural objects, the differences are too great between the things being compared. Similarly, if we apply what Hume is saying to Paley's argument comparing a watch to a world or an eye to a telescope, the differences between the objects being compared are too great and the argument is severely weakened. Hume uses his own bad analogy (sometimes called the architect's argument) to make his point. He explains that if we were to see a house, we would conclude it had a builder or architect because we know this from experience, but saying a house resembles a universe and inferring that it had a similar cause would be far from perfect.

Hume writes 'The dissimilitude is so striking, that the utmost you can here pretend to is a guess, a conjecture, a presumption concerning a similar cause; and how that pretension will be received in the world, I leave you to consider'.

David Hume – *Dialogues Concerning Natural Religion*

Why only similarities in some of the properties in our analogy?

Here we see Hume make another criticism of teleological arguments based on the comparison of human-made to natural things. He questions why, when we compare the Universe to houses and machines, etc., do design arguments only use the similarities in 'some' of their circumstances to infer the similarity of their causes. Design arguments propose that because two things share one thing in common such as complexity, they must also share another quality in common, that of being designed. The problem is that if that was the case, then following the same logic, many absurd qualities could be attributed to the Universe, for example:

- Watches are complex
- Watches were created in the fifteenth century
- The Universe is complex
- Therefore, the Universe was created in the fifteenth century.

We can also widen this idea out a little and incorporate something that we have already explored in the cosmological argument. That is, very simply, **similar effects do not necessarily arise from similar causes**. In fact, Hume takes it a step further and says that doing this degrades God and gives us an anthropomorphic view of God.

The designer might not be the God of classical theism

Hume refers to this idea on more than one occasion, and from different perspectives in his *Dialogues*. Design arguments are used to prove that God exists as the designer. Hume suggests that the designer suggested is often far from the God of classical theism.

- **An anthropomorphic view of God** – Design arguments use analogy to compare human-made objects and natural objects and suggest that because complex human-made objects have a designer, then complex natural objects require a designer. In following

DON'T FORGET

What is interesting is that Hume wrote his book before Paley, so it is not a direct criticism of Paley's design argument, but rather of design arguments in general.

DON'T FORGET

Just because two things share one quality or circumstance, it doesn't mean they share another quality or indeed cause. Hume makes his point in the form of a question: '[B]ut can you think, Cleanthes, that your usual phlegm and philosophy have been preserved in so wide a step as you have taken, when you compared to the universe houses, ships, furniture, machines, and, from their similarity in some circumstances, inferred a similarity in their causes?'

this line of reasoning Hume suggests that the analogy provides a very human or anthropomorphic view of God, which if anything discredits God. This is because the complexity in human-made objects comes from a human designer, so arguing for the same complexity in natural things leaves us with a very 'human-type God'.
- **An inferior deity** – Hume explains this as part of his *Dialogues*:
'*This world, for aught he knows, is very faulty and imperfect, compared to a superior standard; and was only the first rude essay of some infant deity, who afterwards abandoned it, ashamed of his lame performance: it is the work only of some dependent, inferior deity; and is the object of derision to his superiors: it is the production of old age and dotage in some superannuated deity; and ever since his death, has run on at adventures, from the first impulse and active force which it received from him.*'
- **A team of Gods** – Hume suggests that human-made things such as houses require a team of designers. Would we not infer this when we think of a world, meaning a team of Gods rather than the God of classical theism? As Hume says, 'A great number of men join in building a house or ship, in rearing a city, in framing a commonwealth; why may not several deities combine in contriving and framing a world?'

A. J. AYER

A.J. Ayer (1910–1989), the famous British philosopher, argued that we have no idea what designed or 'not designed' universes look like, so how could we possibly claim that this Universe was designed by a God. As Ayer exclaimed, 'until we can say what the world would have to be like, to be not designed, we cannot conclude that the world is designed'.

Ayer also attacks **a posteriori argument in general** in his book *Language, Truth, and Logic*. He explains that we cannot say that God exists because any a posteriori argument at best can only lead us to the conclusion that **God probably exists**.

EVOLUTION

Evolution is covered as a topic in the Origins section of the Higher; you can have a look at page 111 to gain a deeper understanding of this scientific theory. It is important for us to know a little bit about it for this unit as it is one of the key criticisms put forward against the design argument. As scientific materialist Richard Dawkins explains, 'Once you understand how Darwinism works, then you could easily see that that's a far better, far more parsimonious, far more scientific explanation than intelligent design'.

The theory of evolution suggests that all living organisms came from a common ancestor and have gradually changed over time. Scientific materialists (such as Richard Dawkins) explain that it is the theory of evolution by natural selection that gives the appearance of design in our Universe. **Evolution is often described as a blind process, which means that things can appear designed without any need for a designer God.**

DON'T FORGET

Scientists such as Richard Dawkins explain that evolution is what gives the appearance of design in our Universe.

One of the scientific arguments from ID proponent Michael Behe is 'irreducible complexity', which, as we explored earlier, means that every part of that biological system is vital for the system to work. So, the system can't be made any less complex and therefore natural selection is defeated. A very straightforward criticism comes from Ker Than, currently Director of Science Communications at Stanford University. He explains that '[a] necessary – and often unstated – flipside to this is that if an irreducibly complex system contains within it a smaller set of parts that could be used for some other function, then the system was never really irreducibly complex to begin with'.

DON'T FORGET

Many scientists would claim that these systems set out by Behe as irreducibly complex really aren't and many of the parts within these systems are found elsewhere in other biological systems.

THINGS TO DO AND THINK ABOUT

1. Create a set of flash cards for each of the criticisms of the teleological argument below. Make sure you explain the criticism and any key thinkers involved.
    - David Hume
        - Disanalogy.
        - Why only similarities in some of the properties in our analogy?
        - The designer might not be the God of classical theism.
    - A. J. Ayer.
    - Evolution.
    - Arguments against the Intelligent Design movement.

THE EXISTENCE OF GOD

THE STRENGTHS AND WEAKNESSES OF THE COSMOLOGICAL AND TELEOLOGICAL ARGUMENTS

Cosmological Argument — Strengths

- As it is an posteriori argument it is based on empirical evidence, gained through the senses by observing the Universe around us.

- The cosmological argument is straightforward in that the chains of cause and effect exist in our Universe and there is nothing we observe that would conflict with this idea of causation, motion or contingency. Taking this further our experiences tell us that things in our Universe do not cause themselves so they must have a cause, which would eventually lead to a first cause.

- The cosmological argument seems compatible with modern scientific theories such as the Big Bang. As yet scientists have no evidence for the cause of the Big Bang, so the case can be made that God, as the first cause, caused the Big Bang.

- Infinite regress is also something that is not very widely accepted and the cosmological argument provides and alternative to this.

- According to Leibniz and the principle of sufficient reason, the Universe itself must have an explanation and the cosmological argument gives a straightforward explanation for the Universe.

Cosmological Argument — Weaknesses

- Because the Cosmological Argument is an inductive argument it can never really prove that God exists but only that God probably exists.

- Any human reasoning can only be applied to our known Universe so to make any claims about what might exist beyond our Universe is unreasonable.

- To some the cosmological argument seems compatible with the Big Bang. However, scientists such as Stephen Hawking argue that the Big Bang was inevitable due to the laws of gravity, with no need for a creator God.

- Experience of things within our Universe tells us that we cannot infer something is true of the whole because it is true of the parts of the whole. So it makes very little sense to say that because objects within the Universe have a cause that the Universe itself has a cause.

- Even if the cosmological argument is successful in proving that there is a first cause, there are any number of things that the first cause could be that is not the God of classical theism.

Teleological Argument — Strengths

- As it is an posteriori argument it is based on empirical evidence, gained through the senses by observing the Universe around us.

- It is pretty clear that complex human-made objects have been designed by a designer. It is therefore logical to suggest that complex natural objects, that give the appearance of design, also require a designer.

- The regularity of our Universe suggests that it has been designed or fine-tuned to be like this rather than it simply just happening this way by chance. If there were small changes to some of the natural constants in our Universe then life would never have developed.

- The intelligent design movement argues there are biological systems that exist that are irreducibly complex. It is argued these systems could not have adapted from earlier, simpler systems. This for many disproves evolution through natural selection, suggesting a designer.

- Many things in our Universe have a purpose for their existence. Our experience of our world tells us that things do not create their own purpose but rather are given that purpose by design, suggesting a designer.

The existence of God: The strengths and weaknesses of the Cosmological and Teleological arguments

Teleological Argument — Weaknesses

- Even if we can conclude that our Universe was designed we are still left with the question of who or what the designer may be. The God of classical theism is one option, but it is not the only option.
- Many problems arise when you try to argue an analogy between human-made and natural objects. As Hume pointed out, the difference between the two is too great.
- There are things in our world that seem badly designed, or certainly not the work of an all-powerful, all-knowing and all-loving God.
- As the Teleological Argument is an inductive argument it can only try to 'persuade us' that God exists rather than actually 'prove' that God exists. This means that at its very best the argument will leave us with the conclusion that god probably exists, not that God exists.
- Evolution gives us the scientific understanding of how the appearance of design could take place through a blind natural process.

CAN EITHER RELIGIOUS OR NON-RELIGIOUS ARGUMENTS PROVIDE CONCLUSIVE PROOF ABOUT THE EXISTENCE OF GOD?

This chapter has looked at the different arguments for and against the existence of God. It is now our job to look at that evidence in detail, using our skills of analysis (starting with how we compare, connect and draw out possible consequences from the evidence and viewpoints) before making a reasoned judgement (evaluating) on whether God exists. The three main responses to the question are:

- God exists – Some may respond that God exists. For our purposes within this unit of the course we would usually label these people as religious, we could also call them Theists. They would believe that the arguments we have presented here could be used to say that it is very probable that God exists. They would argue that the arguments presented, such as the cosmological and teleological arguments (or other arguments you may have looked at in class), are stronger than the criticisms of those arguments.
- God doesn't exist – Some may respond that God doesn't exist. For our purposes within this unit of the course we would usually label these people as non-religious, we could also call them Atheists. They would be of the opinion that the criticisms of the cosmological and teleological arguments that we have explored here (or the criticisms of other arguments you have studied) outweigh the arguments themselves and would argue that it is very probable that God does not exist.
- We can't be certain – Some would believe that the evidence does not allow us to be certain either way. We would label those people as being Agnostic. The evidence presented isn't conclusive either way so you are simply in the position of not knowing.

Your job is to not just try and align yourself with a particular position, but to be able to reason why it is that you take that position over the other positions that are available.

THINGS TO DO AND THINK ABOUT

1. Use the diagrams to create a set of flashcards that outline the strengths and weaknesses of the cosmological and teleological arguments.

2. Take some time to think about the three perspectives above: (a) God exists, (b) God doesn't exist and (c) We can't be certain either way. Create three large mind-maps using what you have learnt in this chapter for each perspective, so you have a complete overview of the unit.

3. Use your mind-maps created in question 2 to help you answer the following 20-mark questions:
   'To what extent do you agree with religious arguments for the existence of God?'
   'To what extent do you agree with the non-religious challenges to the existence of God?'

   Things to consider when answering the questions:
   - Have you included enough KU, A and E?
   - Are you referring back to the question in your answer?

INDEX

Abrahamic religions 34, 35, 115
Adverse Childhood Experiences (ACEs) 52–53, 54–55, 56
Animism 9
Anthropic Principle 120, 122
Aquinas, Thomas 116–117, 118, 119, 120–121, 124
asceticism 12
assisted dying 90–93
    see also euthanasia
atonement theory 40
autonomy
    end-of-life decisions 90–91, 93, 94–95, 98–101
    organ donation 82–83
Ayer, A.J. 125

Behe, Michael 123, 125
Big Bang theory 106–107, 119
    evidence 106–107
    see also origins, of Universe
brain dumps 7
British Medical Association (BMA)
    assisted dying 93, 95, 97
    embryo research 74, 79, 81
    end-of-life (palliative) care 101
    organ donation 85
Buddhism 4, 8–31
    assisted dying 96
    beating heart donation 87
    dependent origination 10, 19
    Dhamma (teachings) 26–27
    Five Aggregates (Khandas) 15
    Five Precepts 8, 24–25, 65
    Four Noble Truths 8, 13, 15, 64
    Mahayana tradition 21
    Nature of Human Beings 8, 13
        Kamma 8, 13, 17, 27, 65
        Tanha 8, 16–17, 21
        Three Root Poisons 8, 16–17, 18, 20, 21
    Nibbana (enlightenment) 8, 10, 11, 12, 13, 20–21
    Noble Eightfold Path 8, 12, 13, 21, 22–23, 28, 64
    palliative care 100
    practices 22–31
        devotion 8, 30–31
            Buddhanussati (mindfulness) 30
            festivals 30–31
            Puja 30
            retreats 30, 31
        meditation (Samadhi/Vipassana) 8, 12–13, 22–23, 28–29
    Punna 24, 27
    Samsara (cycle of life/death/rebirth) 8, 17, 18–19, 21
    Sangha (community) 8, 26–27
    Sila (Moral Conduct) 24–25
    Six Realms 18–19
    Theravada tradition 12, 21, 28, 30
    Three Marks of Existence 13, 14–15
        Anatta (no self) 11, 14–15
        Anicca (impermanence/change) 14
        Dukkha (un-satisfaction/suffering) 11, 14, 15, 21
    Twelve Nidanas 18, 19

Christianity 4, 9, 32–49
    afterlife 42
    assisted dying 92, 96
    beliefs
        Ascension 41, 43
        atonement 40
        characteristics of God 34–35
        concept of service and care to others 39
        God as creator 34–35
        Incarnation 38
        Jesus 35, 38–41
        miracles 39
        Resurrection 41, 43
        sanctity of life 76, 79
        Trinity of God (Father, Son and Holy Spirit) 35
        ultimate sacrifice 40
        Virgin Birth (immaculate conception) 38
    Christian action and community 46–47
    Eucharist/Holy Communion 32, 33, 49
    Gospels 34, 35, 44–45
    Heaven and Hell 42–43
    Judgement 42–43
    nature of human beings 34–43, 35, 36–37
        free will 35, 36
        humans as images of God 36
        sin (original) 35, 36–37
        stewards 35, 36
    New Testament 32, 37, 44–45
    Old Testament 32–33
    palliative care 100
    parables 43, 44–45
    practices 44–49
        prayer 48
    Sermon on the Mount 44–45
    see also existence of God; origins, of life; origins, of the Universe
Church of Scotland
    assisted dying 92, 96
    organ donation 84
    palliative care 100
    therapeutic use of embryos 79, 81
Classical Theism 114–115, 127
Copleston, Frederick 118
Cornell notes 6, 15
cosmic background radiation 106
cosmological arguments, existence of God 114–119, 126
cosmological redshift 107
Craig, William Lane 116, 117
crime *see* morality

Darwin, Charles 111, 123
Dawkins, Richard 125
Day Age Creationism 105
dependent origination, Buddhism 14, 19
disanalogy 124
doctrine of double effect (euthanasia) 95
dual coding 7, 17, 27
Dyson, Freeman 122

Egoism, organ donation 85
embryos, morality 72–81
end of life
    morality 90–101
    see also assisted dying; autonomy; euthanasia; palliative care
environment, morality 52–53, 64
euthanasia 94–97
    see also assisted dying
evolutionary theory *see* origins, of life
exam structure 4–5
existence of God 114–127
    circular logic 118
    cosmological arguments 114–119, 126
    teleological arguments 114, 120–125, 126–127

First Cause argument 116
flashcards 6